Raleigh House

COOKBOOK II

Martha Johnson

Copyright © 1995

Raleigh House
Kerrville, Texas
all rights reserved

FIRST PRINTING   AUGUST 1995   5000 COPIES

Library of Congress Catalog Card Number 95-69559

International Standard Book Number 0-9631037-1-7

Additional copies may be obtained by addressing
Raleigh House Cookbook II
P.O. Box 2182
Kerrville, Texas 78029-2182

Printed in the USA by

WIMMER
The Wimmer Companies, Inc.
Memphis • Dallas

Dedication and Thanks

This cookbook is dedicated, with love, as a legacy to my family, especially to my twenty-three great grandchildren. This is a milestone as I will be ninety years old and looking forward to greeting my twenty-fourth great grandchild soon after this book is printed.

My sincere thanks to my family and friends for their contribution of recipes and also their willingness to sample the many recipes tested.

I also want to express my appreciation to Everett Williams, my computer mentor, without whom this Raleigh House Cookbook II could never have been completed.

My family's life has revolved around food in more than the usual way! My first cookbook, Raleigh House, was written at the urging of family and friends. Raleigh House II, my second cookbook, is my own labor of love — the love of good food and my family!

My restaurant, in the Hill Country at Kerrville, Texas, was named for my husband, Raleigh W. Johnson. He was a manufacturer's representative for commercial kitchen equipment. Our son, Raleigh W. Johnson, Jr. continued with the business after his father's death. Now, his two sons, Raleigh W. Johnson III and David Johnson, are carrying on the tradition — a third generation.

The interest and support of my entire family helped immeasurably in getting Raleigh House Restaurant off to a good start thirty-nine years ago. James R. Graves, my son-in-law, owned a commercial air conditioning business and came to my aid promptly when a crisis occurred in that area. My son advised me concerning needed equipment and other phases of the restaurant industry. My brother, Robert Robinson, came to help after he retired and made sure that everything was running smoothly in the "front of the house." My grandchildren and then my great grandchildren also had a part in Raleigh House in many ways. I made matching uniforms for them to wear.

Since I was open only in the summer, my main staff was composed of college students. Their enthusiasm and interest made them popular with the customers.

The first waitress I had was from Fredericksburg. She was a loyal, caring friend as well as an employee for twenty-six years until she had to retire because of her health. She often suggested that I write about the interesting experiences of the Raleigh House years. Perhaps, some day, I will write a personal journal for pasterity. In the meantime, I hope you will enjoy this book as much as I have enjoyed writing it.

Table of Contents

Appetizers

Raleigh White Johnson, Senior

Bleu Cheese Dip

This is the easiest dip you can ever make.

1	(3 ounce) package cream cheese
1	(3 ounce) package Bleu cheese
¼	cup butter, softened
1	tablespoon brandy

Combine cream cheese, Bleu cheese and butter. Beat at medium speed in a mixer until smooth. Add brandy, mixing well. Serve with crackers or sliced apples or pears.

Yield: 1 cup

Broccomole

This can be made with either fresh or frozen broccoli.

2   cups raw broccoli pieces, flowerets and peeled stems, or 1 (10 ounce) package frozen broccoli cuts
2   teaspoons salt
¼   cup commercial sour cream
1 to 2 tablespoons grated onion
1   tablespoon mayonnaise
2   teaspoons fresh lemon juice
¼   teaspoon curry powder or to taste

Cook broccoli, uncovered, in 1″ water with salt, until barely tender. Drain well. Place sour cream, onion, lemon juice, mayonnaise and curry powder in jar of blender. Add broccoli and push down into sour cream. Cover and blend to a puree, stopping several times to push down sides with spatula. Taste and add more salt, if necessary. Serve with crackers or Doritos.

Yield: About 2½ cups

I have served this as a dressing placed on top of sliced tomatoes.

Dill Dip

If Beau Monde seasoning is not available in your area, combine 1½ teaspoons ground celery seeds, ¾ teaspoon onion powder and ¾ teaspoon salt. Use 1 teaspoon for this recipe. Store remainder of mixture in an airtight container.

⅔   cup mayonnaise
⅔   cup sour cream
1   tablespoon dried dillweed
1   tablespoon grated onion
1   teaspoon Beau Monde seasoning

Combine all ingredients. Serve immediately or cover and refrigerate up to 2 days. Serve in a hollowed cabbage head or bowl with assorted fresh vegetables.

Yield: 1⅓ cups

Cheese Straws Olé

2	cups (8 ounces) shredded Monterey Jack cheese	½	cup yellow cornmeal
½	cup margarine, softened	1	teaspoon chili powder
1	cup flour	½	teaspoon salt
		½	teaspoon ground cumin

Mix cheese and margarine in mixer, gradually add remaining ingredients, mixing until mixture is no longer crumbly and can be shaped into a ball. Use a cookie press with a star-shaped disk to make dough in "ribbons" on ungreased cookie sheet. Bake at 375° about 8 minutes or until lightly browned. Remove from oven and cut into 2″ pieces with a sharp knife while still warm. Remove to wire rack to cool, then pack in a tightly covered container.

Yield: About 8 dozen

Italian cheese straws may be made by this recipe, substituting Mozzarella cheese for the Monterey Jack, 1½ cups flour for the flour and cornmeal and 2 teaspoons Italian seasoning for the chili powder and cumin. Add a dash of white pepper.

Cream Cheese Mold

This mold can also be used for dessert garnished with strawberries. A delicious ending especially when served with wine, port or champagne.

1	(8 ounce) package cream cheese, softened	1	envelope unflavored gelatin
1	(3 ounce) package cream cheese, softened	¼	cup water
		1	cup slivered almonds, toasted and coarsely chopped
½	cup butter, softened	1	teaspoon grated lemon rind
½	cup sour cream	½	teaspoon almond extract
2	tablespoons sugar		Strawberries for garnish, if desired

Combine cream cheese and butter and beat at medium speed in a mixer until smooth. Add sour cream and sugar and mix. Combine water and gelatin in a small saucepan; let stand 1 minute. Cook and stir over very low heat until gelatin melts. Add to cream cheese mixture, stirring well. Add almonds, lemon rind and almond extract. Spoon into a 1-quart mold that has been rubbed lightly with mayonnaise. Chill until firm. Unmold on serving platter and garnish with strawberries, if desired. Serve with melba toast or crackers.

Yield: 4 cups

Eggplant Dip

Rena Kyriakides gave this recipe to me when I was visiting Athens, Greece many years ago.

1	eggplant (a little over 2 pounds)	2	teaspoons lemon juice
¼	cup grated onion	½	cup olive oil
1	tablespoon olive oil	1	teaspoon salt
2	tablespoons flour	½	teaspoon sugar
½	cup cold water	½	teaspoon pepper
		¼	cup vinegar

Bake eggplant in a 350° oven until covered with wrinkles, turning from side to side. Remove from oven and cool slightly; but do not let get cold. Peel and put meat into a blender or food processor. Blend to a puree, then drain on paper towels as it must not be juicy. Set aside. Place the 1 tablespoon olive oil, flour and water in a small saucepan and boil until the consistency of cream, stirring constantly. Remove from stove and cool. In blender, put in order given the lemon juice, the ½ cup olive oil and the salt. Blend and add the cream mixture by spoonfuls quickly. Blend until it is like mayonnaise. Add eggplant, onion, sugar, pepper and vinegar. Chill in the refrigerator for 3 to 4 hours in a covered container.

I have also used this in a salad. Place a thick slice of tomato on lettuce-lined salad plate and top with a scoop of the eggplant dip. No additional dressing is needed.

Tortilla Dip

1	cup mayonnaise	2	(4 ounce) cans chopped green chilies, undrained
1½	cups grated Parmesan cheese		
1	cup (4 ounces) grated Monterey Jack cheese	¼	teaspoon ground cumin
		⅛	teaspoon chili powder

Combine all ingredients and spoon into a 1-quart baking dish. Bake at 350° for 20 minutes. Serve hot with tortilla chips.

Yield: 3 cups

Helpful Hint: *1 pound eggplant — 2½ cups diced.*

Mushrooms in Cream Cheese Pastry

These can also be frozen, unbaked. Make turnovers, then brush with egg yolk wash. Freeze in single layer on cookie sheet, then transfer to airtight containers. Freeze up to 4 weeks. To serve: bake frozen turnovers at 400° until golden brown.

Filling:

½	pound fresh mushrooms chopped very fine	¼	teaspoon salt
⅓	cup finely chopped onion	¼	teaspoon freshly ground pepper
2	tablespoons unsalted butter	¼	cup dairy sour cream
2	tablespoons flour	1	egg yolk
1	tablespoon dry sherry or vermouth	1	tablespoon water

Sauté mushrooms and onion in butter until juices have evaporated. Sprinkle with flour; stir to mix well. Add sherry, salt and pepper; cook over medium heat, stirring constantly, until mixture is almost dry. Add sour cream and cool. Using just half of the pastry at a time, roll out a little less than ⅛" thick. Cut with 3" fluted round cookie cutter. Put 1 slightly rounded teaspoon of mushroom filling in center of each circle. Fold in half and press edges to seal. Mix egg yolk with water and brush on tops of turnovers. Bake in a pre-heated 400° oven on ungreased cookie sheets until golden brown. Serve warm.

Pastry:

½	cup unsalted butter, softened	2	teaspoons snipped fresh chives
1	(3 ounce) package cream cheese, softened	1½	cups flour
		½	teaspoon salt

Beat butter and cream cheese in bowl until smooth, stir in chives, if used. Add flour and salt; mix to form a stiff dough. Divide in half; refrigerate wrapped in plastic wrap, 30 minutes. Work with only half of the dough at a time, leaving other half in refrigerator.

Yield: 26 to 28

Helpful Hint: *Ever wonder what to do when you do not have fresh onion, etc.?*
1 tablespoon instant minced onion — 1 medium onion
2 tablespoons onion flakes — 1 medium onion
1 tablespoon celery flakes — ¼ cup chopped celery
⅛ teaspoon garlic powder — 1 clove garlic

Escargots Italienne

This is a delicious appetizer not too difficult to fix.

24	canned snails, drained	½	teaspoon dried basil
1	cup dry white wine or vermouth		Salt
			Pepper
6	shallots, minced	¼	cup butter (½ stick)
3	cloves garlic, minced		French bread, sliced, toasted and buttered
6	tablespoons (¾ stick) butter		Minced parsley for garnish
4	tomatoes, peeled seeded and chopped		

In a non-aluminum saucepan, reduce the wine over high heat to ⅔ cup. Add the snails and simmer them, covered, for 8 minutes. Drain the snails, reserving the wine and transfer them to a bowl. In a large skillet, sauté the shallots and garlic in the 6 tablespoons butter, for 2 minutes. Add the tomatoes, basil, salt and pepper to taste and simmer the mixture until almost all the liquid has evaporated. Add the reserved wine and boil the sauce over moderate heat, stirring constantly, for 5 minutes. Reduce heat to very low and keep sauce warm. In a skillet, sauté the snails in the ¼ cup butter for 3 minutes. Add the snails to sauce along with juices. To serve: Place a slice of French bread on each of 6 plates and divide the snails on them. Garnish with parsley.

Yield: 6 first course servings

The sauce can be made ahead and the snails pre-cooked and both refrigerated. To serve, sauté the snails, heat the sauce, combine and serve.

Raspberry Brie in Rye

2	(7″) round loaves rye bread	½	cup seedless raspberry jam
1	(15-ounce) round Brie	⅓	cup sliced almonds

Using a serrated knife, slice off about ½″ from top of bread loaf. Reserve top. Place Brie on top of 1 loaf of the bread and trace around outer edge of cheese with knife. Remove cheese. Using traced mark as guide, cut bread vertically 2″ deep; remove bread, leaving a 5″ x 2″ cavity. Cut bread top, trimmings and remaining loaf of bread into 1″ or 2″ cubes; set aside. Remove rind from top of cheese and place cheese in bread cavity; spread with jam and sprinkle with almonds. Bake at 325° for 15 or 20 minutes or just until soft. Serve immediately with bread cubes.

Yield: 6 servings

Whole wheat round bread may be substituted if the rye is not available. Strawberry jam may be substituted, if desired.

Strawberry Brie

1	(12 ounce) wedge of Brie cheese	1½	teaspoons brown sugar, packed
2	tablespoons strawberry jam	3	tablespoons sliced almonds
1	tablespoon Chambord liqueur	1	tablespoon honey

Remove rind from the top of Brie, then slice horizontally in half. Mix jam and liqueur. Spread the jam mixture over bottom half. Top with remaining half of Brie. Mix almonds and honey and spread over, then sprinkle with brown sugar. Bake in a 325° oven about 15 minutes or just until softened.

Yield: Scant 2 cups

Zucchini Carrot Spread

This is a nutrition-packed spread. I like to serve it on whole wheat crackers.

1	(8 ounce) container whipped cream cheese	1	tablespoon chopped parsley
½	cup grated carrot	¼	teaspoon garlic salt
½	cup grated zucchini		Dash white pepper

Combine all ingredients; chill at least 1 hour. Serve on melba toast, whole wheat crackers or in celery stalks.

Yield: 1½ cups

Mushroom Cream Cheese Dip

I concocted this for unexpected guests when I had some mushrooms left over from beef Wellington.

8	ounces cream cheese, room temperature	1	teaspoon minced garlic
6	ounces fresh mushrooms, minced	2	tablespoons dry sherry or vermouth
2	tablespoons olive oil	¼	teaspoon salt
1	teaspoon finely minced onion	½	teaspoon dried thyme leaves, crushed

Sauté onion and garlic in olive oil until limp. Add mushrooms and simmer 1 or 2 minutes, or until tender. Remove from heat and add sherry, salt and thyme. Let cool slightly, then mix with cream cheese. If mixture is too heavy for a dip, add a little cream or sour cream to right consistency, or serve with a butter knife for spreading.

Yield: About 2 cups

Mascarpone cheese may be used instead of the cream cheese, if desired. This also makes a delicious sandwich.

Scallops with Vermouth

This is a deliciously rich appetizer. An intermezzo would be in order before rest of menu.

2¼ pounds bay scallops	1 cup whipping cream
¼ cup butter, melted	1 teaspoon lemon juice
1¼ cups dry vermouth	¼ teaspoon salt
Pinch saffron (optional)	¼ teaspoon white pepper

Wash scallops well to remove any sand. Drain on paper towels, then cook with butter in a large skillet over medium heat, stirring constantly, about 3 minutes or until just opaque. Drain and set aside. Discard drippings; set aside. Add vermouth and saffron to skillet. Bring to a boil over medium heat, and cook until mixture is reduced by half. Add whipping cream and next 3 ingredients. Cook over medium low heat until mixture thickens, stirring occasionally. Add scallops and cook over low heat just until heated. Serve from a chafing dish with cocktails or make a first course by placing in ramekins or scallop shells; top with grated Parmesan and warm until bubbly in the oven.

Yield: 10 to 12 appetizer servings

Shrimp Dill Pâté

½ cup cold tomato juice	2 tablespoons lemon juice
2 envelopes (2 tablespoons) unflavored gelatin	½ teaspoon salt
1 cup boiling tomato juice	½ teaspoon Worcestershire sauce
2 cups dairy sour cream	1 cup cooked shrimp or equivalent canned shrimp
1 tablespoon dried dillweed	

Add cold tomato juice to gelatin in blender container; cover and blend at low speed until gelatin is softened. Add boiling tomato juice; run blender on low until gelatin is dissolved. If gelatin granules cling to side of container, stop blender and use spatula to push into liquid. Add remaining ingredients except shrimp and blend on high. Continue blending until smooth. Stop blender and add shrimp. Turn blender on and off until shrimp are chopped. Pour into a 5 cup mold or bowl that has been lightly rubbed with mayonnaise. Chill until firm, about 3 hours. Unmold and serve as a spread for melba toast or crackers.

Yield: 5 cup mold

Tortillas Au Gratin

This may be fixed a little ahead of time, refrigerated, then baked before serving.

8 ounces Monterey Jack cheese, grated	8 (8-inch) flour tortillas
8 ounces Cheddar cheese, grated	2 tablespoons butter or margarine, melted
½ cup sliced green onions	Sour cream
4 ounce can chopped green chilies, drained	Picante sauce

Combine cheeses, set aside. Combine onion and green chilies and set aside. Layer 4 tortillas into each of two 8″ round cake pans. Sprinkle ⅔ cup of cheese mixture and 2 heaping tablespoons onion-chilie mixture between each tortilla. Brush top tortilla in each stack with melted butter. Bake at 400° for 20 minutes or until cheese melts and tops of tortillas are brown. Cool 5 minutes, then turn out on plates and cut into wedges. Serve immediately with sour cream and picante sauce.

Yield: 12 to 14 servings

Spicy Pecans

These are handy to keep on hand as they keep well in metal containers. They are also delicious to serve with cocktails.

4 cups (1 pound) pecan halves	3 tablespoons sugar
3 tablespoons Kahlúa	½ teaspoon salt
1 tablespoon vegetable oil	⅛ teaspoon red pepper
¼ cup chili powder	

Pre-heat oven to 300°. Combine nuts, liqueur and oil in large bowl; toss to combine. Add chili powder, sugar, salt and red pepper; toss until well coated. Spread nuts in jelly roll pan and bake 25 minutes, stirring frequently. Remove from pan and loosen nuts from pan with metal spatula. Cool in pan on wire rack. Serve to guests or pack in decorative boxes for friends.

Yield: 4 cups

Breads

Martha and her brother, Robert Robinson

Baking Powder Biscuits

2	cups flour, sifted before measuring	½	teaspoon salt
4	teaspoons baking powder	½	cup shortening
		¾	cup milk, about

Pre-heat oven to 450°. Sift flour with baking powder and salt into medium bowl. Cut shortening into flour mixture with pastry blender or 2 knives until mixture resembles coarse cornmeal. Make a well in the center. Pour in ⅔ cup of milk all at once. Stir quickly around the bowl with a fork. If mixture seems too dry, add a little more milk, to form a dough just moist enough (but not wet) to leave sides of bowl and form a ball. Turn out dough onto lightly floured board to knead. Gently pick up dough from side away from you; fold over toward you; press out lightly with palm of hand. Give the dough a quarter turn. Repeat ten times. Gently roll out dough, from center, to ½" thickness. With floured 2½" biscuit cutter, cut straight down into dough, being careful not to twist cutter. Place on ungreased cookie sheet; bake 12 to 15 minutes in a 425° oven.

Yield: 8 (2½") biscuits

Banana Bread

This recipe uses self-rising flour which simplifies the mixing somewhat, and makes a delicious, tender bread.

¾	cup sugar	1	teaspoon baking soda
½	cup shortening	1¾	cups self-rising flour
2	large eggs	3	tablespoons sour cream
2	very ripe medium bananas, sliced	1	teaspoon vanilla

Mix self-rising flour and soda. Set aside. Cream sugar, shortening and eggs in electric mixer until fluffy. Add ½ cup of the flour, then sliced bananas, one at a time, beating well after each addition. Then add the remaining flour alternately with the sour cream. Beat in the vanilla. Bake in a greased and floured loaf pan in a 350° oven about 45 to 50 minutes or until a wood pick inserted in the center comes out dry. Let cool before cutting.

Yield: 1 large loaf

Boston Brown Bread Muffins

These muffins are steamed, not baked. They are similar to Boston brown bread, non-sweet, and not as light as other muffins. Notice that there are no eggs in this recipe which is why they do not rise as much, and cups need to be filled almost to the top.

½	cup flour	½	teaspoon allspice
½	cup whole wheat flour	1	cup buttermilk
½	cup yellow cornmeal	½	cup molasses
1	teaspoon baking soda	½	cup dark raisins
½	teaspoon salt	½	cup chopped nuts (optional)

Grease twelve 2½" muffin-pan cups. In large bowl, combine flours, cornmeal, baking soda, salt and allspice; stir in buttermilk and molasses, blending well. Stir in raisins and nuts. Spoon batter into muffin-pan cups, filling each almost to the top; cover pan tightly with foil. Place muffin-pan in 14" x 9" roasting pan; place roasting pan over burner on top of the stove. Carefully pour boiling water to come halfway up sides of muffin-pan cups. Cover roasting pan tightly with additional foil. Steam over low heat about 45 minutes or until pick inserted in center comes out clean. Remove pan from water bath; cool 5 minutes. Serve warm or at room temperature.

Yield: 12 muffins

These muffins are cooked on top of the stove, which releases oven space.

Broccoli Cornbread

This is Evelyn Sterling's recipe. It is easy to prepare and delicious!

2	packages Jiffy cornbread mix	1	(10 ounce) package frozen
4	eggs		chopped broccoli, thawed and
1	stick margarine, melted		squeezed dry, but not cooked
1	medium onion, minced	8	ounces low fat cottage cheese

Mix all ingredients lightly with a fork just until dry ingredients disappear. Bake in a greased 9" x 13" baking pan at 400° about 25 minutes or until wooden pick inserted in the center comes out clean. Leftovers can be frozen and heated in the microwave.

Yield: 9" x 13" pan

Buttermilk Biscuits

½ cup shortening   ¾ cup buttermilk
2 cups self-rising flour

Cut shortening into flour with pastry blender, two knives or the tips of your fingers until mixture is crumbly. Add buttermilk, stirring with a fork until dry ingredients are moistened. If mixture seems dry, add a little more buttermilk to form a dough just moist enough (but not wet) to leave the sides of the bowl and form a ball. Turn dough out on lightly floured board to knead. Pick up dough from side away from you; fold over toward you; press out lightly with palm of hand. Give the dough a quarter turn. Repeat 6 or 7 times. Gently roll out dough, from center (rolling back and forth toughens biscuits), to ½" thickness. Cut with floured cutter making sure you do not twist as you cut. Place on an ungreased baking sheet, close together if you wish a higher biscuit; apart if you like a crustier one. Bake in a pre-heated 425° oven about 12 to 15 minutes.

Yield: 12 biscuits

Carrot Bread

3 cups flour   3 eggs, beaten
¾ teaspoon salt   1 cup vegetable oil
1 teaspoon baking powder   2 cups grated carrots
1 teaspoon baking soda   1 (8 ounce) can crushed
2 cups sugar   pineapple, drained
1 teaspoon ground cinnamon   1 teaspoon vanilla
1 cup chopped walnuts or
   pecans

Combine first 6 ingredients; stir in nuts of your choice. Combine remaining ingredients; add to flour mixture, stirring just until dry ingredients are moistened. Spoon batter into 2 greased and floured 8½" x 4½" x 3" loaf pans. Bake at 350° about an hour or until done in center when tested with a toothpick. Cool slightly, then remove from pans to a wire rack. This bread slices better the next day.

Yield: 2 loaves

Save and freeze juice from pineapple. It can be used the same as lemon juice to keep sliced peaches and apples from turning dark.

Cheese Muffins

For a brunch or coffee, serve mini-muffins in several varieties. Omit the cheese and cayenne. Instead add ½ cup crumbled crisp-cooked bacon or add 1 tablespoon grated orange rind and ½ cup white raisins to the dry ingredients, then continue recipe.

2	cups flour, sifted before measuring	¼	teaspoon cayenne pepper
¼	cup sugar	1	cup milk
3	teaspoons baking powder	⅓	cup vegetable oil (reduce to ¼ cup if adding bacon)
½	teaspoon salt	1	egg
½	cup grated sharp cheese		

Pre-heat oven to 400°. Grease bottoms of 14 (2½″) muffin cups. Sift flour again with sugar, baking powder and salt into large bowl. Stir in cheese and cayenne pepper. Make a well in the center, then add milk, oil, and egg in that order. Mix lightly with a fork until dry ingredients are moistened. Do not overmix. Quickly dip batter into muffin cups, filling slightly more than half full. Bake 20 to 25 minutes or until cake tester comes out clean when inserted in center. Serve hot. If using mini-muffin tins, bake only until they test done in center, about 10 minutes.

Yield: 14 muffins

Another variation would be dropping ½ a rounded teaspoonful of preserves of your choice on the uncooked batter. The muffin will rise, but not entirely cover the preserves, making an attractive service; particularly if you use several kinds of preserves.

Chocolate Chip Muffins

These are good enough to be eaten for dessert. They would also be delicious for a coffee, brunch, luncheon or a snack anytime.

2	cups flour	⅓	cup butter or margarine (⅔ stick), melted
1	tablespoon baking powder	½	cup milk
½	teaspoon salt	½	cup sour cream
⅓	cup sugar	1	cup chocolate chips
⅓	cup brown sugar, packed	½	cup chopped nuts
1	egg, beaten		

Pre-heat oven to 375°. Sift flour, baking powder, salt and sugars together into a mixing bowl. Add the butter, milk, egg, and sour cream. Mix gently with a fork until ingredients are just mixed. Fold in chocolate chips and nuts. Spoon into greased muffin tins and bake about 20 to 25 minutes or until firm in center when pressed with your finger.

Yield: 18 muffins

Dried Cherry Muffins

½	cup unsalted butter, softened	1	teaspoon baking soda
¾	cup sugar	½	teaspoon salt
2	large eggs	1	cup buttermilk
1	tablespoon frozen orange	⅔	cup chopped dried cherries
	juice, undiluted	½	cup chopped pecans
2	cups flour		

Beat butter in electric mixer until creamy; gradually add sugar and beat until fluffy. Add eggs, one at a time, beating after each addition. Add orange juice. Sift flour, soda and salt together and add to butter mixture alternately with buttermilk, beginning and ending with flour mixture. Mix at medium speed until just blended after each addition. Fold in cherries and pecans. Spoon into greased or sprayed muffin pans, filling ¾ full. Bake in a pre-heated 400° oven about 20 minutes or until firm when pressed in the middle with your finger. Remove from pans while hot and serve.

Yield: 12 muffins

Dried cranberries may be substituted.

Chocolate Chip Coffee Cake

One of my great grandchildren's favorites.

2	cups flour	¾	cup milk
1½	cups sugar	½	teaspoon vanilla
½	cup margarine, room	½	teaspoon almond extract
	temperature	6	ounces (1 cup) mini semi-sweet
3	teaspoons baking powder		chocolate morsels
2	eggs		Powdered sugar

Combine first 4 ingredients in mixing bowl; mix at low speed until mixture is fine crumbs. Remove 1 cup of crumb mixture and set aside. Add eggs, milk, almond and vanilla extracts to remaining crumb mixture; mix just until blended. Fold in chocolate morsels. Pour batter into a greased 11"x 7"x 1½" pan. Sprinkle with reserved crumb mixture. Bake in a pre-heated 350° oven about 35 minutes or until cake tests done when pick is inserted in center. Cool slightly, then dust with powdered sugar. If you are freezing cake, remove waxed paper, then wrap in foil.

Yield: 11 " x 7 " x 1½ " pan

If you wish to freeze this cake, line bottom of pan with waxed paper. Bake, cool, then remove from pan and wrap with foil. To heat, place foil package on cookie sheet and heat in 300° oven about 20 minutes or until warm. Dust with powdered sugar.

Creamed Corn Muffins

This is an updated recipe from Revolutionary days.

1¼	cups flour	1	cup milk
1	cup cornmeal	¼	cup vegetable oil
1	tablespoon baking powder	2	eggs, lightly beaten
1	teaspoon salt	1	(16½ ounce) can creamed corn
¼	cup sugar		

Pre-heat oven to 400°. Lightly coat sixteen 2½" muffin pan cups with non-stick vegetable spray. Mix together flour, cornmeal, baking powder, salt and sugar in a large bowl. Add milk, oil and eggs. Mix with a fork until all ingredients are moistened. Stir in creamed corn. Spoon batter into prepared cups, filling almost to the brim. Bake in a 375° oven for 25 minutes or until puffed and pick inserted in the center comes out clean. Cool for 10 minutes before taking out of the pan.

Yield: 16 muffins

Cornmeal Pancakes, Johnson

These are exceptionally light pancakes. The trick is not to overmix. This recipe was from my mother-in-law who was a very good cook. She served them with creamed salt pork. They were one of my husband's favorite breakfast dishes.

2	cups self-rising flour	2	eggs, beaten
½	cup cornmeal	3	cups buttermilk
2	teaspoons baking soda	¼	cup vegetable oil

Combine flour, cornmeal and soda in a large bowl; make a well in center of mixture. Combine eggs, buttermilk and oil; add to dry ingredients, stirring with a fork until dry ingredients disappear. Scrape sides and bottom of bowl with a rubber spatula to be sure ingredients are mixed. For each pancake, ladle ¼ cup batter onto hot lightly greased griddle. Turn pancakes when tops are bubbly and cook until bottoms are lightly brown. Serve with syrup or honey butter.

Honey Butter:

1	cup butter or margarine, softened	3	tablespoons honey
		¼	teaspoon cinnamon

Beat butter or margarine until creamy. Add honey and cinnamon. Refrigerate. Makes 1 cup.

Yield: 24 (4") pancakes

If you do not have self-rising flour, simply add 1½ teaspoons baking powder and ½ teaspoon salt to each cup of regular flour.

Dried Cherry Scones

¾ cup dried cherries	½ cup butter or margarine, room
1 cup boiling water	temperature
3 cups flour	1 egg, separated
3 tablespoons sugar	½ cup sour cream
1 tablespoon baking powder	¾ cup half-and-half
½ teaspoon salt	1 teaspoon almond extract
½ teaspoon cream of tartar	

Soak cherries in the boiling water for 10 minutes, drain. In large bowl, combine flour, sugar, baking powder, salt and cream of tartar. Cut in butter or margarine to make coarse crumbs. Set aside. In small bowl, combine egg yolk, sour cream, half-and-half and extract. Add to flour mixture along with cherries. Stir with a fork until a dough is formed. Turn out on a floured board and knead gently with tips of your fingers 5 or 6 times. Divide dough in half and shape into 2 balls. Roll each ball into a circle a half inch thick. Cut into 6 wedges. Repeat with second ball. Place on greased cookie sheet. Brush with slightly beaten egg white, then sprinkle with sugar. Bake in a 400° oven 15 to 20 minutes. Serve warm.

Yield: 12 scones

Chopped dried apricots or peaches may be used if dried cherries are not available.

Dried Cherry Sour Cream Muffins

1 cup sour cream	1½ cups flour
¼ cup frozen orange juice,	2 teaspoons baking powder
undiluted and thawed	1 teaspoon baking soda
1 large egg	½ teaspoon salt
⅓ cup brown sugar, packed	½ teaspoon almond extract
¼ cup granulated sugar	1 cup (about 4 ounces) dried tart
½ stick butter, melted and cooled	cherries, chopped

In a small bowl, whisk together the sour cream, orange juice, egg, sugars, almond extract and butter until well mixed. In a second bowl, sift the flour, baking powder, soda, and salt. Add the sour cream mixture and stir with a fork until just combined. Fold in cherries and spoon batter into vegetable-sprayed muffin tins. Bake on the middle shelf of a pre-heated 400° oven about 15 to 20 minutes or until a tester placed in center comes out clean. Serve hot.

Yield: 12 muffins

German Pancake, Elenora

Actually, this rich pancake looks much like a soufflé and behaves like one. So, as soon as it is done, rush the pancake to the table and serve.

4	tablespoons (½ stick) butter	½	teaspoon salt
½	cup flour	4	eggs
½	cup evaporated milk (not condensed milk)		

Pre-heat oven to 400°. Melt butter in 10″ oven-proof skillet. Combine flour, milk and salt in mixing bowl; add eggs, one at a time, whipping after each addition. Pour egg mixture into skillet and cook over medium heat until bottom is golden brown. Loosen from bottom of pan. Make a criss-cross slash with knife through pancake and place in oven. Bake until puffed and golden brown, 12 to 15 minutes. Serve with lemon slices, confectioner's sugar and syrup or with sour cream and fresh fruit.

Yield: 2 generous servings

This pancake is delicious with the addition of fresh strawberries or peaches on top. The eggs are the leavening.

Green Chilie-Cheese Cornbread

This goes well with a Mexican supper.

1	cup flour	1	(8½ ounce) can cream-style corn
1	cup cornmeal		
4	teaspoons baking powder	1	(4 ounce) can chopped green chilies, drained
¼	teaspoon salt		
4	ounces sharp Cheddar cheese, grated	⅓	cup milk
		⅓	cup vegetable oil
		2	large eggs

In a medium bowl, stir together flour, cornmeal, baking powder and salt. Add milk, oil and eggs. Beat with a fork until egg yolks and whites are mixed. Then add cheese, corn and chilies. Mix with a spoon just until ingredients are mixed. Do not overmix. Turn into a greased 9″ square pan and bake in a pre-heated 400° oven about 30 to 35 minutes or until done in center. Cut into squares and serve hot.

Yield: 9 servings

Gingerbread Scones with Lemon Sauce

These can be served warm or cold. I like them warm.

6	tablespoons sugar	¼	teaspoon ground cloves
2	cups flour, divided	¾	stick margarine
¾	cup oats, old-fashioned or quick	⅓	cup milk
		⅓	cup raisins or currants
4	teaspoons baking powder	2	eggs, slightly beaten
1	teaspoon ginger	¼	cup molasses
1	teaspoon cinnamon		

Pre-heat oven to 425°. In a large bowl, combine sugar, 1¾ cups of the flour, oats, baking powder, ginger, cinnamon and cloves. Cut in the margarine with a pastry cutter or fork until crumbly. In a medium bowl, combine milk, currants or raisins, molasses and eggs. Mix well. Add milk mixture to flour mixture and mix until dry ingredients are moistened. Sprinkle remaining ¼ cup of flour on board. Turn mixture on board and knead gently with fingers 5 or 6 times. Pat dough to a ¾" thickness. Cut into squares or triangles. Lay trimmings on top of each other, press together and roll out to make additional scones. Extra kneading will make scones tough. Place scones on ungreased cookie sheet. Bake 9 to 10 minutes or until light brown. Serve with lemon sauce.

Lemon Sauce:

¾	cup ricotta cheese, room temperature	2	tablespoons frozen lemonade concentrate, thawed
		½	cup lemon yogurt (optional)

While scones are baking, place ricotta cheese and lemonade concentrate in blender or food processor. Blend on high speed or process until smooth. Add the lemon yogurt only if you wish a thinner sauce.

Yield: 12 to 20 scones

Oil the measuring cup you are using for the molasses and it will come out readily.

Hazelnut Scones with Lemon Curd

I love hazelnuts. They are plentiful in Greece and are sold on street corners, toasted, in little bags. I ate my fill while there. Perhaps that is why hazelnut-flavored Frangelico is one of my favorite liqueurs.

2	cups flour	¾	cup chopped, blanched hazelnuts
2	teaspoons baking powder		
¼	teaspoon salt	2	large eggs, beaten
½	cup sugar	½	cup whipping cream
⅓	cup butter	1½	tablespoons Frangelico

Combine first 4 ingredients in a bowl; cut in butter with a pastry blender or the tips of your fingers until mixture is crumbly. Add hazelnuts; make a well in the center and set aside. Combine eggs, whipping cream and liqueur, then add to dry ingredients, mixing just until dry ingredients are moistened. Roll or pat dough to ½ inch thickness on floured board. Cut in desired shapes, squares or triangles. Place on parchment or foil-lined cookie sheets about 1″ apart. Pile any scraps of dough on top of each other and lightly press together. Cut out additional scones. Bake on middle shelf of a pre-heated 400° oven for 15 to 20 minutes or until golden brown. Cool and serve with lemon curd.

Lemon Curd:

5	large eggs	½	cup lemon juice
1½	cups sugar	½	cup butter
1	tablespoon grated lemon rind		

Melt butter in heavy saucepan, (not aluminum), add lemon juice, rind and sugar. Cook, over medium-low heat, stirring constantly, until sugar is dissolved. Add a little of the hot mixture to eggs. Mix, then add to rest of sugar mixture. Cook, stirring constantly, until thick. Cool and serve with scones. Yield: 2½ cups. Lemon curd keeps beautifully in the refrigerator. Use it also on pound cake, waffles or whatever suits your fancy.

Yield: 12 to 18 scones

To toast and skin hazelnuts, place in one layer in a baking pan. Bake in a 350° oven for 10 to 15 minutes, or until the skins blister. Wrap in a kitchen towel and let them steam for 2 minutes. Rub the nuts with the towel to remove the skins.

Holiday Cranberry Muffins

I like to make these for Thanksgiving or Christmas breakfast.

4	tablespoons butter, melted and cooled	¾	cup sugar
1	cup firm unblemished cranberries, washed and patted dry	4	teaspoons double-acting baking powder
		½	teaspoon salt
2¾	cups flour	1	cup milk
		1	egg, slightly beaten

Pre-heat oven to 400°. Butter or spray a 12-cup muffin tin (each cup should be about 2½" across at the top). Either chop the cranberries coarsely or chop in a food processor and set aside. Combine the flour, sugar, baking powder and salt and sift into mixing bowl. Mix in milk at low speed, then stir in the egg and melted butter. Fold in the cranberries by hand and stir until well combined. Spoon about ⅓ cup of the batter into muffin cups, filling them ⅔ full. Bake on middle shelf of 375° about 30 minutes or until firm when pressed in center with your finger. Serve warm.

Yield: 12 muffins

The batter can be made the night before and refrigerated, covered.

Kahlúa Date-Nut Bread

This bread makes delicious sandwiches when filled with softened cream cheese.

1	cup pitted dates, chopped	1	large egg, beaten
½	cup Kahlúa	2	cups flour
½	cup warm water	1	teaspoon salt
1	teaspoon grated orange rind	1	teaspoon soda
⅔	cup firmly packed brown sugar	⅔	cup chopped pecans or walnuts
2	tablespoons shortening		

Combine dates, Kahlúa, water and orange rind and set aside. Cream sugar and shortening until light and fluffy; add egg and mix well. Sift flour, salt and soda; add to creamed mixture alternately with date mixture. Stir in pecans. Pour into a greased and floured 9"x 5"x 3"loaf pan. Bake at 350° for 1 hour or until bread tests done in middle. Remove from pan and let cool on rack before cutting.

Yield: 1 loaf

Kona Banana Bread

This has been a family favorite for four generations. It is almost more a cake than a bread. It is delicious for breakfast, lunch or dinner.

1	cup shortening	2½	cups flour
2	cups sugar	1½	teaspoons baking soda
4	eggs	1	teaspoon salt
1½	cups mashed ripe bananas		

Cream shortening and sugar in mixer bowl. Add eggs, one at a time, beating after each addition. Stir in bananas. Sift dry ingredients together and add to banana mixture. Mix only until blended. Pour into a greased 13" x 9" x 2" baking pan. Bake at 350° for 30 minutes or until pick inserted in center comes out clean. Cut into squares and serve hot with plenty of butter.

Yield: 12 to 15 servings

Mammy's Cornbread

This recipe dates back over fifty years and was in a children's cookbook. It is a family standby.

¼	cup sugar	1	cup flour
2	tablespoons butter, softened	¼	teaspoon salt
1	egg	¾	cup cornmeal
1	cup milk	4	teaspoons baking powder

Cream butter and sugar. Add egg and milk. Sift dry ingredients and add. Mix just until moistened. Do not beat in mixer. Place in a greased 9" pie tin or cake pan. Bake in a 350° oven about 45 minutes or until it tests done in middle. Cut into 8 pieces.

Yield: 8 servings

Scotch Oatmeal Muffins

This is my Aunt Carrie's recipe.

1	cup quick oats	½	teaspoon soda
1	cup buttermilk	1	egg, slightly beaten
1	cup flour	⅓	cup brown sugar, packed
1½	teaspoons baking powder	⅓	cup vegetable oil
½	teaspoon salt		

Soak oats in buttermilk for 15 minutes or longer. Sift together flour, baking powder, salt and soda; stir into oat mixture. Add egg, brown sugar and oil; stir with a fork until just blended. Fill greased muffin tins ⅔ full. Bake at 400° for 20 to 25 minutes. Serve hot with plenty of butter.

Yield: 12 large muffins

Mexican Hushpuppies

These can accompany a Mexican dinner or can serve as appetizers.

¾	cup yellow cornmeal	1	(4 ounce) can chopped green
½	cup flour		chilies, drained
2	teaspoons baking powder	1	tablespoon minced onion
¼	teaspoon salt	1	egg
⅛	teaspoon red pepper	½	cup milk
1	cup (4 ounces) grated		Vegetable oil
	Monterey Jack cheese		

Combine first 8 ingredients in a large bowl; make a well in center of mixture. Beat egg and milk together and add to dry ingredients, stirring just until moistened. Pour oil to a depth of 3" into a Dutch oven; heat to 375°. Carefully drop batter by rounded tablespoonfuls into hot oil. Fry a few at a time 3 to 4 minutes or until golden brown, turning once. Drain on paper towels or brown paper. Serve immediately.

Yield: About 2 dozen

Pecan Muffins

These muffins have a surprise in the middle — a cube of cream cheese.

2	cups flour	1	cup sour cream
1	tablespoon baking powder	⅓	cup butter, melted
½	teaspoon salt	1	(3 ounce) package cream
½	teaspoon baking soda		cheese, cut into 12 cubes
⅔	cup sugar	1	cup chopped pecans
1	egg, beaten		

Sift flour, baking powder, soda, salt and sugar into mixing bowl. Add sour cream, the beaten egg and melted butter. Add chopped pecans. Stir with a fork until just combined. Spoon into greased muffin cups, filling only ⅓ full. Place a cube of cream cheese in center, then add the rest of the batter, filling ⅔ full. Bake in a pre-heated 350° oven about 20 to 25 minutes or until muffins are firm in the center when lightly pressed with a finger.

Yield: 12 muffins

Helpful Hint: 8 ounces cream cheese — 1 cup
3 ounces cream cheese — 6 tablespoons

Quick Molasses Brown Bread

This is a heavy, non-sweet bread, similar to steamed brown bread only much easier and quicker. Delicious served with baked beans.

1	cup flour	1	egg
1¼	teaspoons soda	1	cup buttermilk
¾	teaspoon salt	½	cup molasses
¾	cup dry bread crumbs	½	cup dark raisins
3	tablespoons soft margarine		

Sift flour, soda and salt together. Add bread crumbs and mix well. Cut in margarine. Beat egg and combine with buttermilk, molasses and raisins. Add to dry ingredients and stir until just mixed. Pour into a well greased, 2 quart ring mold or 8"tube pan. Bake at 400° for about 30 to 35 minutes or until toothpick inserted in center comes out clean.

Yield: 8" tube pan or ring mold

Scotch Sweet Walnut Scones

3½	cups flour	4	eggs
5	teaspoons baking powder	½	cup milk
1	teaspoon salt	1	tablespoon maple syrup
2	tablespoons sugar	½	cup walnuts, finely chopped
¾	cup (1½ sticks) softened butter or margarine	1	teaspoon sugar

Pre-heat oven to 425°. Grease 2 large cookie sheets. In medium bowl with fork, mix flour, baking powder, salt and 2 tablespoons sugar. Cut butter in until mixture resembles coarse crumbs. In a small bowl with fork, beat eggs. Reserve 2 tablespoons for brushing on scones. Stir milk and maple syrup into remaining beaten eggs. Stir milk mixture into flour mixture just until ingredients are moistened. Turn out on floured board and lightly roll into a 15"x 9"rectangle. With knife or pastry cutter, cut dough in 3"squares; cut each square into a triangle. Place 1"apart on cookie sheets. In cup, stir walnuts with 1 tablespoon sugar. With pastry brush, brush tops of scones with reserved egg; sprinkle with walnuts. Bake scones in a 400° oven for 10 to 15 minutes or until golden. Cool scones and wrap in foil. Just before serving, heat foil-wrapped scones in 425° oven about 10 minutes to heat through.

Yield: 30 scones

These scones can be frozen wrapped in foil. Reheat in a 425° oven in the foil for 15 minutes.

Skillet Cornbread

I bake this in a sectioned iron skillet so each piece has a crust. Serving from the skillet is a great way to keep it piping hot.

1	cup yellow cornmeal	1	cup buttermilk
½	cup flour	½	cup whole milk
½	teaspoon salt	1	large egg
½	teaspoon baking soda	½	cup oil
2	teaspoons baking powder		

Pre-heat oven to 450°. Grease an 8″iron skillet or an 8″square or round cake pan with either bacon grease or shortening. Heat in oven until piping hot. Combine dry ingredients; mix well, then add buttermilk, milk, egg and oil. Mix with a fork only until dry ingredients disappear. Pour batter into hot pan and bake about 20 minutes or until golden brown. Cut into squares if in cake pan, into wedges if baked in skillet.

Yield: 6 servings

Super Popovers

Popovers are a versatile bread. They can be split and spread with mustard, butter or mayonnaise then filled with a slice of cheese and a rolled up slice of ham. They can also be filled with creamed chicken for a luncheon entrée.

6	eggs	2	cups flour
2	cups whole milk	¾	teaspoon salt
6	tablespoons butter, melted		

Break eggs into mixer bowl; beat until frothy. Beat in milk and butter, then slowly add flour and salt. Batter should be light but not foamy. If it becomes lumpy, strain it. If popovers are to be baked immediately, pre-heat oven to 400°. Generously oil custard cups (6 or 4 ounce size) or popover pans or even oven-proof coffee cups, filling each to within ½″ of the top. Arrange individual cups on cookie sheet for easier handling. Bake until very dark brown and well-done, about 1 hour for 6 ounce cups, 45 minutes for 4 ounce cups. When done, cut 2 small slits in the top of each to release steam, then bake another 5 minutes. Remove from oven. Release sides and edges from cups with a small knife and remove popovers. Serve hot, but do not cover them or they will become soggy. Leftover popovers can be reheated in a moderate oven.

Yield: 8 to 10 popovers

Batter may be made ahead and stored in a covered container in the refrigerator. Stir with a long-handled spoon before pouring into custard cups or popover pans. Half the recipe can be made for 4 or 5 popovers.

Sour Cream Biscuits

This recipe makes a delicious rich, tender biscuit.

2	cups flour, sifted before measuring	1	teaspoon sugar
3	teaspoons baking powder	½	cup shortening
½	teaspoon soda	½	teaspoon salt
		1	cup dairy sour cream

Pre-heat oven to 425°. Sift flour with rest of dry ingredients into a medium bowl. Cut in shortening until mixture resembles cornmeal. Add sour cream, stirring with a fork only until mixture is moistened. Turn dough out on floured board. Knead about 9 times, to form a soft, smooth dough. Gently roll out dough, from center, to ¾" thickness. With floured 2½" biscuit cutter, cut straight down into dough, being careful not to twist cutter. Place on ungreased cookie sheet; bake 10 to 12 minutes in a 400° oven. Serve hot.

Yield: 8 (2½") biscuits

Wild Rice Pancakes

For a gourmet breakfast, try these pancakes with blueberry syrup, or pure maple syrup and melted butter. Rice can be cooked the night before and refrigerated.

¼	cup wild rice	2	tablespoons sugar
½	teaspoon salt	3	teaspoons baking powder
1½	cups water	1	teaspoon baking soda
2	eggs	½	teaspoon salt
2	cups buttermilk	4	tablespoons butter, melted
2	cups flour		

Follow the quick-soak method to prepare ¼ cup wild rice for cooking. Cook wild rice in boiling, salted water until soft and partially puffed. Sift together the flour, sugar, baking powder, soda and salt into mixing bowl. Beat the eggs, buttermilk and melted butter together. Make a well in flour mixture, add the egg mixture and mix with a fork until dry ingredients disappear. Gently fold in rice. Drop by ¼ cup onto a hot lightly greased griddle. Turn only once. Do not overmix these pancakes.

Yield: 16 to 18 pancakes

Whole Wheat Muffins

This is a tender, delicious muffin.

1½ cups whole wheat flour
½ cup unbleached flour, sifted
before measuring
4 teaspoons baking powder
½ teaspoon salt

¼ cup brown sugar, packed
1 egg, beaten
1½ cups milk
¼ cup vegetable oil

Combine dry ingredients and mix well. Combine brown sugar, egg, milk and oil. Add to dry ingredients all at one time. Stir quickly with a fork until dry ingredients are just combined. Mixture will be lumpy. Fill greased muffin cups ⅔ full and bake at 425° about 20 to 25 minutes or until muffins are firm when pressed lightly in the center.

Yield: 12 muffins

Sour Milk Muffins

The name muffin means "little muffs" — to warm the fingers. This recipe will come in handy if you want to use up sour milk. Buttermilk may also be used.

2 cups flour, sifted before
measuring
¼ cup sugar (may be increased to
½ cup for sweeter muffin)
2 teaspoons baking powder

½ teaspoon baking soda
½ teaspoon salt
1 cup sour milk or buttermilk
¼ cup oil
1 egg

Sift dry ingredients into a bowl. Add sour milk, oil and egg in that order. Mix with a fork until dry ingredients are moistened. Do not overmix. Fill greased or sprayed muffin cups ⅔ full. Bake in a pre-heated 400° oven about 20 to 25 minutes.

Yield: 12 muffins

Zucchini-Pecan Bread

A delicious nutritious bread.

3	cups flour	2	zucchini (1 pound)
1	teaspoon salt	2	eggs, slightly beaten
2	teaspoons baking powder	1	cup sugar
1	teaspoon baking soda	¾	cup honey
2	teaspoons cinnamon	1	cup vegetable oil
1	cup chopped pecans	2	teaspoons vanilla

Combine first 5 ingredients; stir in pecans. Wash zucchini in salt water to remove grit, then grate enough to make 2 cups. Combine zucchini and remaining ingredients; add to flour mixture, stirring just enough to moisten dry ingredients. Spoon batter into 2 greased and floured 9"x 5"x 3"loaf pans. Bake in pre-heated 350° oven for 45 to 55 minutes or until a wooden pick inserted in the middle comes out clean. Cool in pans 10 minutes; remove from pans and cool completely on wire rack.

Yield: 2 loaves

BREADS / yeast

Refrigerator Rolls

These are potato rolls, but are made with potato flakes. This dough makes delicious cinnamon rolls. Dough will keep in the refrigerator for 3 to 5 days.

⅔	cup shortening	1	package dry yeast
½	cup sugar	½	cup warm water (105°)
2	teaspoons salt	½	teaspoon sugar
⅔	cup potato flakes	2	eggs
½	cup water		6 to 8 cups flour
1	cup milk, scalded		

Sprinkle potato flakes over water in a small bowl and set aside. Place shortening, sugar and salt in mixer bowl. Add hot milk. Mix until shortening is melted. Add potato mixture. Cool to lukewarm. Place warm water and the ½ teaspoon sugar in small bowl, sprinkle yeast over and let set until yeast foams up. Add to mixer bowl, along with eggs and 3 cups flour. Mix at high speed for 5 minutes, then add enough additional flour to make a soft, but not sticky dough. Turn out on floured board and knead until dough is elastic. Cover and let rise in a warm draft-free place until a little more than doubled. Make into whatever shape roll you desire, place on greased cookie sheets and let rise again until a little more than doubled. Bake at 400° until golden brown.

Yield: 40 to 48 rolls

Be sure to use the potato flakes, not potato buds.

Basic White Bread

2	cups milk	½	teaspoon sugar
3	tablespoons sugar	2	packages dry yeast
1	tablespoon salt	6 to 6½ cups bread flour
¼	cup butter or margarine	2	tablespoons melted butter or
¼	cup water (105° to 115°)		margarine

In small saucepan, heat milk just until bubbles form around edge of pan. Add sugar, salt and ¼ cup butter, stirring until butter is melted. Pour into mixer bowl and cool to lukewarm. Place water in a small bowl with the ½ teaspoon sugar, sprinkle yeast over and let dissolve and foam. Add half of the flour to mixing bowl and beat at medium speed 2 minutes. Add dissolved yeast and mix. Gradually add remaining flour to make a soft but not sticky dough. Beat at high speed 3 minutes. Turn dough out on lightly floured board. Cover with a towel and let rest 10 minutes. Knead by folding dough toward you, then pushing down and away from you with heel of hand. Give dough a quarter turn; repeat kneading until dough is smooth and elastic. Place in the same mixing bowl, lightly oiled. Turn over to oil other side. Cover over with a towel and let rise in a warm draft-free place until doubled in bulk. It has risen enough when two fingers poked in dough leave an indentation. Turn dough out onto floured board and let rest 10 minutes. Stretch or roll dough until it is about 27 inches long — 3 times as long as the pan you are going to bake it in. Fold dough into thirds, from opposite direction, pressing with fingers to break any air pockets. Seal edges and ends by pinching together. Roll under palm of hand to smooth loaf. Place, seam side down, in a greased 9" x 5" x 3" loaf pan. Brush top of loaf with melted butter. Cover with a towel; let rise in a warm draft-free place until double. Bake in a pre-heated 400° oven for 40 to 50 minutes or until loaf sounds hollow when rapped with knuckles. Remove from pan immediately and cool on wire rack away from drafts.

Yield: 2 loaves

Amish Friendship Bread

This is a very sweet bread. Like sourdough bread, it is made from a starter. Give a cup of the starter to two friends, keeping 1 cup for yourself. Make bread with remainder of starter. This bread freezes well. Delicious with cream cheese.

Amish Friendship Bread Starter:

2	envelopes dry yeast	2	cups flour
¼	cup warm water (105°)	2	cups milk
1	cup sugar, divided		

Day 1. Sprinkle yeast over warm water in a non-metal bowl. Add 1 tablespoon sugar and let stand until yeast foams up well. Combine rest of sugar, flour and milk in a 4 quart non-metal container. Stir in yeast with a wooden spoon. Cover loosely with a towel and let set in a warm, dry place for 24 hours. Days 2, 3, 4, stir daily with a wooden spoon, keep covered and in a cool place, but do not refrigerate.

Day 5 additions:

½	cup sugar	1	cup milk
1	cup flour		

Mix well and let stand 24 hours. Day 6, 7, 8, 9, stir with a wooden spoon.

Day 10 additions:

½	cup sugar	1	cup milk
1	cup flour		

Stir well and fill three 1 cup containers. Keep one for yourself. Give the other two, with recipe, to friends, then use what is left to make your bread according to directions below. Use your one cup as a starter for more bread.

Bread:

Remains of starter		½	teaspoon salt
1	cup oil	½	teaspoon baking soda
½	cup milk	1	cup chopped nuts (optional)
3	eggs	1	large box instant vanilla pudding
1	teaspoon vanilla		
2	cups flour	1	teaspoon cinnamon and ¼ cup sugar for sprinkling on top of bread
1	cup sugar		
1½	teaspoons baking powder		
2	teaspoons cinnamon		

Continued on next page

Place starter in large bowl, then add next 4 ingredients. Mix thoroughly. In separate bowl mix flour, sugar, baking powder, cinnamon, salt, baking soda, nuts and vanilla pudding. Add dry ingredients to milk mixture and mix thoroughly. Pour into 2 large well-greased loaf pans that have been sprinkled with the mixed sugar and cinnamon. Sprinkle additional cinnamon and sugar on top. Bake in a pre-heated 350° oven for 50 minutes or until bread tests done in center. Let cool 10 minutes then turn out of pan on wire rack to cool completely.

Yield: 2 loaves

Keep your cup of starter alive for future bread making.

Chocolate Butter-Pecan Coffee Cake

This is a variation of the usual cinnamon-sugar coffee cake.

Coffee Cake:
1	recipe Sour Cream Rich Dough (RECIPE IN INDEX)	¼	cup cocoa

Make Sour Cream Rich Dough, adding cocoa with the butter, sour cream, etc. Punch down dough, divide in half. Roll half of dough on lightly floured board into a 12" x 9" rectangle.

Filling:
8	tablespoons sugar	10	tablespoons finely chopped
2	teaspoons ground cinnamon		pecans, divided
4	tablespoons butter, melted and cooled, divided		

Mix sugar and cinnamon. Brush dough with 2 tablespoons melted butter; sprinkle with 4 tablespoons cinnamon-sugar mixture and 3 tablespoons pecans. Roll up dough, jelly roll style, starting at long edge; pinch seam to seal. Transfer to greased cookie sheet, seam-side down. Make a ring, pressing edges together. Using scissors or sharp knife, cut roll at 1½" intervals; twist each section slightly so that cut surface faces up. Repeat steps with remaining half of dough, remaining butter, 4 tablespoons cinnamon-sugar mixture and 3 tablespoons pecans. Let rise, covered, until a little more than doubled.

Glaze:
3	tablespoons light corn syrup	1	tablespoon boiling water

Mix syrup and boiling water; brush lightly over tops of cakes. Sprinkle with rest of cinnamon-sugar and rest of pecans. Bake in a pre-heated 350° oven about 25 to 30 minutes or until cakes sound hollow when tapped. Remove cakes to wire racks and cool completely before serving.

Yield: Two 14" coffee cakes

Chocolate Sticky Buns

Chocolate lovers will love these.

Buns:

1	package dry yeast	½	cup (1 stick) butter or
⅓	cup 105° water		margarine, softened
⅓	cup sugar	¾	cup hot milk
1	teaspoon salt	3½	cups flour
		1	egg

Dissolve yeast in warm water. Combine sugar, salt and butter or margarine in mixing bowl. Add the hot milk and beat until margarine is melted. Cool to lukewarm. Add 1½ cups flour to mixture and beat at medium speed for 3 minutes. Add egg and yeast mixture. Beat at medium speed 3 minutes. Blend remaining 2 cups flour and beat until dough is elastic. Cover with a towel and let rise to double in a draft-free place. When dough has risen, divide in half. Roll each half to a 14" x 9" rectangle. Brush lightly with melted margarine. Sprinkle with half the filling. Roll up as for a jelly roll from 9" side. Seal edges firmly. Cut into 9 equal pieces. Place in one of the prepared 9" cake pans. Repeat with remaining dough. Cover and let rise in a warm place until doubled in bulk. Bake at 350° for 35 minutes. Turn out of pan immediately onto serving plate.

Filling:

1	cup sugar	2	teaspoons cinnamon
2	tablespoons cocoa		

Mix all ingredients together for filling and set aside.

Topping:

1	stick butter or margarine	3	tablespoons cocoa
1	cup brown sugar, packed	1	cup coarsely chopped pecans
¼	cup white corn syrup		

Melt butter or margarine in a heavy saucepan; add the brown sugar, corn syrup and cocoa. Bring to a boil and cook for 1 minute. Divide the syrup into two 9" round cake pans and sprinkle pecans on top.

Yield: 18 buns 2 cake pans

Cream Cheese Coffee Cake

The ingredients for Sour Cream Rich Dough cannot be halved. Make the dough, let it rise and use half for this recipe; or double the recipe for the filling and make 2 coffee cakes.

Filling:

2	tablespoons dried currants	1	tablespoon all-purpose flour
1	tablespoon cognac (optional)	1	egg yolk
1	(8 ounce) package cream cheese, room temperature	½	teaspoon pure vanilla
		¼	teaspoon grated lemon rind
⅓	cup sugar	¼	teaspoon grated orange rind

Combine currants and cognac in small bowl and let stand one hour. Combine cream cheese, sugar and flour in mixing bowl; beat until light and fluffy. Beat in egg yolk, vanilla, lemon and orange rinds; fold in currants and cognac. Refrigerate, covered, but remove in time to bring to room temperature before using.

Glaze:

2	tablespoons light corn syrup	3	tablespoons finely chopped nuts of your choice
1	tablespoon boiling water		

Mix corn syrup and water and brush lightly over top of dough. Sprinkle with nuts and bake in a pre-heated 350° oven about 25 to 30 minutes or until golden brown. Cool completely before serving.

Coffee Cake:

½   recipe Sour Cream Rich Yeast
Dough (RECIPE IN INDEX)

Roll dough on lightly floured board into an 18"x 9"rectangle. Place rectangle with the 9"edge facing you. Spread top two thirds of dough with cream cheese filling, leaving a 2"border. Fold unspread third over center then cover with top third to make 3 layers of dough and 2 layers of filling. Pinch seam and ends to seal. Transfer dough to buttered cookie sheet, using a wide metal spatula. Make 8 evenly spaced cuts through dough with pastry scraper or sharp knife, starting each cut at sealed edge and ending 1" from folded edge. Spread strips apart slightly, leaving them attached to folded edge. Let rise in a warm, draft-free place until doubled.

Yield: 14 " coffee cake

Another alternative would be to make a different variety of sweet bread out of remaining half of the dough. Cakes freeze well.

Croissants, Raleigh House

Dough must remain chilled as you work with it. Place in freezer for 10 to 15 minutes or in refrigerator about 30 minutes, if butter begins to soften.

2	envelopes dry yeast	2	teaspoons salt
1	teaspoon sugar	2	cups (4 sticks) unsalted butter,
¾	cup warm water (105° to		well chilled and cut into
	115°)		½-inch pieces
3¾	cups unbleached flour, divided	1	egg beaten with 1 tablespoon
½	cup milk		milk for glaze
2	tablespoons sugar		

Combine water and sugar in medium bowl, add yeast and let dissolve. Add ¾ cup flour with milk and sugar and whisk until smooth. Cover bowl with plastic wrap. Let stand in a warm area, about 75°, 1½ to 2 hours to mature. About halfway through rising process, batter will bubble up and then sink down; if preparation is to be discontinued at this point, stir bubbles out of batter and refrigerate up to 24 hours; maturing process will continue. Combine remaining 3 cups flour and salt in large bowl. Add well-chilled butter and mix, flattening butter pieces slightly with just the tips of your fingers, working quickly so butter does not get warm. (If yeast mixture is not ready to use, refrigerate flour mixture.) Add yeast batter to flour mixture and fold in carefully with spatula, moistening flour without breaking up butter pieces; dough will be crumbly. Turn dough out on lightly floured board. Pat down and roll into 18" x 12" rectangle. Using a metal spatula, fold right ⅓ of dough toward center, then fold left ⅓ over to cover (like a business letter). Dough will be slightly rough. Lift folded dough off board, scrape board clean and sprinkle lightly with flour. Repeat patting, rolling and folding dough 3 more times. Wrap dough in plastic and chill at least 45 minutes or up to 24 hours. To shape croissants, pat dough into rough rectangle. Cut in half lengthwise through the center, then crosswise into thirds, making 6 equal pieces. Place 5 pieces in the refrigerator. Roll out remaining piece on well-floured board into 5½" x 14" rectangle. Using pastry cutter or long sharp knife, divide dough in half crosswise to make two 5½"x 7" pieces. Cut each piece diagonally to form a total of 4 triangles. Using rolling pin, gently roll from shortest side of 1 triangle, until dough measures 7" across. Gently roll from longest side to point until dough measures 8" across. Holding point of triangle with one hand, loosely roll dough up from base to point with other hand. Transfer croissant tip side down to ungreased rimmed cookie sheet. Curve both ends down slightly, forming a crescent. Repeat with remaining dough. Brush croissants with egg beaten with milk. Set aside, uncovered, in a warm, draft-free place and let rise until double, about 1 to 2 hours; reglaze with egg mixture once during rising. Reglaze croissants again with egg mixture, then bake in a pre-heated 450° oven on middle shelf, about 12 to 15 minutes. Let cool

Continued on next page

slightly before serving. Croissants can be cooled completely, then wrapped airtight and frozen. Reheat unthawed croissants at 375° for 10 minutes.

Yield: 24 croissants

Croissants can be made over a period of several days; note stopping places in basic recipe. When rolling out dough, lift frequently and sprinkle flour over board to prevent sticking. With flat pastry brush, remove excess flour from dough after rolling.

Prune-Raisin Crescents

These are served at room temperature. Delicious for a brunch or coffee.

Filling:

½	the recipe of Sour Cream Rich Dough (in Index)	2	tablespoons unsalted butter, softened
1	cup pitted prunes	1	tablespoon light brown sugar, packed
¼	cup raisins	¼	teaspoon grated lemon rind

Make dough and let rise. Combine prunes, raisins and enough water to cover, in small saucepan. Heat to boiling, then reduce heat to simmer. Cook, covered, 10 minutes. Drain well. Puree prune-raisin mixture in blender or food processor. Stir in brown sugar and lemon rind until smooth. Divide dough in 2 equal pieces. Roll each piece on lightly floured surface to a 12" circle, cut each into 8 equal wedges. Spread a slightly rounded tablespoonful of prune filling over each wedge leaving ½" border on all sides. Roll up, starting at wide end. Place on buttered cookie sheet, with tip of wedge down. Let rise, loosely covered, in a warm, draft-free place, until doubled.

Glaze:

1	egg yolk	Powdered sugar
1	tablespoon heavy cream	

Mix egg yolk and cream; brush lightly over tops of crescents. Bake in a pre-heated 350° oven about 15 minutes or until golden brown. Cool completely on wire racks. Sprinkle powdered sugar over tops and serve.

Yield: 16 crescents

In making the sour cream dough, the ingredients cannot be halved for this recipe. Either double filling and make 32 crescents or use other half of dough to make a different recipe.

Kahlúa Cinnamon Rolls

This is another delicious bread for breakfast, coffees or brunches.

Kahlúa Pan Syrup:

¼ cup butter
⅓ cup light brown sugar, packed

1 tablespoon light corn syrup
¼ cup Kahlúa

Place all ingredients in small saucepan. Bring to simmer. Reserve ⅓ cup syrup to spoon over baked rolls. Turn remainder into 9" round cake pan.

Rolls:

1 teaspoon sugar
¼ cup very warm water
1 package dry yeast
⅓ cup boiling hot milk
¼ cup shortening

¼ cup granulated sugar
½ teaspoon salt
2¼ cups flour, divided
1 large egg, beaten

Soften yeast in water with 1 teaspoon sugar added. Combine hot milk, shortening, sugar and salt in mixing bowl. Add 1 cup flour and beat well. Cool to lukewarm then add egg, yeast and remaining flour and mix to moderately stiff dough. Turn out on floured board. Knead 4 or 5 times or until elastic. Place back in lightly oiled mixing bowl, turning over to oil both sides. Cover and let rise until double in bulk. Meanwhile, prepare filling. When dough has risen, turn out on a lightly floured board and roll to a 16"x 12"rectangle. Spread with filling. Roll up like a jelly roll, starting from long side. Cut into 12 slices about 1½"in diameter. Arrange slices in a 9" round cake pan prepared with the syrup. Press slices slightly to flatten. Let rise until double. Bake at 375° for 20 to 25 minutes. Remove from oven. Let rolls stand in pan 5 minutes, then turn out upside down onto serving plate. Spoon reserved Kahlúa pan syrup over top.

Spiced Raisin Sugar Filling:

¼ cup softened butter
⅓ cup granulated sugar
¾ teaspoon cinnamon

1 tablespoon Kahlúa
⅓ cup coarsely chopped raisins

Beat first 3 ingredients together, then add Kahlúa and raisins.

Yield: 12 rolls

Rapid Rise Whole Wheat Bread

This bread is very good and takes less time than usual. It is made with Fleischmann's Rapid Rise yeast and requires only one rising.

3½ to 4½ cups whole wheat flour
¼   cup brown sugar, firmly
     packed
2   tablespoons shortening
1½   teaspoons salt

1   package Fleischmann's Rapid
     Rise yeast
1½   cups hot water (125° to 130°)
Vegetable oil
Melted butter or margarine

Mix 2 cups of the flour, brown sugar, shortening, salt and yeast in mixer bowl. Add hot water and beat at low speed 1 minute, scraping bowl several times. Add 1½ cups more flour and beat at high speed 2 minutes. Stir in enough of the remaining flour to make dough easy to handle. Dough should be soft but not sticky. Turn dough out on floured board and knead about 5 minutes or until smooth and elastic. Cover dough with mixing bowl and let rest 10 minutes. On lightly floured board stretch or roll dough until it is about 27 inches long — 3 times as long as the pan you are going to bake it in. Fold dough into thirds, from opposite direction, pressing with fingers to break any air pockets. Seal edges and ends by pinching together. Roll under palm of hand to smooth shape of loaf. Place, seam side down in a greased 9"x 5"x 3"loaf pan. Brush top of loaf with melted butter. Cover with a towel; let rise in a warm draft-free place until double. When a finger poked into dough leaves an indentation, rising is sufficient. Sides of dough should reach top of pan. Bake in a pre-heated 400° oven for 40 to 50 minutes or until loaf sounds hollow when rapped with knuckle. Remove from pan immediately and cool on wire rack away from drafts.

Yield: 1 loaf

1 cup halved raisins or 1 cup toasted nuts, finely chopped, may be added, if desired. Add them to dough before the second addition of flour.

Sour Cream Rich Dough, Landry

This dough takes longer to rise than most yeast dough. Having all ingredients at room temperature gets the best results. I use Fleischmann's Active Dry yeast in a 4 ounce jar. It is convenient for this recipe as it takes more than one envelope.

Dough:

1	package plus 1 teaspoon dry yeast (3¼ teaspoons)	½	cup sour cream
¼	cup very warm water (105° to 115°)	½	cup sugar
		1½	teaspoons salt
3	eggs	1	teaspoon vanilla
½	cup butter, melted and cooled to room temperature	4½ to 5 cups flour	

Dissolve yeast in water in a small bowl. Beat eggs in mixing bowl; add butter, sour cream, sugar, salt and vanilla and beat until thoroughly mixed. Add dissolved yeast and mix. Add 2 cups flour and beat until smooth and dough "ribbons". Gradually add as much of the remaining flour as needed to make a soft, but not sticky dough. Beat until elastic in mixer, then turn out on floured board and knead for 2 minutes, Adding as much flour as needed to prevent sticking. Shape into a ball. Put a little vegetable oil in bottom of mixer bowl and place dough in it, turning over so ball is oiled. Cover with a towel and let rise in a draft-free place. I use one of my kitchen cupboards. When dough is more than doubled, make into rolls or any of the following recipes. Bake in a 350° oven about 15 minutes for rolls.

Yield: About 4 dozen rolls

If you are adding flavors of your own choosing in following recipes, add them after phrase "thoroughly mixed". The protein in flour helps stabilize the yeast. I find that bread rises faster and has more volume with protein-rich flour.

Stollen

I like to bake this for Christmas.

1	envelope dry yeast	2	eggs, beaten
1	cup warm whole milk	3½	cups flour
¼	cup sugar	½	cup sliced blanched almonds
½	cup (1 stick) butter, melted	¼	cup diced candied orange peel
1	teaspoon salt	¼	cup candied cherry halves
½	teaspoon ground cardamom	¼	cup yellow raisins, plumped in
4	tablespoons ground almonds		hot sherry or brandy

Dissolve yeast in warm milk in bowl. Add sugar, butter, salt, cardamom and almonds, combine. Set aside 2 tablespoons of the beaten egg. Add remainder of egg to bowl along with 2 cups flour; beat at high speed until smooth. Add remaining flour gradually, beating until a soft, pliable dough is formed. Turn out on floured board and knead until smooth, about 10 minutes. Add sliced almonds, orange peel, cherries and raisins to dough and knead until evenly distributed. Place dough in a lightly oiled bowl, Turn it over so it is oiled on both sides and cover with a towel. Let rise in a warm, draft-free place until double, about 1½ hours. Punch dough down and roll into a 12" circle. Fold almost in half; gently press edges together. Place on greased cookie sheet. Brush top with melted butter. Let rise for 1 hour or until doubled. Brush with reserved egg. Bake in a pre-heated 350° oven about 30 minutes. Remove to a wire rack to cool. Dust with powdered sugar or spread with a thin powdered sugar glaze before serving.

Yield: 1 Stollen

Whole Wheat Croissants, Raleigh House

2 envelopes dry yeast	1½ tablespoons honey
¾ cup warm water (105° to 115°)	1¾ cups unbleached flour
1 teaspoon sugar	2 teaspoons salt
1¾ cups whole wheat flour, divided	2 cups (4 sticks) unsalted butter, chilled and cut into ½" pieces
½ cup milk	1 egg, beaten with 1 tablespoon milk

Combine yeast, sugar and water in a bowl and stir until yeast dissolves. Add ¾ cup whole wheat flour with milk and honey and whisk until smooth. Cover bowl with plastic wrap. Let stand in a warm place for 1½ to 2 hours to mature. About halfway through rising process, batter will bubble up then sink down; if preparation is to be discontinued at this point, stir bubbles down and refrigerate up to 24 hours; maturing process will continue. Combine remaining whole wheat flour with 1¾ cups unbleached flour and 2 teaspoons salt in a large bowl. Add well-chilled butter and mix, flattening butter pieces slightly with only the tips of your fingers. (Refrigerate if yeast mixture is not ready). Pour yeast batter into flour mixture and carefully fold in using rubber spatula, just moistening flour without breaking up butter pieces; dough will be rough and crumbly. Turn dough out on floured board. Pat down and roll into an 18" x 12" rectangle. Using a metal spatula, fold right ⅓ of dough toward center, then fold left ⅓ over to cover (like a business letter). Dough will be slightly rough. Lift folded dough off board, scrape board clean and sprinkle lightly with flour. Repeat patting, rolling and folding dough three more times. Wrap dough in plastic and chill at least 45 minutes up to 24 hours. Follow the directions in Croissants, Raleigh House, for shaping and baking.

Yield: 24 croissants

Cheese Croissants may be made by sprinkling freshly grated Swiss or Cheddar cheese over center of each croissant before rolling up.

Cakes
& Frostings

Betty Ann Graves, daughter and Martha
Fall of 1994

Almond Lemon Cake

This cake has brandy in it. Cake can be glazed or just dusted with powdered sugar.

Cake:

1 cup fine dry bread crumbs	¼ teaspoon ground mace
3 eggs, room temperature	½ to ⅔ cup cognac or brandy
1 cup superfine sugar	1 cup whole blanched almonds,
2 tablespoons grated lemon rind	ground

Generously butter 8" springform pan. Coat with some of the bread crumbs. Tap out excess and reserve.

Beat eggs in mixing bowl until foamy; gradually add sugar. Continue beating until mixture is very light and tripled in volume. Beat in lemon rind and mace. Fold in remaining bread crumbs alternating with cognac. (Use enough cognac to make a medium-stiff batter.) Fold in almonds. Pour batter into prepared pan; smooth top. Bake in a 350° oven about 35 minutes or until a wooden pick inserted in center of cake comes out clean. Cool on wire rack for 10 minutes; remove sides of pan. Cool completely. Wrap cake in plastic wrap; let stand at cool room temperature overnight to mellow flavors and improve texture. Ice with lemon icing.

Lemon Icing (optional):

1 cup powdered sugar	2 to 3 tablespoons fresh lemon juice

Place sugar in small bowl. Gradually stir in 1 tablespoon lemon juice. Continue adding lemon juice, whisking constantly, until icing has consistency of heavy glaze. Dribble over cake.

Yield: 8" cake (8 to 10 servings)

If you do not have superfine sugar on hand, just put regular sugar in a blender. Blend a few seconds, then measure.

Apple Pecan Cake

This is similar to the pear cake in my first cookbook, but has a frosting made with dark brown sugar. Special!

Cake:

4½ cups raw apples, peeled and chopped
Lemon juice
1½ cups salad oil
2 cups sugar
2 large eggs

2½ cups all-purpose flour, sifted before measuring
1 teaspoon salt
1 teaspoon baking soda
2 teaspoons baking powder
1 teaspoon vanilla
1½ cups pecans, chopped

Prepare apples and toss them with a little lemon or pineapple juice to keep them from darkening, set aside. Beat sugar, eggs and oil in mixer bowl. Mix well at low speed until creamy and smooth. Sift flour again with salt, soda and baking powder. Add flour to creamed mixture a little at a time, mixing at medium speed after each addition. Add vanilla and mix. Remove beaters and fold in apples and nuts by hand. Bake in a greased 13"x 9"x 2" pan in a 350° oven for 55 to 60 minutes or until cake tests done in center. Let cool in pan, then spread with brown sugar frosting.

Brown Sugar Frosting:

1 stick butter or margarine
⅛ teaspoon salt
⅓ cup evaporated milk, undiluted

1 cup dark brown sugar, firmly packed
2 to 2½ cups powdered sugar

Combine margarine, salt, milk and brown sugar in heavy saucepan. Heat over medium heat, stirring constantly, until sugar is dissolved. Add enough powdered sugar to make of spreading consistency. (Place a little frosting on cake at first to test.)

Yield: 13 " x 9 " x 2 " pan

Banana Cake with Lemon Frosting

This is my son's favorite birthday cake. The lemon frosting is a nice contrast to the blandness of the bananas.

Cake:

2¼ cups cake flour, sifted before measuring
2½ teaspoons baking powder
½ teaspoon baking soda
½ teaspoon salt
1¼ cups sugar
½ cup shortening
1 cup mashed ripe bananas
1 teaspoon pure vanilla
2 eggs
½ cup buttermilk

Pre-heat oven to 350°. Grease and flour two 8″ x 1½″ square cake pans or a 13″ x 9″ x 2″ baking pan. Sift dry ingredients into large bowl of electric mixer. Add shortening, bananas and vanilla and beat until just combined, then continue beating, scraping sides and bottom of bowl occasionally. Add eggs and buttermilk and beat 2 minutes longer at medium speed. Pour batter into prepared pans and bake layers for 30 to 35 minutes; Bake oblong pan for 40 to 45 minutes or until done when tested in center with toothpick. Cool in pans 10 minutes, then remove from pans to cool thoroughly on wire racks. Ice with lemon frosting.

Lemon Frosting:

½ stick margarine
2 cups powdered sugar
2 tablespoons lemon juice
2 tablespoons milk
2 teaspoons grated lemon rind

Cream margarine and sugar together. Gradually add lemon juice, milk and lemon rind. Beat frosting until it reaches spreading consistency.

Yield: 13″ x 9″ x 2″ pan

This cake is very perishable and must be refrigerated. If I am planning to remove cake from pan before icing it, I always line the bottom of the pans with greased waxed paper for easier removal.

Helpful Hint: *A pastry blender is great to chop avocado, hard boiled eggs or any soft foods.*

Basic Pound Cake

Always use fresh ingredients. Check date on bottom of baking powder can. Eggs should always be large — 2 ounces in the shell. Eggs and butter should be at room temperature before using. Spoon flour lightly into measuring cup, then level off with a knife.

2¼ cups cake flour
1   teaspoon baking powder
¼   teaspoon salt
1   cup (2 sticks) butter or
     margarine

¾   cup sugar
1½   teaspoons vanilla extract
4   large eggs, separated

Heat oven to 350°. Grease and flour 9"x 5"x 3"loaf pan or use a Teflon-coated pan. If using a Pyrex pan, reduce oven temperature to 325°. Sift flour, baking powder and salt into a small bowl; set aside. In large bowl of mixer, beat butter, sugar and vanilla until very fluffy, scraping sides and bottom of bowl once. The longer you beat the butter and sugar, the better for the cake. Separate eggs, adding each yolk as it is separated to butter mixture and beating thoroughly to blend; set egg whites aside in second large bowl. At low speed, beat flour mixture into butter mixture until just blended. Beat egg whites at high speed until stiff but not dry. Fold ⅓ of beaten egg whites into batter with rubber spatula to lighten, then blend in remaining whites. Spoon batter into prepared pan and bake 50 to 65 minutes or until wooden pick inserted in center comes out clean. Cool cake in pan 20 minutes, then remove to wire rack to cool completely.

Yield: One 9 " x 5 " loaf pan

Cake flour is preferable for this cake, but you can use all-purpose flour. Use 2 tablespoons less per cup. Or, you can make your own version of cake flour. For every cup you use, whisk 2 tablespoons cornstarch into ¾ cup all-purpose flour.

Buttermilk Chocolate Cake

The chocolate pecan topping is put on top of unbaked cake. When cake is done, it is ready to eat.

Cake:

½	stick margarine	½	teaspoon salt
3	tablespoons cocoa	¾	teaspoon soda
½	cup boiling water	¼	cup buttermilk
1	cup sugar	1	teaspoon vanilla
1	cup flour	1	egg

Mix margarine, cocoa and boiling water in mixing bowl. Cool, then add flour, sugar, salt and soda that have been sifted together. Mix, then add vanilla, buttermilk and egg and mix until smooth. Pour batter into a greased and floured 9" cake pan. Sprinkle topping over unbaked batter. Bake in a pre-heated 350° oven about 25 to 30 minutes or until cake tests done in center.

Topping:

4 ounces sweet chocolate, grated	½ cup chopped pecans

Mix grated chocolate and pecans and sprinkle over unbaked cake.

Yield: 9" cake pan

Yellow Cake

This is a useful cake to make as it can be iced with a frosting of your choice or, if made in a 13" x 9" x 2" pan, cut into squares and serve as a dessert with a sauce or fruit.

3	cups sifted cake flour (sifted before measuring), or use sifted regular flour and remove 2 tablespoons from each cup, which equals cake flour	¾	cup (1½ sticks) margarine, room temperature
2½	teaspoons baking powder	1½	cups sugar
1	teaspoon salt	3	eggs
		1	teaspoon vanilla
		1	cup milk

Pre-heat oven to 350°. Grease and flour two 9"x 1½" square cake pans. (I usually line bottom of pans with waxed paper). Sift flour with baking powder and salt. In large bowl of electric mixer, beat margarine, sugar, eggs and vanilla at high speed until light and fluffy. With rubber scraper, scrape sides and bottom of bowl twice during mixing. At low speed, beat in flour mixture alternately with milk, beginning and ending with flour. Beat only until smooth. Pour batter into pans; bake 30 to 35 minutes, or until surface springs back when lightly touched with fingertip.

Yield: Two 9" x 1½" pans

Carrot Cake

This cake can also be baked in two 9" cake pans for a layer cake.

Cake:

2	cups sugar	1½	cups oil
2	cups flour	2	teaspoons cinnamon
4	eggs	½	teaspoon salt
3	cups grated carrots	1	teaspoon baking powder
1	teaspoon vanilla	2	teaspoons baking soda

Mix all dry ingredients together in a mixing bowl. Add oil, eggs, vanilla and carrots; blend well. Bake in a 13"x 9"x 2"baking pan in a pre-heated 350° oven for 30 minutes or until done in the center. Frost with cream cheese frosting.

Cream Cheese Frosting:

1	cup chopped pecans, optional	1	stick butter or margarine
1	pound box powdered sugar	1	teaspoon vanilla
8	ounces cream cheese		

Cream the cheese and butter, then add the sugar, vanilla and pecans. Blend well. If not of spreading consistency, add a little milk.

Yield: 13 " x 9 " x 2 " cake

I sometimes pour about 1 cup frozen orange juice, thawed but undiluted, over this cake while it is still in the pan to make a tasty glaze, instead of frosting it.

Helpful Hint: *1 pound carrots — 2½ cups diced or shredded.*

Cherry Almond Cake

This cake should be made the day before serving as flavor improves.

Cherry Almond Cake:

2   cups sugar
2   cups flour
½   teaspoon salt
2   eggs, beaten
1   (16 ounce) can sour red
     cherries, drained but saving
     juice

4   tablespoons butter or
     margarine, melted
2   teaspoons soda
2   teaspoons water
1   cup chopped nuts, optional
½   teaspoon almond extract

Pre-heat oven to 350°. Grease a 9"x 13" pan. Mix sugar, flour and salt in mixer bowl. Combine eggs and cherry juice and add to dry ingredients and mix, then add butter, almond extract and soda mixed with water. Fold in cherries and nuts. Place in prepared pan and bake about 35 minutes. Remove from oven and pour glaze over hot cake.

Glaze:

1½ cups sugar
2   tablespoons flour
1   teaspoon almond extract
2   tablespoons butter or
     margarine

1½ cups hot water
Whipped cream for garnish
     (optional)

Combine ingredients in saucepan. Cook, stirring, until thick, then pour over hot cake. When cake is cool, garnish with whipped cream, if desired.

Yield: 16 servings

Chocolate Buttermilk Cake

This is a delicious cake for a party. It is rich but not too expensive.

Cake:

2	cups flour	2	eggs
2	cups sugar	½	cup buttermilk
2	sticks margarine	1	teaspoon soda
1	cup water	1	teaspoon vanilla
¼	cup cocoa		

Sift flour and sugar together in mixing bowl. In a saucepan, boil margarine, water and cocoa together. Add to sifted dry ingredients. Mix together, then add the eggs, buttermilk, soda and vanilla. Beat until smooth. Pour into greased or sprayed jelly roll pan, 15" x 10½" x 1". Bake in a pre-heated 400° oven about 20 minutes or until done in center when tested. Frost while warm with chocolate frosting.

Chocolate Frosting:

1	stick margarine, softened	1	teaspoon vanilla
⅓	cup cocoa	4 to 6	tablespoons milk
1	pound powdered sugar, sifted to get any lumps out		

Place margarine, cocoa, powdered sugar, vanilla in mixing bowl. Add 4 tablespoons milk and enough more to make icing of spreading consistency. Ice cake, then cut into 40 to 48 squares.

Yield: 40 to 48 squares

Variations: Add 1 teaspoon cinnamon to batter and frosting, add miniature marshmallows and chopped nuts to frosting, spread cake with raspberry or strawberry preserves before frosting.

Chocolate Upside-Down Cake

This cake is moist and rich. It also freezes well. It is from a church cookbook published in the early twentieth century.

Cake:

3 tablespoons butter or margarine
1 cup sugar
1 egg yolk, unbeaten
2 squares unsweetened chocolate, melted
¾ cup milk

1 egg white, beaten stiff but not dry
1 cup flour
1 teaspoon baking powder
1 teaspoon pure vanilla
⅛ teaspoon salt

Cream butter and sugar in mixer bowl until light. Add egg yolk and beat well. Place unwrapped chocolate on microwave-proof dish. Microwave on high 1½ minutes. Squares will retain some of their original shape. Remove from microwave and stir until completely melted. Add to butter mixture. Sift flour, baking powder and salt together. Add to butter mixture alternately with milk, beginning and ending with flour mixture. Beat egg white in small bowl with hand mixer until firm peaks remain when beater is lifted. Gently fold into batter. Prepare pan with topping.

Topping:

4 tablespoons butter or margarine
4 tablespoons brown sugar, packed

1 cup white corn syrup
¾ cup chopped pecans or nuts of your choice

Melt butter and sugar together, add corn syrup and nuts. Cover the bottom of either a 10″ deep pie plate or 10″ round cake pan with the butter mixture. Spoon in the cake batter and smooth top. Bake in a pre-heated 350° oven about 45 minutes or just until cake is done in center when tested. Remove from oven and let set about 5 or 10 minutes, then place a cake plate over top of cake and invert. Serve warm or cold with whipped cream or ice cream.

Yield: 8 servings

Favorite Chocolate Cake, Cynthia

This cake is very rich and delicious. It is simple to make as the base is a cake mix. The sour cream icing is delicious, too.

Cake:

1	package Duncan Hines chocolate cake mix	½	cup Crisco oil
1	(3½ ounce) package instant vanilla or chocolate pudding mix	4	eggs
		1	teaspoon pure vanilla
		1	cup Hershey's chocolate syrup
1	cup water	1	cup chocolate chips

Combine cake mix, oil, pudding mix, water, eggs, and vanilla. Blend to moisten, then beat at medium speed of electric mixer, scraping bowl occasionally. Pour about ¾ of batter into well-greased and floured 10″ tube pan or large Bundt pan. Mix chocolate syrup with rest of batter. Stir in chocolate chips. Spoon over batter in pan. Bake in a pre-heated 350° oven about an hour or until cake tests done. Cool in pan 10 minutes then turn out on serving plate. When completely cool, ice with chocolate sour cream icing.

Sour Cream Icing:

1	stick butter or margarine	1	cup sour cream
4	ounces unsweetened chocolate, broken up	2	teaspoons vanilla
		¼	teaspoon salt
4	cups powdered sugar		

In top of double boiler, melt butter and chocolate over barely simmering water. Remove and cool to lukewarm. Add powdered sugar and salt, then blend in sour cream and vanilla Beat in mixer until smooth. If you want to "gild the lily" you can garnish with toasted chopped pecans or almonds.

Yield: 16 to 18 servings

Filled Chocolate Cake

Filled with whipped cream and frosted with a rich chocolate frosting, this makes an attractive as well as delicious dessert.

Cake:

1 cup cocoa	2¾ cups flour
2 cups boiling water	2 teaspoons baking soda
1 cup margarine, softened	½ teaspoon baking powder
2½ cups sugar	½ teaspoon salt
4 eggs	1½ teaspoons pure vanilla extract

Combine cocoa and boiling water, stirring until smooth, set aside. Cream margarine; gradually add sugar, beating well at medium speed in electric mixer. Add eggs, one at a time, beating well after each addition. Add vanilla. Combine flour and next 3 ingredients; add to creamed mixture alternately with cocoa mixture, beginning and ending with flour. Pour batter into 3 greased and floured 9" round cake pans. Bake at 350° for 20 minutes or until a wooden pick inserted in the center comes out clean. Cool in pans 10 minutes, then remove and cool completely. Spread whipped cream filling between layers. Ice with perfect chocolate frosting.

Whipped Cream Filling:

1 cup whipping cream	¼ cup sifted powdered sugar
1 teaspoon vanilla	

Beat whipping cream and vanilla until foamy; gradually add powdered sugar, beating until soft peaks form. Spread between layers of cake.

Perfect Chocolate Frosting:

1 cup (6 ounces) semi-sweet chocolate morsels	1½ sticks margarine or butter
½ cup half-and-half	2½ cups sifted powdered sugar

Combine first 3 ingredients in a heavy saucepan; cook over medium heat, stirring, until chocolate melts. Remove from heat; add powdered sugar and mix well. Beat at low speed of mixer until frosting holds its shape. Add a few more drops of half-and-half if needed to make of spreading consistency. Ice top and sides of cake.

Yield: 3 layer cake

Glazed Buttermilk Cake

This batter is too much for baking in a Bundt pan as it is apt to rise over the top. When this happens, cake will rise, then sink in the middle. Always use a large tube pan, or remove enough batter to make a small pan or 2 cup cakes before pouring in.

Cake:

3	cups sugar	¼	teaspoon soda
2	sticks margarine or butter	¼	teaspoon salt
6	eggs, separated	1	teaspoon baking powder
1	teaspoon lemon extract	1	cup buttermilk
3	cups flour		

Cream sugar and butter thoroughly. Add egg yolks, one at a time, and beat at high speed until fluffy. Add lemon flavoring. Sift together flour, soda, salt and baking powder 3 times. Add buttermilk, alternately with flour mixture, beginning and ending with flour. Beat egg whites until they hold firm peaks, but are not dry. Fold into cake mixture. Place in a well greased and floured tube pan. Bake at 350° for 50 to 60 minutes. Let cool 10 minutes, then remove cake and place on serving plate to cool completely. Pour glaze over cooled cake gradually, letting it sink in before pouring more.

Lemon Glaze:

1	egg, beaten		Juice and grated rind of two
2	tablespoons flour		lemons
1	cup sugar	½	stick margarine or butter

Combine ingredients in a saucepan (not aluminum) and cook over medium to low heat, stirring constantly, until mixture is slightly thickened. Pour over cooled cake.

Yield: Tube Pan

I sometimes bake this cake in a 16" ring mold for teas. It cuts into 40 pieces which are easier to fit onto a tea-size plate.

Hazelnut Cake

This cake is delicious with just a dusting of powdered sugar. This type of cake used to be called a "ground-nut" cake. 2 cups hazelnuts will make 2¾ cups when ground and lightly measured in the cup. I use my coffee grinder for the grinding.

6	large eggs, separated	¼	teaspoon cream of tartar
1	tablespoon fresh lemon juice	½	teaspoon salt
1	cup sugar	2¾	cups finely ground hazelnuts,
½	cup flour		skins removed
2	teaspoons baking powder		Whipped cream garnish (optional)
2	teaspoons freshly grated lemon		Raspberries or strawberries for
	rind		garnish (optional)

Beat egg yolks and lemon juice in electric mixer until thick and pale, then add ¾ cup of sugar, a little at a time, beating until well mixed. Sift flour and baking powder together and add to the yolk mixture along with the grated lemon rind. In another bowl, beat the egg whites until they are foamy, add the cream of tartar and salt and beat mixture until it holds soft peaks. Add the remaining ¼ cup sugar, a tablespoonful at a time, and beat until the mixture holds stiff peaks. Fold the egg whites gently but thoroughly into the yolk mixture. Sprinkle the ground hazelnuts over the top and fold them in gently but thoroughly. Pour the mixture into an ungreased 10"x 4½"tube pan with a removable bottom. Bake on the middle rack of a pre-heated 350° oven for 45 to 50 minutes, or until a tester comes out clean. Invert the pan onto a rack or on a bottle and let cool completely before removing from pan. Serve with whipped cream and berries of your choice.

Yield: 10" tube pan

Toast hazelnuts in one layer in a baking pan in a 350° oven about 10 minutes or until skins blister. Wrap in a kitchen towel. Let steam for 1 minute. Rub nuts in towel to remove skins. Let them cool.

Jam Pecan Cake

This cake can be made with any variety of preserves or jam you prefer. Cake can be made ahead and frozen, then thawed and glazed.

Cake:

1	cup butter or margarine, softened	1	teaspoon soda
2	cups sugar	½	teaspoon ground cinnamon
6	eggs, room temperature	½	teaspoon ground cloves
1	cup buttermilk	1	cup blackberry jam or jam of your choice
4	cups flour, sifted before measuring	1	cup chopped pecans (optional)
½	teaspoon salt	1	teaspoon vanilla

Pre-heat oven to 350°. Grease and flour three 9" square or round cake pans. Cream butter; gradually add sugar, beating at medium speed until light and fluffy. Add eggs, one at a time, beating after each addition. Combine flour, salt, baking soda and spices. Gradually add to butter mixture alternately with buttermilk, beginning and ending with flour. Combine at medium speed. Remove beater and fold in jam, pecans and vanilla. Pour batter into prepared pans. Bake until tester inserted in center comes out clean. Cool, even tops of cake with serrated knife, if needed. Place one layer on shallow-rimmed serving plate, spoon some of the glaze over top. Repeat with remaining layers and glaze, allowing glaze to drip down sides and form a well around cake. Serve within 4 hours of assembly.

Glaze:

3	cups sugar	1	stick butter
1	cup whipping cream or evaporated milk	1	cup jam

Combine sugar, whipping cream and butter in heavy saucepan over medium heat. Cook, stirring constantly, until syrup reaches 240° or soft ball stage. Remove from heat, add jam. Cool for 30 minutes before pouring over cake. Should be eaten same day after glaze is added.

Yield: 12 servings

When I entertained my church guild, I made this cake in a 15" x 11" x 2½" sheet cake pan. It cut into 40 squares - 8 cuts across and 5 cuts down.

Kahlúa Swirl Cake

This cake has Kahlúa in the batter and also in the glaze. Delicious! Be sure to use the correct pan size. This recipe calls for a 9" tube pan (9 cup size).

Cake:

2	cups sifted flour (sifted before measuring)	½	cup softened butter or margarine
1	teaspoon baking powder	2	large eggs
¾	teaspoon baking soda	1	teaspoon vanilla
¾	teaspoon salt	¾	cup sour cream
½	teaspoon mace	⅓	cup Kahlúa
1¼	cups sugar		

Resift flour with baking powder, soda, salt and mace. Combine sugar, butter, eggs and vanilla in large mixing bowl. Beat 2 minutes on medium speed. Mixture may look curdled. On lowest speed, blend flour mixture alternatley with sour cream and Kahlúa, starting and ending with flour mixture. Spoon ⅓ of batter into a greased and floured 9" tube pan (9 cup capacity). Cover with ½ of streusel filling and second ⅓ of batter. Add rest of filling and rest of batter. Bake in a pre-heated 350° oven for 45 minutes or until cake tests done in middle. Remove from oven and let cool 10 minutes. Invert onto a cake rack and cool to lukewarm. Spoon on glaze.

Streusel Filling:

⅓	cup brown sugar, packed	⅓	cup chopped pecans
¼	teaspoon cinnamon	¼	teaspoon mace

Mix all ingredients and set aside.

Glaze:

2	tablespoons butter	1	tablespoon Kahlúa
¾	cup sifted powdered sugar, measured after sifting		

Mix all together until smooth. Spread on cake.

Yield: 9" cake

Recipes suitable for a 10 inch tube pan (16 cups), won't always fit in a 12 or 13 cup Bundt pan. If pan is too small, the batter will run over the sides and the cake will fall; if pan is too big, the sides will shield the batter and slow the baking.

Norwegian Toskakake

This recipe was a favorite one of Gladys Andersen, a dear Norwegian friend. The whipping cream broiled topping makes this cake extra special. There are some of her recipes in my first cookbook.

Toskakake:

3   eggs, room temperature
1   cup sugar
1½ cups flour
1½ teaspoons baking powder

¾   cup (1½ sticks) unsalted butter, melted
3   tablespoons whole milk
1   teaspoon vanilla

Butter a 10" springform pan. Beat eggs and sugar in mixing bowl until pale yellow and fluffy, about 6 minutes. Sift flour and baking powder together and fold into egg mixture. Add melted butter, milk and vanilla and beat at low speed just until smooth. Spoon into prepared pan. Bake in a pre-heated 350° oven about 30 to 35 minutes or until tester comes out clean. Just before cake is done, prepare topping.

Topping:

⅓   cup unsalted butter
½   cup sugar

½   cup whipping cream
½   cup slivered blanched almonds

Melt butter in a heavy skillet over low heat. Mix in sugar and cream and cook, stirring, until sugar dissolves. Increase heat to high and bring to a boil. Let boil vigorously exactly 2½ minutes. Immediately pour hot topping over cake, sprinkle with nuts and continue baking until topping is bubbly and brown. Be sure to watch carefully. Cool on rack and serve from the pan warm or at room temperature. This cake needs no garnish.

Yield: 6 to 8 servings

Peachy Cake

Cake:

2	sticks butter or margarine	2	cups flour
1	cup sugar	1	teaspoon baking powder
2	eggs	1	teaspoon baking soda
1	(29 ounce) can sliced peaches, drained	1	teaspoon cinnamon
		1	teaspoon vanilla

Grease and flour a 15"x 8"x 2"pan. Cream butter with sugar and vanilla then add eggs, one at a time, beating well after each addition. Puree peaches in blender to make 2½ cups. Sift dry ingredients together. Add to creamed mixture alternately with peaches, beginning and ending with flour. Bake at 350° 35 to 40 minutes or until cake tests done in center. Remove from oven and cool, then spread with Orange Frosting.

Orange Frosting:

1	stick butter or margarine, room temperature	3	tablespoons frozen orange juice, thawed, undiluted
3	cups powdered sugar		

Beat all ingredients in mixer until well creamed and fluffy.

Yield: 15 " x 8 " x 2 " pan

This can also be made in a 13" x 9" x 2" pan , a slightly thicker cake. This is a handy recipe when fresh peaches are out of season.

Peanut Butter Cake

This is my great-grandchildren's favorite.

2¼	cups flour	3	eggs, beaten to blend
2	cups lightly packed dark brown sugar	1	teaspoon vanilla
		1	teaspoon baking powder
1	cup smooth peanut butter	½	teaspoon baking soda
1	stick butter or margarine, room temperature	1	cup semi-sweet chocolate chips
1	cup whole milk		

Pre-heat oven to 325°. Grease bottom only of 12"x 8"x 2"baking pan. Combine first 4 ingredients in large mixing bowl and blend until crumbly. Set aside 1 cup of flour mixture. Add next 5 ingredients to remaining flour mixture and blend well. Spoon batter into pan and sprinkle with reserved flour mixture. Top with chocolate chips. Bake until tester inserted in center of cake, comes out clean. Let cool slightly , then cut into squares and serve.

Yield: 12 to 15 servings

I sometimes use the chunky peanut butter.

Tipsy Apple Cake

If you have any cake left over, try breaking it up in chunks and layer in parfait glasses with whipped cream.

4	cups baking apples, peeled, cored and chopped	¼	teaspoon ground cloves
		2	cups sugar
6	tablespoons brandy	½	cup salad oil
2	cups flour	2	eggs
2	teaspoons cinnamon	1	cup walnuts or pecans, chopped
2	teaspoons baking soda		
1	teaspoon nutmeg	1	cup dark raisins, coarsely chopped
1	teaspoon salt		

Place chopped apples in a bowl and pour as much brandy over them as they will absorb. Sift together flour, cinnamon, baking soda, nutmeg, salt and cloves. Toss flour mixture into soaked apples. In mixer bowl, beat together sugar, oil and eggs. Combine with flour mixture and mix well. Remove beaters and stir in nuts and raisins. Pour into a greased 13"x 9"x 2"baking pan. Bake in a pre-heated 325° oven for 1 hour or until done in center. Serve warm or cold with whipped cream.

Yield: 13 " x 9 " x 2 " cake

This cake is delicious served warm with hard sauce.

Pear Upside-Down Cake

The combination of the ginger-flavored cake and bland pears is delicious.

Topping:

¾   stick butter, melted   4   medium-size firm pears
1   cup light brown sugar, packed

Butter the sides of a 10"x 2¾"springform pan or a 10"x 3"cake pan. In a small bowl, mix the brown sugar and butter together, then spread evenly in the prepared pan. Peel the pears and cut them in half lengthwise. Scoop out cores with a spoon. Place them in a skillet with 1 inch of water. Bring to a boil, then lower heat and simmer, uncovered, until they are barely tender. Drain in colander. To flatten pears, cut ¼" off the rounded side of each pear half. Place 2 of the pieces in the center of pan, then arrange the halves, core-side up on the bottom of prepared pan, like the spokes of a wheel, stem-side toward the middle. Chop the rest of the pear pieces coarsely and reserve.

Cake:

2½ cups flour
1½ teaspoons baking soda
1   teaspoon ground cinnamon
1   teaspoon ground ginger
¼   teaspoon ground cloves
1   teaspoon salt
½   cup dark molasses

½   cup honey
¾   cup hot water
1   egg
½   cup granulated sugar
1   stick butter or margarine, melted

Pre-heat oven to 350°. Sift the flour, soda, cinnamon, ginger, cloves and salt on a piece of waxed paper. Combine molasses, honey and hot water and mix well. In mixing bowl, beat the sugar, melted butter and egg. Beat well. Add flour mixture alternately with the molasses-honey mixture beginning and ending with flour mixture. Fold in reserved chopped pears and dribble over pear-lined pan. Bake in the middle of the oven about an hour or until a wooden pick inserted in the center comes out clean. Let cool 5 or 10 minutes, then place a serving plate over top of pan and invert. If using springform pan, remove sides. Cut into wedges and serve warm or at room temperature.

Yield: 8 or 10 servings

Raisin Pecan Pound Cake

This is an old-fashioned version of pound cake. It is baked in a loaf pan.

2¼	cups cake flour	4	large eggs
¼	teaspoon baking soda	¼	cup milk
¼	teaspoon salt	¾	teaspoon fresh lemon juice
1	cup (2 sticks) butter or margarine	¾	cup golden raisins, chopped
¾	cup sugar	½	cup pecans, chopped

Heat oven to 350°. Grease and flour a 9″ x 5″ x 3″ loaf pan. In small bowl, mix flour, soda and salt; set aside. In another small bowl mix milk and lemon juice and let set for 10 minutes. It will look curdled. In large bowl of electric mixer at high speed, beat butter and sugar at least 5 minutes until fluffy and sugar no longer seems grainy, scraping bowl once. Add milk mixture and blend. Separate eggs, adding each yolk as it is separated to butter mixture and beating thoroughly to blend. Set egg whites aside in second large bowl. At low speed, beat flour mixture into butter mixture until just blended. Add raisins and pecans. With clean beaters and with mixer at high speed, beat egg whites until stiff, but not dry. Using rubber spatula, gently add ⅓ of beaten egg whites into batter to lighten, then fold in rest of egg whites. Spoon batter into prepared pan. Bake 60 to 65 minutes; remove from pan and cool completely.

Yield: Sixteen ½″ slices

Special Pecan Cake

Pecans toasted in butter are what make this cake exceptionally delicious.

Cake:

2   cups chopped pecans, divided
2½   sticks butter, divided
2   cups sugar
4   large eggs
3   cups flour

2½   teaspoons baking powder
½   teaspoon salt
1   cup whole milk
2   teaspoons pure vanilla

Toast the 2 cups pecans in ½ stick butter in a 300° oven, stirring frequently. Set aside ⅔ cup for the icing. Cream sugar with remaining butter, add eggs, one at a time, beating well after each addition. Sift flour, baking powder and salt together and add to creamed mixture alternately with the milk, beginning and ending with flour. Stir in vanilla and 1⅓ cups toasted pecans. Grease and line three 9″ round cake pans with circles of waxed paper, greasing them lightly. Place batter in prepared pans and bake in a pre-heated 350° oven for 25 to 30 minutes or until a toothpick inserted in the middle comes out clean. Let set 10 minutes before turning out of pans onto a wire rack to cool completely. Remove waxed paper then ice with pecan frosting.

Butter Pecan Frosting:

1   stick butter
2¼   cups sugar
1½   cups evaporated milk,
     not condensed milk

⅔   cup pecans reserved from
     cake recipe
1   teaspoon vanilla

Combine butter, sugar and milk in a saucepan. Bring to a boil and continue to boil for 2 minutes, stirring constantly. Remove from heat and beat until creamy. Blend in pecans and vanilla. Spread between layers, then cover top and sides completely.

Yield: 9″ layer cake

I usually specify pure vanilla as it gives a better flavor to cakes as well as desserts.

Super Buttermilk Cake

This cake is very light and of a sponge-cake consistency. It can be used as is, without the glaze, with a topping of fruit and whipped cream, or a dessert sauce. It is also delicious with just the glaze.

Cake:

2	cups flour	2	cups sugar
½	teaspoon soda	4	large eggs
½	teaspoon baking powder	1	teaspoon pure vanilla
Pinch salt		1	cup buttermilk
2	sticks margarine		

Sift dry ingredients together. Cream margarine with 2 cups sugar, vanilla and eggs, one at a time. Beat until fluffy. Add sifted flour mixture alternately with buttermilk beginning and ending with flour. Pour into a greased and floured 13"x 9"x 2"baking dish. Bake in a pre-heated 350° oven for 40 to 45 minutes or until it tests done in center. Pour warm glaze over cooled cake in pan. This cake must be served from the pan.

Glaze:

1 cup heavy cream or evaporated milk, not condensed	2½ tablespoons sugar

Heat the sugar and cream in a saucepan, stirring, until hot. Do not boil.

Yield: 13" x 9" x 2" cake

Evaporated milk may be substituted for whipping cream, if you want to cut calories.

White Cake

This is the first cake my mother taught me how to make. I think I was about 11 years old. It was iced with old-fashioned boiled icing in recipe section of this book. If you do not have cake flour, substitute sifted flour less 2 tablespoons from each cup.

Cake:

¾ cup egg whites (about 6)
2¾ cups sifted cake flour (sifted before measuring)
3 teaspoons baking powder
½ teaspoon salt

1½ cups sugar, divided
¾ cup (1½ sticks) butter
1 teaspoon vanilla extract
½ teaspoon almond extract
1 cup milk

Place egg whites in mixing bowl and let warm to room temperature, about 1 hour. Pre-heat oven to 350°. Grease and flour two 9"x 1½" square cake pans. Sift flour with salt and baking powder; set aside. At high speed beat egg whites until foamy. Gradually beat in ½ cup sugar, beating well after each addition. Then beat until soft peaks form when beater is raised. Set aside. In large bowl of electric mixer, cream butter with rest of sugar, vanilla and almond extracts until light and fluffy. At low speed, beat in flour mixture, alternately with milk, beginning and ending with flour mixture. Beat in egg whites at low speed just until batter is smooth, about 1 minute. Pour batter into prepared pans, bake 25 to 30 minutes or until surface springs back when touched with finger tip. Cool in pans 10 minutes. Remove and let cool completely on wire racks. Frost with old-fashioned boiled icing or icing of your choice.

Yield: Two 9" cake pans

This cake can also be made in a 13" x 9" x 2" baking pan. Notice that this recipe requires two mixing bowls. I always buy an additional bowl at the time I purchase my mixers to simplify matters.

Chocolate Cream Frosting

This is another staple recipe of mine. A vanilla cream frosting can be made by eliminating the cocoa. My mother sometimes dipped the measuring spoon into almond extract, then measured the vanilla in the same spoon.

1	pound powdered sugar	¼	teaspoon salt
5	tablespoons cocoa	¼	cup milk (about)
¾	stick margarine, softened	1	teaspoon vanilla

In mixer bowl, combine powdered sugar and cocoa. Mix well, then add salt, softened margarine, vanilla and milk. Beat until creamy and light. Add a little more milk, if needed, to make of spreading consistency. Try a little on your cake to see if it spreads easily without running off cake.

Yield: 2 layer or 13″ x 9″ cake

I often make this same recipe with sour cream instead of the milk. However, add sour cream gradually as it may not seem enough at first, but thins after beating. Sour cream can be used for both the chocolate and vanilla frostings.

Coffee Frosting

This is a delicious frosting. Brown sugar as well as coffee is one of the ingredients.

1½	cups firmly packed brown sugar	1	teaspoon instant coffee granules
½	cup water	3	egg whites
⅛	teaspoon cream of tartar		Pinch salt

Combine first 3 ingredients in a heavy 2-quart saucepan. Cook over medium heat, stirring constantly, until mixture begins to boil and sugar dissolves. Cook, stirring often, until mixture spins a thread 6″ to 8″ long when dropped from the tip of a spoon or candy thermometer reaches 240°. Remove from heat, add coffee granules, stirring until granules dissolve. Beat egg whites at medium speed with an electric mixer until foamy. Continue to beat, slowly adding syrup mixture in a thin stream. Add salt and beat at high speed until stiff peaks form and frosting is thick.

Yield: 4 cups

Cream Cheese Glaze

This glaze can be used on pound cakes or whatever, when a thick icing is not desired.

3   ounces cream cheese, softened   Dash salt
2 to 2½ tablespoons milk   1½ cups powdered sugar, sifted to
1   teaspoon vanilla   prevent lumps

Beat cream cheese at medium speed until fluffy. Add milk, vanilla and salt. Beat until smooth. Add powdered sugar gradually, beating until smooth. Mixture should be fairly thin. Either dribble or spoon over cake.

Yield: 1 cup

Old-Fashioned Boiled Frosting

This is my mother's recipe that I used to frost the very first cake I ever made.

2   egg whites (¼ cup)   1   teaspoon vinegar
2   cups sugar   1   teaspoon vanilla
⅛   teaspoon salt   1   cup water

In bowl of electric mixer, let egg whites warm to room temperature. In medium saucepan, combine sugar, salt and vinegar with 1 cup water. Cook stirring, over medium heat, until sugar is dissolved and syrup is clear. Continue cooking over medium heat, without stirring, to 242° on a candy thermometer, or until a little spins a thin thread, 6" to 8" long, when dropped from the tip of a spoon. Meanwhile, with mixer at medium speed, beat egg whites until soft peaks form when beater is lifted. With mixer at high speed, gradually pour hot syrup in a thin stream over egg whites, beating constantly. Add vanilla and continue beating until stiff peaks form and frosting is thick enough to spread.

Yield: 8" or 9" two layer cake

Penuche Frosting

This is a fool-proof frosting and one I use often on spice cakes, gingerbread or yellow cakes. This is for a 2-layer cake or a 13" x 9" x 2" cake.

⅔   cup margarine (1⅓ sticks)
1⅓   cups brown sugar, firmly
      packed
⅔   cup milk

⅛   teaspoon salt
1   teaspoon vanilla
1   pound powdered sugar

Melt margarine in heavy saucepan, add brown sugar and salt. Cook over low heat, stirring constantly, until sugar is melted. Slowly add milk, bring to a boil and boil 2 minutes. Remove from heat and add vanilla. Sift powdered sugar into a large bowl, then pour hot brown sugar mixture over, beating until well combined. Ice cake. If frosting thickens too much, add a little more milk for spreading consistency.

Yield: Frosting for 8" layer cake

Seafoam Frosting

2   egg whites (¼ cup)
1½   cups brown sugar, firmly
      packed
¼   teaspoon cream of tartar

⅓   cup water
Dash salt
1   teaspoon vanilla

In top of double boiler, combine egg whites, sugar, cream of tartar, water and salt. Cook over rapidly boiling water (water in bottom should not touch top of double boiler), beating constantly with portable electric mixer at medium speed, until soft peaks form when beater is lifted — about 7 minutes. Remove from boiling water, add vanilla, and continue beating until frosting is thick enough to spread — about 2 minutes.

Yield: 13" x 9" x 2" layer cake

Seven-Minute Frosting can be made from this recipe by substituting granulated sugar for the brown sugar.

Cookies

Raleigh White Johnson, Jr.
Martha's son

Almond Apricot Macaroons

These are delicious. The apricots give a slightly tart taste.

1⅓ cups (8 ounces) slivered almonds
1⅓ cups powdered sugar
Pinch salt
¼ teaspoon pure vanilla extract
¼ teaspoon almond extract
1 egg white
⅓ cup coarsely chopped walnuts or pecans
3 tablespoons finely chopped dried apricots

Position knife blade in food processor bowl; add almonds. Process 2 or 3 minutes or until almonds form a fine powder that begins to hold together, stopping occasionally to scrape down the sides. Add powdered sugar and next 3 ingredients; process until blended. With processor running, add egg white, blending until mixture forms a ball. Transfer to a bowl and stir in nuts and apricots. Shape into 1" balls and place about 1" apart on a lightly greased or parchment covered cookie sheet. Bake at 350° for 10 to 12 minutes. Cool on a wire rack. Store in an airtight container.

Yield: 2 dozen

Almond-Filled Wafers

These wafers are very delicate and should be handled carefully.

Wafers:

1 cup butter, softened
2¼ cups flour
⅓ cup whipping cream
½ cup granulated sugar

Cream butter until light and fluffy. Gradually add flour alternately with whipping cream, beginning and ending with flour. Shape dough into a ball; cover and chill 2 hours. Divide dough in half; place remaining portion in the refrigerator. Roll dough ⅛" thick on a lightly floured board. Cut with a 1½" round cutter. Use a ¼" to ⅜" cutter to cut out heart or other decorative design in center of half of the cookies. Sprinkle both sides of cookies with granulated sugar and place on lightly greased or parchment covered cookie sheets. Repeat with remaining dough. Bake at 375° for 7 to 9 minutes or until lightly browned. Cool on wire racks. Spread solid cookies with frosting, place cut-out cookie on top. Store in a tightly covered container.

Frosting:

½ stick butter, softened
¾ cup powdered sugar
½ teaspoon almond extract
1 or 2 drops of coloring, optional

Combine all ingredients until creamy.

Yield: About 4½ dozen

Almond Meringues

The addition of the lemon juice and almonds make these meringues special.

1	tablespoon butter, softened	½	teaspoon strained fresh lemon
3	egg whites, room temperature		juice
¾	cup sugar	1	teaspoon grated lemon rind
⅛	teaspoon vanilla	1	cup slivered blanched almonds

Pre-heat oven to 250°. Lightly coat two cookie sheets with the softened butter and set aside. In mixer bowl, beat the egg whites until they froth. Gradually add the sugar and vanilla and continue to beat until whites form stiff, but not dry, peaks. With a rubber spatula, fold in the lemon juice, lemon rind and almonds. Drop the meringue by teaspoonsful onto the buttered cookie sheets, letting it mound naturally, leaving at least an inch between each mound. Bake on middle shelf of the oven for 40 minutes, then transfer cookies to wire racks and cool at room temperature. Place in tightly covered container. As with most meringues, do not make on a damp, humid day.

Yield: About 4 dozen

Amaretto Balls, Vivian

These delectable cookies may be made ahead and frozen in a tightly covered container.

1	cup vanilla wafer crumbs	2	tablespoons white corn syrup
¾	cup chopped pecans or	⅓	cup amaretto
	almonds		Powdered sugar for coating
1	cup powdered sugar		

Mix vanilla wafer crumbs, nuts and powdered sugar in bowl of mixer. Add corn syrup and liqueur, blending to make a stiff dough. Roll into ¾" to 1" balls and then roll into sifted powdered sugar. Place in a single layer on waxed paper. Cover and chill overnight. Store in tightly covered container.

Yield: About 35 balls

I chop my nuts in a food processor. They should be fairly fine but not a meal. This recipe can be doubled or tripled.

Applejacks

Another recipe from Sturbridge Village.

1 cup light brown sugar, packed	½ teaspoon salt
½ cup shortening	1 teaspoon nutmeg
1 egg	1 cup chopped unpeeled apples
1½ cups flour	Rum
½ teaspoon soda	

Cream sugar and shortening, add egg, then dry ingredients beating until well blended. Stir in apples. Drop in balls on greased pan. Bake at 375° for 12 to 15 minutes. As soon as they come from the oven, sprinkle each cookie with 4 or 5 drops rum.

Yield: About 3 dozen

Aunt Ethel's Filled Cookies

This is another recipe from my neighbor, Vivian Surles. It is a little trouble to make but is well worth it. This recipe dates back several generations.

Cookies:

1 cup sugar	2½ cups flour
½ cup shortening or margarine	½ cup buttermilk
1 egg	½ teaspoon salt
1 teaspoon baking powder	1 teaspoon vanilla
½ teaspoon soda	

Cream sugar and shortening, then beat in egg. Add buttermilk and vanilla, then dry ingredients. Store, covered, in the refrigerator overnight. Next day, roll out dough ⅛" thick and cut with a small biscuit cutter. Place a scant teaspoon of the filling on each cookie. Moisten the edges and place another cookie on top. Pinch edges together. Bake at 350° for 10 to 12 minutes. Cool completely, then spread with a thin icing made of powdered sugar and a little milk. If you wish to make a smaller cookie, you may place filling on half of one cookie and then fold over in a half moon shape and bake.

Filling:

1 cup raisins or dates (cut dates in pieces)	1 tablespoon flour
	½ cup sugar
½ cup chopped nuts, black walnuts are the best	½ cup water
	¼ teaspoon cinnamon

Place ingredients in a saucepan and boil, stirring constantly, until smooth and very thick. Cool overnight for easier handling before filling cookies.

Yield: About 24 cookies

Bitsy's Sugar Cookies

Bitsy Kostelecky is a friend of my neighbor, Vivian Surles. This sugar cookie is one of the best I have ever tasted. In addition, it is easy to make and uses margarine and shortening instead of butter.

½	cup margarine	1	teaspoon vanilla
½	cup shortening	2¼	cups flour
1	cup sugar	½	teaspoon baking powder
1	egg	½	teaspoon soda

Cream margarine, shortening, sugar and vanilla together in mixer. Add egg, flour, soda and baking powder. Mix well. Shape into 1″ balls. Place on greased cookie sheet and flatten with a water glass dipped in granulated sugar. Bake in a 350° oven for 10 to 12 minutes or until light brown. Remove to a wire rack and cool. Store in a tightly covered container.

Yield: 6 to 7 dozen

My Mother used to dip her sugar cookies, which she rolled out, in sugar. This recipe accomplishes the same with the glass dipped in sugar.

Bourbon Brownies

These are rich and delicate, so cut them carefully.

4	(1 ounce) squares of unsweetened chocolate	2	cups sugar
1	cup butter or margarine	1½	cups flour
4	large eggs	½	teaspoon salt
		2	tablespoons bourbon

Combine chocolate and butter or margarine in small heavy saucepan; cook over low heat, stirring constantly, until chocolate melts. Cool 10 minutes. Beat eggs in mixer until pale and thick; gradually add sugar, beating well. Add chocolate mixture, flour, salt, and bourbon. Beat at low speed 1 minute. Spoon into a lightly greased, floured 12″ x 9″ x 2″ pan. Bake in a 350° oven for 25 to 30 minutes or until a toothpick inserted in center comes out clean. Do not overbake. Cool on rack 10 minutes, then cut into bars with a thin knife. Dust with powdered sugar, if desired.

Yield: 4 dozen

Brown Sugar Shortbread

This can also be baked in an earthen shortbread pan.

1	cup butter, softened	2	cups flour
¾	cup firmly packed dark brown sugar	2	teaspoons praline liqueur

Beat butter at medium speed in mixer until creamy; gradually add brown sugar, beating until light and fluffy. Add liqueur, then flour, (dough will be stiff). Firmly press dough into a well-greased, floured 9" round cake pan. Bake at 300° for about 1 hour or until tester comes out dry when inserted in the middle. Let cool 15 minutes, then loosen edges and invert onto cookie sheet. Cut into wedges with a sharp knife.

Yield: 9" round cake pan

Cake Mix Cookies

Use plain cake mix, not the butter or pudding kind, for this recipe. The box should contain at least 18 ounces.

Cake mix of your choice	½	cup oil
2 eggs		

Mix ingredients well, then add nuts, etc. Drop by teaspoonsful onto ungreased cookie sheet 2" apart. Bake at 350° for 8 to 10 minutes according to size of cookie.

Yield: About 3 dozen

I have made these with a cake mix and added a variety of nuts, chocolate or peanut butter chips, raisins or Heath's Bits O' Brickle with equal success. Use whatever fits with the flavor cake mix.

Chewy Praline Squares

A great dessert after a Mexican supper.

2	large eggs	1½	cups flour, sifted before measuring
2	cups light brown sugar, packed		
2	sticks butter, melted	1	teaspoon vanilla
		1	cup chopped pecans

Beat eggs and sugar in mixer bowl until light colored. Stir in the butter, then add flour gradually. Add vanilla and pecans. Pour into a greased 8"x 11"pan. Bake at 350° for 30 to 35 minutes or until toothpick inserted in the middle comes out dry but with a few crumbs sticking to it. Cool on rack and cut into squares.

Yield: 3 dozen

Caramel Cookies

This cookie freezes well. It can be cut into 48 small squares, if serving at a tea.

Cookie Dough:

1	cup plus 2 heaping tablespoons flour	2	tablespoons sugar
1	stick butter or margarine		Pinch salt

Cream the 1 cup flour, butter, sugar and salt. Spread in a 6" x 12" pan. Bake in a 325° oven about 20 minutes, but do not let brown.

Second Layer:

2	eggs, well beaten	½	teaspoon baking powder
1½	cups brown sugar, firmly packed		Pinch salt
1	teaspoon vanilla	1	cup chopped pecans

Mix together the eggs, pinch of salt, brown sugar, vanilla and the remaining flour, baking powder and nuts. Pour over baked dough and return to oven. Bake at 325° for 35 minutes. Cool before cutting.

Yield: 24 cookies

Chewy Caramel Squares

2	sticks margarine	1	teaspoon baking powder
1	pound light brown sugar	¼	teaspoon salt
½	cup granulated sugar	1	cup chopped walnuts or
4	eggs		pecans (optional)
1	teaspoon vanilla		Confectioners sugar
2	cups flour		

Heat margarine and brown sugar in a saucepan until margarine is melted. Remove from heat and place in bowl of mixer. Add sugar, eggs, and vanilla. Mix well. Sift together flour, salt and baking powder. Add to first mixture and blend well. Add nuts, if desired. Spread in a greased and floured cookie sheet with 1" sides. Bake at 300° for 35-40 minutes or until toothpick inserted in center comes out with a few crumbs sticking to it. Cool 20 minutes. Cut into squares and sprinkle with sifted confectioners sugar while still warm. Let cool completely before removing from pan to a covered container. These will freeze.

Yield: 32 squares

Chewy Chocolate Pan Cookies

This is an easy way to make cookies for a crowd.

1¼	cups margarine or butter	¾	cup cocoa
2	cups sugar	1	teaspoon baking soda
2	eggs	½	teaspoon salt
2	teaspoons vanilla	12	ounces (2 cups) chocolate or
2	cups all-purpose flour		peanut butter chips

Heat oven to 350°. Grease a 15½"x 10"x 1"jelly roll pan. In large mixer bowl, beat margarine or butter and sugar until light and fluffy. Add eggs and vanilla and beat well. Combine flour, cocoa, baking soda and salt; gradually blend into creamed mixture. Stir in chips. Spread batter into prepared pan; bake 20 minutes or until just set. Cool completely and cut into bars or squares.

Yield: 15½ " x 10 " x 2 "

I have also made these as individual cookies using the chocolate chips for chocolate lovers.

Chocolate Buttermilk Squares

Squares:

2	cups flour	2	eggs
2	cups sugar	½	cup buttermilk
2	sticks margarine	1	teaspoon soda
1	cup water	1	teaspoon vanilla
¼	cup cocoa		

Sift flour and sugar in mixer bowl. Boil together the margarine, water and cocoa. Add to flour and sugar, then add eggs, buttermilk, soda and vanilla. Beat until smooth. Heat oven to 400°. Pour batter into a greased cookie sheet with 1"sides. Bake for about 20 minutes until done in center. Frost while warm.

Chocolate Frosting:

1	stick softened margarine	¼	teaspoon salt
1	pound powdered sugar, sifted	1	teaspoon vanilla
	if lumpy	4 to 6	tablespoons milk
6	tablespoons cocoa		

Mix all ingredients in mixer, then spread on warm cake. Cut into squares.

Yield: 40 small squares

Nuts and miniature marshmallows may be added to frosting, if desired. Also a "Black Forest" touch may be given by spreading raspberry or cherry preserves over cake before frosting.

Chocolate Marshmallow Rice Krispy Cookies

These are made with chocolate bark, an easy snack. My great grandchildren love to make and eat these.

2	pounds chocolate bark	2	cups mini marshmallows
1	cup creamy peanut butter	3	cups Rice Krispies
2	cups dry roasted peanuts		

Place broken chocolate bark in a 13" x 9" pan. Heat in a 200° oven for 10 minutes. When soft, stir in remaining ingredients. Drop silver dollar-size dollops on waxed paper and cool to room temperature until firm, about 1 hour. Store in covered container.

Yield: About 5 dozen

Chocolate Meringue Bars

This recipe can be used for dessert by making larger pieces and serving with a scoop of ice cream.

Bars:

4	tablespoons butter	1	teaspoon cold water
4	tablespoons vegetable shortening	1	teaspoon vanilla
½	cup sugar	1¾	cups flour
½	cup light brown sugar, firmly packed	¼	teaspoon salt
3	egg yolks	1	teaspoon baking soda
		1	(6 ounce) package chocolate chips

Sift flour, soda and salt together. Cream butter, shortening, sugar and the ½ cup brown sugar in mixing bowl. In separate bowl, beat egg yolks, water and vanilla. Add to butter mixture alternately with flour. Spread into a vegetable sprayed 12"x 7" oblong pan. Sprinkle with chocolate chips.

Topping:

3	egg whites	1½	cups brown sugar, loosely packed

Beat the egg whites until firm peaks form, then add the 1½ cups brown sugar one tablespoon at a time. Spread meringue over chocolate chips making sure to touch all edges of the pan to keep meringue from shrinking. Bake in a 325° oven for 30 to 35 minutes or until done in center. Cool before serving. Cut into bars of size desired.

Yield: 12 to 24 bars

Chocolate Oat Bars

Bars:

1	cup quick-cooking oats	⅓	cup flour
½	cup light brown sugar, firmly packed	½	stick margarine or butter, melted
½	cup pecans, chopped fairly fine	¼	teaspoon baking soda
		¼	teaspoon salt

Pre-heat oven to 350°. Place ingredients in bowl of mixer. Beat at low speed until well mixed. Pat mixture into bottom of a floured 8" x 8" baking pan. Bake 10 minutes. Set aside.

Second Layer:

1	(1 ounce) square unsweetened chocolate	1	teaspoon pure vanilla
1	stick of margarine or butter	1	large egg
½	cup sugar	⅔	cup flour
2	tablespoons whole milk	¼	teaspoon baking soda
		¼	teaspoon salt

Melt chocolate and margarine or butter in a small saucepan over low heat. Remove from heat and stir in sugar, milk, vanilla, egg, flour, soda and salt. Mix until smooth and pour over baked layer; bake 30 minutes longer or until toothpick inserted in center comes out clean. Cool and cut into 2" x 1½" bars.

Yield: About 20 bars

Chocolate Shortbread

2⅓	cups flour	1¾	cups powdered sugar
⅓	cup cocoa	1	square unsweetened chocolate
⅛	teaspoon salt	1	teaspoon vanilla
1	cup butter, divided		

Put chocolate and ¼ cup (½ stick) of butter in a heavy small saucepan. Place over low heat until chocolate is melted. Set aside to cool. Beat remainder of butter, sugar and vanilla in bowl of mixer until light and fluffy. Add melted chocolate and mix. Sift flour, salt and cocoa together, then add to creamed mixture. Beat until blended and smooth. Divide dough into quarters. Roll each quarter between waxed paper to ¼" thickness. Cut into squares or triangles. Re-roll any scraps by laying them on top of each other. If kneaded with hands, dough is apt to become tough. Bake on an ungreased cookie sheet in a 350° oven about 10 to 12 minutes or until just firm to the touch. Cool and store in a tightly covered container.

Yield: Forty 3" cookies

Congo Squares

⅔ cup shortening
1   pound light brown sugar
3   eggs
1   teaspoon vanilla
2¾ cups flour

2½ teaspoons baking powder
½   teaspoon salt
1   cup chopped nuts
6   ounces semi-sweet chocolate
      chips

Cream shortening and sugar. Add eggs, one at a time, beating after each addition. Add vanilla. Sift together flour, baking powder and salt; add to creamed mixture. Stir in nuts and chocolate chips. Bake in a greased 9"x 13"x 2"pan at 350° about 35 to 40 minutes or until just done in center. Cut into bars.

Yield: 4 dozen squares

Gingerbread Boys

This recipe calls for a large gingerbread cutter. One Christmas, I used a 3" gingerbread boy cutter and packaged them in small boxes for my great grandchildren. I decorated them with currants for the eyes and a tiny bit of candied cherry for the nose.

¾ cup dark corn syrup
½   pound butter or margarine
1   cup sugar
1   tablespoon cider vinegar
1   egg

5   cups of flour
1½ teaspoons baking soda
1   teaspoon ginger
1   teaspoon cinnamon
¼   teaspoon salt

Heat corn syrup to boiling, then pour over butter or margarine in a mixing bowl. Add the sugar and vinegar and beat until smooth. Blend in the egg. Sift together the flour, baking soda, ginger, cinnamon and salt. Add to the corn syrup mixture and mix. Cover and chill in the refrigerator for several hours or overnight. Remove ¼ of the dough at a time. Roll out on floured board to ¼" thick. Cut with a large gingerbread boy cutter. Place on greased cookie sheet. Bake 10 to 12 minutes at 350°. Frost with powdered sugar frosting. Decorate with raisins for eyes and buttons. Use a part of a candied cherry for nose.

Powdered Sugar Icing:

2   cups powdered sugar, sifted
      after measuring
1   teaspoon vanilla

Dash salt
Milk enough to make of spreading
      consistency

Mix all ingredients together until smooth.

I did not ice the small gingerbread boys.

4 O'Clocks

Another recipe from Old Sturbridge Village. Original recipe said, "Stamp each cookie with a butter print in flower pattern to make the 4 O'Clocks." These old-fashioned flowers were in my Grandmother Eastman's garden.

½	cup sugar	1	teaspoon soda
½	cup butter	½	teaspoon salt
1	egg	1	tablespoon lemon juice
1 to 1½ cups flour		1	teaspoon grated lemon rind

Cream butter and sugar until very light. Add beaten egg, then lemon rind. Start with 1 cup flour, sifted with the soda and salt, add to first mixture. Add lemon juice. Then add up to ½ cup additional flour, beating between additions. Dip fingers in sugar and pinch off balls of dough, rolling each ball in sugar; arrange on greased cookie sheet, 2" apart. Bake at 375° for 12 to 15 minutes. This recipe makes large flat cookies, spreading as they bake.

Glazed Brownies

Brownies:

½	cup shortening	2	(1 ounce) squares unsweetened chocolate, melted
1	cup brown sugar, packed		
2	eggs	½	cup chopped pecans
½	cup flour	1	teaspoon vanilla
⅛	teaspoon salt		

Pre-heat oven to 350°. Cream shortening and sugar, then add eggs and beat well. Sift flour with salt and add to sugar mixture. Add melted chocolate, pecans and vanilla. Spread in greased 9" x 9" square pan. Bake about 20 minutes or until barely done in middle. Spread with glaze and cut before completely cold with a thin knife.

Glaze:

1	cup powdered sugar, sifted before measuring	1	tablespoon whole milk
2	tablespoons white corn syrup	¼	teaspoon vanilla

Combine all ingredients and stir until well blended. Spread on brownies.

Yield: 12 to 15 squares

You may substitute a little oil of peppermint for the vanilla and add a little green coloring to the glaze, if desired.

Honey Brownies

I like to cook with honey. This recipe comes from Sue Bee Honey.

1½	cups flour	½	cup honey
1	teaspoon baking powder	1	egg
½	teaspoon salt	1	teaspoon vanilla
½	cup soft shortening	½	cup nuts
½	cup brown sugar, packed		

Pre-heat oven to 350°. Mix all ingredients except nuts in mixer until smooth, then stir in nuts. Spread into a greased 8"x 8" pan. Bake 25 to 30 minutes or until a slight imprint remains when touched with a finger. Do not overbake. Before cooling, cut into 15 bars, five cuts across and three cuts down.

Yield: 15 bars

Honey is sold by weight. A 12-ounce jar equals an 8-fluid ounce measuring cup. Granulation does not affect the taste or purity of honey. It never spoils. Honey can be measured easily by using the same cup used for the oil or by coating a cup with spray.

Palmiers

This is a favorite French pastry of mine made a little simpler with mock French pastry.

1	cup cold unsalted butter, no substitutions	½	cup sour cream
1¾	cups flour	1	teaspoon grated lemon peel
			Sugar

With pastry blender or two knives, cut butter into flour in a large bowl until mixture resembles coarse crumbs. Stir in sour cream and lemon peel until well blended. Place on waxed paper and shape into a 4½" square. Wrap and refrigerate at least 2 hours or overnight. Divide dough into quarters. Sprinkle 2 tablespoons sugar on board. Roll one quarter on sugared surface, turning frequently, into a 12"x 5" rectangle. Keep remaining dough refrigerated. On long edge, lightly mark center (do not cut through dough). From each short side, roll up, jelly roll fashion, toward center until edges just meet (scroll fashion). Wrap well in waxed paper. Repeat with rest of dough, forming 3 more scrolls, using more sugar as needed. Wrap all the scrolls and either refrigerate 2 to 3 hours or freeze 20 minutes.

Pre-heat oven to 375°. Line cookie sheets with foil or parchment. Place ¼ cup sugar on waxed paper. Cut each scroll crosswise into ¼" slices; dip each side in sugar. Place 2½"apart on cookie sheet. Bake 10 minutes or until edges are golden brown. Turn cookies with spatula and bake 2 or 3 minutes more, until both sides are golden brown. Immediately transfer to wire rack. Store in tightly covered container, placing waxed paper between single layers.

Yield: 80 cookies

Molasses Chews

I love molasses, so I had to include this recipe. Yes, this is another Sturbridge recipe.

1	cup white sugar	¼	cup molasses
1	cup brown sugar	4	cups sifted flour
1	cup shortening	1	teaspoon salt
2	eggs	1½	teaspoons baking soda
2	teaspoons vanilla	1	cup flaked coconut

Cream sugars and shortening, add beaten eggs, vanilla, molasses, flour sifted with soda and salt and coconut. Form small balls on greased cookie sheet. Bake 12-15 minutes at 375°.

Mother's One Cup Cookies

1	cup margarine, softened	1	teaspoon baking soda
1	cup granulated sugar	1	cup quick oatmeal, uncooked
1	cup light brown sugar, packed	1	cup chopped nuts of your
3	eggs		choice
1	cup peanut butter	1	cup raisins
2	cups flour	1	cup chocolate chips

Cream margarine and sugars in mixer until light and fluffy. Add eggs, one at a time, beating after each addition. Add peanut butter, then flour mixed with the soda. Mix well. Add remaining ingredients, one at a time, mixing at low speed after each addition. Drop heaping teaspoonsful onto lightly greased cookie sheet. Bake in a 350° oven for 10 minutes. Cool and pack in covered container.

Yield: About 5 dozen

Lumberjacks

This is a large soft cookie, 24 to a cookie sheet. A recipe I got many years ago in a pamphlet from Old Sturbridge Village.

1	cup sugar	1	teaspoon baking soda
1	cup shortening	1	teaspoon salt
1	cup dark molasses	2	teaspoons cinnamon
2	eggs	1	teaspoon ginger
4	cups sifted flour		

Cream the sugar and shortening, add molasses and eggs, then dry ingredients. Have at hand a small bowl of sugar. Dipping the fingers into the sugar, pinch off a ball of cookie dough, about walnut-sized. Dip the ball into the sugar, arrange on a greased cookie sheet. Bake in a 350° oven 12-15 minutes.

Yield: 4 dozen

Oatmeal Pecan Cookies

These cookies call for toasted oatmeal and pecans which gives a special flavor.

1½	cups butter, divided	1	large egg
3	cups regular or quick-cooking oats, uncooked	1	teaspoon vanilla
		1½	cups flour
1	cup chopped pecans or walnuts	1	teaspoon baking soda
		½	teaspoon salt
¾	cup firmly packed brown sugar	1	teaspoon ground cinnamon
½	cup granulated sugar	1	cup raisins

Melt ½ cup of the butter in a 15"x 10"x 1"jelly roll pan in a 400° oven. Remove from oven; add oats and pecans, stirring to coat. Bake at 400° for 15 to 20 minutes, stirring occasionally, until lightly browned. Set aside to cool. Beat remaining cup of butter at medium speed in mixer until soft and creamy. Gradually add sugars, beating well, then beat in egg and vanilla. Combine flour and next 3 ingredients; add to butter mixture, mixing well. Stir in raisins and oat mixture. Drop by rounded tablespoons onto lightly greased cookie sheets; bake at 375° for 10 to 12 minutes or until lightly browned. Cool 1 minute; then remove to wire racks to cool completely.

Yield: 5 dozen

Pecan Cookies

These cookies can be dropped by scant teaspoonsful, then flattened with the bottom of a glass dipped lightly in flour, if you do not want to roll them out.

Cookies:

½	cup butter, softened	1	cup flour
⅓	cup sugar	1	cup finely chopped pecans
1½	teaspoons grated orange rind		

Cream butter; gradually add sugar and beat until light and fluffy. Add orange rind, flour and pecans; mix well. Cover and chill 1 hour or more. Roll dough ⅛"to ¼" thick on a lightly floured board. Cut with a 2"cutter. Place on ungreased cookie sheets. Bake in a 350° oven about 7 minutes or until lightly browned. Cool, then spread with icing.

Icing:

1	stick butter, melted	2 to 2½ cups sifted powdered
¼	cup Grand Marnier	sugar

Combine all ingredients in a bowl; beat at medium speed until smooth. Add food coloring, if desired. Yield: 1 cup.

Yield: about 4 dozen cookies

Praline Sand Tarts

Tart:

1 cup margarine, softened	2 cups flour
1 cup powdered sugar, sifted before measuring	½ cup finely chopped pecans
	1 teaspoon vanilla

Cream margarine and sugar in mixer at medium speed. Add flour and mix well. Stir in pecans and vanilla. Shape dough into 1" balls; place about 2" apart on ungreased cookie sheets. Press thumb in center of each cookie to make an indentation. Bake at 375° for about 15 minutes. Do not brown. Cool, then spoon about ½ teaspoon Praline filling into indentation in each cookie.

Praline Filling:

1 stick margarine	2 cups powdered sugar,
1 cup firmly packed brown sugar	sifted if lumpy
Dash salt	½ teaspoon vanilla
½ cup evaporated milk	

Melt margarine in saucepan, add brown sugar and salt; bring to a boil. Boil 2 minutes, stirring constantly. Remove from heat and add milk; bring to a boil and boil 2 minutes. Remove from heat and let cool to lukewarm. Stir in powdered sugar and vanilla; beat until mixture is smooth. Yield: about 1½ cups.

Yield: About 3 dozen

Raisin Gems

I remember these spicy cookies from my childhood.

¾ cup shortening	1 teaspoon cinnamon
1 cup sugar	½ teaspoon cloves
¼ cup molasses	½ teaspoon ginger
1 egg	¼ teaspoon salt
2 cups flour	1 cup raisins
2 teaspoons baking soda	Additional sugar for dipping

Beat shortening and sugar until light and fluffy. Add molasses and egg; beat well. Combine flour, soda, cinnamon, cloves, ginger and salt. Add to molasses mixture; mix well. Stir in raisins. Cover; refrigerate until chilled. Shape into 1" balls; roll in sugar. Place 2" apart on greased cookie sheets. Bake in upper third of a preheated 350° oven for 10 to 12 minutes or until set in middle. Cool 1 minute, then transfer to wire racks.

Yield: About 3 dozen

Raspberry-Filled Brownies

½   cup margarine or butter,
    softened
1   cup sugar
2   large eggs
½   teaspoon vanilla

2   (1-ounce) squares unsweetened
    chocolate, melted
¾   cup flour
1   cup chopped walnuts or
    pecans
⅓   cup raspberry jam

Beat butter in mixer at medium speed until fluffy; add sugar, eggs and vanilla beating well. Add flour and chocolate; stir in nuts. Spoon half of batter into a greased 9"x 9" square pan. Spread jam over batter; top with rest of batter. Bake at 350° about 25 to 30 minutes. Cool and cut into squares.

Yield: 3 dozen small brownies

Walnut Fudge Drop Cookies

Another recipe from Sturbridge Village.

1   cup sugar
¼   cup butter or shortening
2   ounces unsweetened chocolate
2   eggs
1   teaspoon vanilla

½   teaspoon salt
1¾ cups flour
¾   teaspoon soda
1   cup walnuts, chopped

Melt shortening and chocolate over low heat, cool. Beat eggs with salt, add sugar and vanilla. Add the cooled chocolate mixture. Add flour and soda. Combine but do not overbeat. Add walnuts. Drop on greased cookie sheet. Bake 10 minutes at 350°.

Yield: About 4 dozen

White Chocolate Pecan Cookies

Dough may be frozen in a tightly covered container up to six months or can be dropped onto a cookie sheet, frozen; then placed in heavy zip-top bag and stored in freezer. When ready to bake, place frozen mounds on cookie sheet and bake as directed.

½   cup margarine, softened
¾   cup brown sugar, firmly
     packed
2   tablespoons granulated sugar
1   large egg
1½ teaspoons pure vanilla extract
2   cups flour
¾   teaspoon baking soda

½   teaspoon baking powder
⅛   teaspoon salt
6   ounces vanilla-milk morsels or
     6 ounces white chocolate-
     flavored bark, cut into chunks
1½ cups coarsely chopped pecans
     or nuts of your choice

Beat margarine in mixing bowl until fluffy; gradually add sugars, then add egg and vanilla. Mix well at medium speed. Sift flour, soda, baking powder and salt; gradually add to margarine mixture, mixing well. Stir in chocolate and nuts. Drop by rounded teaspoonsful onto lightly greased cookie sheets. Bake at 350° 8 to 10 minutes or until lightly browned. Remove to wire racks to cool. Use your imagination to change recipes — use mint chocolate, peanut butter or vanilla-milk morsels with chocolate dough for instance.

Yield: 5 dozen

If you do not have enough wire racks to cool cookies, place a sheet of waxed paper on table and sprinkle with sugar. Cookies will cool without getting soggy. Use solid shortening or vegetable cooking spray, not butter or margarine to grease pans.

Helpful Hint: *Spritz your spatula with a non-stick spray before removing cookies from the cookie sheet to eliminate sticking and tearing.*

Zucchini Bars

This sweet is packed with nutrition. It contains whole wheat flour, zucchini and white raisins.

Bars:

1¼	cups brown sugar, packed	2	teaspoons baking soda
½	cup margarine, softened	¾	teaspoon cinnamon
2	large eggs	½	teaspoon nutmeg
1	teaspoon vanilla	¼	teaspoon cloves
2	cups whole wheat flour	1½	cups shredded zucchini
½	teaspoon salt	1	cup white raisins

Heat oven to 350°. Grease a 13" x 9" x 2" pan. Mix brown sugar, margarine, eggs, and vanilla in mixer bowl. Add flour, salt, baking soda, cinnamon, nutmeg and cloves. Mix just until dry ingredients disappear, then stir in zucchini and raisins. Spread in prepared pan and bake for 25 to 30 minutes or until toothpick inserted in the center comes out clean. Cool, then frost with Cream Cheese Frosting.

Cream Cheese Frosting:

3	ounces cream cheese, softened	1	teaspoon vanilla
¼	cup plus 2 tablespoons margarine, softened	2	cups powdered sugar

Beat cream cheese, margarine and vanilla until creamy. Add powdered sugar gradually, then beat until smooth.

Yield: 32 bars

Confections

Taken at Texas School Food Service Association meeting
in San Antonio, Texas. I autographed complimentary copies of
Raleigh House Cookbook I.

From left to right:
Raleigh W. Johnson III, Martha Johnson, and David B. Johnson

Bourbon Balls

These are particularly good to serve during the holidays. My family likes them anytime. They keep for several weeks in a covered container in the refrigerator.

4	tablespoons unsalted butter, softened	2	tablespoons bourbon
2	cups powdered sugar, sifted after measuring	2	ounces (⅓ cup) pecans, finely chopped
		8	ounces chocolate almond bark

Cream the sugar and butter together until mixture is light and fluffy. Beat in the bourbon, a tablespoon at a time, then stir in pecans. Mixture should be soft — barely firm enough to form into balls. Add more sugar, if needed. One at a time, pinch off about 1 level tablespoon of the mixture and roll it between the palms of the hands until it forms a ball about 1" in diameter. Place the balls on a cookie sheet lined with waxed paper and refrigerate 30 minutes or until balls are firm. Melt the chocolate almond bark in the top of a double boiler by placing over simmering water that does not touch the bottom of the pan. Stir chocolate almond bark frequently until melted. Remove from heat and let it rest for about 10 minutes, until chocolate is cool but still soft. Remove candies from the refrigerator and, one at a time, spear them with a toothpick. Dip them in the chocolate, coating them thoroughly, then place on a sheet of waxed paper or stick into a piece of Styrofoam until chocolate hardens. Refrigerate at least 2 hours before serving.

Yield: 20 to 30 balls

These can also be made in smaller balls — 1 teaspoon.

Caramelized Almonds

This is a recipe for the microwave.

1	large egg white	2	tablespoons granulated sugar
1	cup sliced almonds		

Beat the egg white in a small bowl until frothy, add the almonds and turn with hands until all are well covered with the egg white. Sprinkle with the sugar and mix until almonds are coated. Spread in a 9" microwave proof pie plate. Microwave on High 2 minutes. Stir, then microwave 6 to 8 minutes longer, stirring every minute until sugar is caramelized and almonds are golden. Cool in pie plate on flat surface.

Yield: 1 cup

Chocolate Caramels

2 (1 ounce) squares unsweetened chocolate	1 cup light corn syrup
½ cup water	1 cup evaporated milk
2 cups sugar	¼ cup butter
	1 teaspoon vanilla

Line a 9" square pan with foil; butter foil. In heavy saucepan, cook chocolate and water, stirring, until chocolate is melted. Add sugar, corn syrup, evaporated milk and butter. Continue cooking, stirring constantly, until mixture boils. Continue cooking, stirring frequently, until candy thermometer registers 240° or until syrup, when dropped into ice water, forms a ball that flattens out when removed from water. Remove from heat; add vanilla. Pour into prepared pan; cool completely. Lift candy and foil out of pan; remove foil. With buttered scissors, cut into 1" squares. Wrap in plastic wrap before storing in container.

Yield: 4 dozen 1" squares

Chocolate Dip

This is an easy dessert, pretty to look at and delicious. An easy substitute for chocolate dipped strawberries.

⅔ cup light corn syrup	1⅓ cups semi-sweet chocolate morsels
½ cup heavy cream	

Place syrup and cream in heavy saucepan. Cook and stir until boiling. Remove from heat; add chocolate morsels and stir until melted. Serve warm as a dip for fresh strawberries or fresh fruit of your choice.

Yield: 1½ cups

Chocolate Strawberry Balls

You may freeze these up to two months.

8 ounces cream cheese, softened	¼ cup strawberry preserves
1 (6 ounce) package semi-sweet chocolate chips, melted	½ cup almonds, toasted and finely chopped
¾ cup vanilla wafer crumbs	

Beat cream cheese at medium speed in mixer until creamy. Add melted chocolate, beating until smooth. Stir in vanilla wafer crumbs and preserves; cover and chill 1 hour. Shape into 1" balls; roll into chopped almonds and chill.

Yield: 4 dozen

Chocolate Fudge

The addition of cornstarch makes a creamier and smoother fudge. Also, buttering the sides of the saucepan keeps the fudge from boiling over.

2	tablespoons cornstarch	2	tablespoons light corn syrup
2	cups sugar	½	stick butter or margarine
½	cup cocoa	1	teaspoon vanilla
⅛	teaspoon salt	½	cup chopped pecans or
⅔	cups whole milk		walnuts

Butter the sides of a 2½ or 3-quart saucepan. Mix the cornstarch, sugar, cocoa, salt, milk, and corn syrup in the pan. Stir over moderate heat until the sugar is dissolved, Try not to splash any of the mixture on the sides of the pan. Bring mixture to a boil. Cover the saucepan for 2 or 3 minutes to dissolve any sugar clinging to the sides of the pan. Uncover and place a candy thermometer in the pan. Boil without stirring, until the thermometer reaches 236° or until a little dropped in a cup of ice water forms a soft ball. Remove pan from heat and add butter but do not stir in. Let cool until pan feels comfortably warm to the palm of your hand. Add the vanilla, incorporate the butter and beat the fudge until it becomes very thick or is thick enough to hold its shape. Quickly stir in the nuts and push into a generously buttered 8″ square pan. When fudge begins to harden, cut into the size pieces you want.

Yield: 36 pieces

Peanut Butter Balls

These are favorites of my family. The recipe was given to me by a friend and neighbor.

2	cups peanut butter	¾	(12 ounce) package semi-sweet
2	cups confectioners sugar,		chocolate chips
	sifted after measuring	1	(1″ x 2½″ x ½″) piece of
			paraffin

Mix peanut butter and sugar. Form into small balls. Refrigerate until firm. Melt chocolate and paraffin and dip the balls in it. I find it easier to spear the balls with a toothpick instead of a fork for dipping. Toothpick can then be placed in a small piece of Styrofoam until chocolate is firm.

Yield: 20 to 30 balls

These are equally good with a coating of chocolate almond bark.

Peanut Butter Fudge

I read recently that peanuts have been found to contain a new chemical called boron that is very beneficial. I am so glad as I have always been fond of peanut butter and peanuts.

4	cups sugar	1	teaspoon vanilla
1	cup milk	1	cup either smooth or chunky
3	tablespoons light corn syrup		peanut butter
3	tablespoons butter or	½	cup coarsely chopped unsalted
	margarine cut into bits		dry-roasted peanuts

In a 2-quart heavy saucepan, combine the sugar, milk, corn syrup and a pinch of salt. Cook the mixture over moderate heat, stirring, until sugar is dissolved, then cook without stirring, until candy thermometer reaches 238°. Remove pan from the heat, add the butter without stirring it into the mixture. Let mixture cool until bottom of pan is comfortably warm to the palm of your hand. Stir in the peanuts, vanilla, and peanut butter. Beat the mixture with a wooden spoon until it begins to lose its gloss. Pour immediately into a buttered 9" square pan. When fudge begins to harden, cut it into squares and let cool completely.

Yield: 2 pounds fudge

Helpful Hint: One cup whole milk can be substituted with 1 cup nonfat dry milk plus 2 teaspoons butter or margarine.

Desserts

Clockwise from top right:
Alice Colvin, Richard Colvin, John Adkins, Jr., and Elizabeth Adkins

Almond Lace Cups

These are very versatile. They can be filled with a mousse, pie fillings, fresh fruit or whatever your taste prefers.

⅔   cup light brown sugar, packed
½   cup light corn syrup
1   stick unsalted butter

1   cup almonds, finely chopped
⅔   cup cake flour

Pre-heat the oven to 325°. In a medium saucepan, bring brown sugar, corn syrup and butter to a boil over moderate heat. Remove from heat and stir in the almonds and flour. Bake 2 cookies at a time. To make each cookie, drop 2 tablespoons of batter onto a nonstick cookie sheet or one lined with parchment or foil, allowing it to spread to 5". Bake in the middle of the oven for about 12 minutes, until golden brown. Let cool for 30 seconds, then carefully remove cookies with a metal spatula. Bake until you have 8 cookies. To form into cups, place cooled cookie on top of a 20 ounce can, an 8 ounce custard cup or whatever size cup you want. Place in a warm oven until cookie softens and droops over can. Let cool until it holds its shape. Remove carefully and, when entirely cool, place in a tightly covered metal container. I like to fill these with a mixture of fresh fruit to make a light dessert after a heavy meal. You will have some cookie dough left over to make some small cookies or 2 or 3 more of the 5" ones.

Yield: 8 cups

Caramel Bread Pudding

This recipe is from an old cookbook of my mother's. It is the fluffiest bread pudding I have ever eaten.

¾   cup light brown sugar, packed
3   slices buttered white, raisin
     or whole wheat bread, cut into
     ½" squares
3   large eggs

1   cup milk
Dash salt
½   teaspoon vanilla
Ice cream, whipped cream,
     or plain cream

Generously butter inside of double boiler top; pour in brown sugar; then add bread squares. Beat eggs with milk, salt and vanilla; pour over bread; do not stir. Cook over boiling water, 1 hour. Serve warm with or without a pitcher of cream.

Yield: 4 servings

For chocolate pudding, melt 1 square chocolate in buttered double boiler top. Stir in brown sugar and ¼ cup milk. Cook over boiling water until sugar dissolves, then add rest of ingredients and remaining ¾ cup milk. Do not stir. Cook as in caramel recipe.

Amaretto Chocolate Pudding

Separate the eggs as soon as you remove them from the refrigerator, but let the whites come to room temperature before whipping them to get higher volume.

2	ounces unsweetened chocolate	1	tablespoon dark rum
2	tablespoons strong coffee	½	cup fine stale bread crumbs
¾	stick butter (6 tablespoons), softened	⅓	cup ground toasted almonds
⅓	cup sugar	4	large egg whites
4	large egg yolks	⅛	teaspoon cream of tartar
1	tablespoon Amaretto	⅛	teaspoon salt
		½	cup Amaretto for drizzling

In the top of a double boiler set over barely simmering water, melt the chocolate in the coffee. In mixer bowl, cream butter and sugar, then beat until fluffy. Add 4 large egg yolks, one at a time, beating well after each addition. Then beat in the chocolate mixture and the Amaretto and rum. Stir in the bread crumbs and almonds. Beat egg whites with cream of tartar and salt until they hold stiff, but not dry, peaks and fold them gently but thoroughly into the chocolate mixture. Turn the batter into a buttered 1-quart mold. Cover tightly with the lid or a double thickness of foil tied with a string. Set the mold in a kettle with a tight-fitting lid. Add enough hot water to come up two thirds of the way up the side of the mold. Steam the pudding, covered with the lid, over moderate heat, for an hour. Drizzle the pudding while still in the mold with the ½ cup Amaretto. Let the mold stand on a rack, uncovered, for 15 minutes, then invert on a serving plate. Serve warm.

Yield: 8 servings

This pudding does not really need a sauce, but can be garnished with unsweetened whipped cream, if desired.

Caramel Plum Cobbler

I like this recipe using plums. It is not as sweet as most cobblers.

2	pounds fresh plums, pitted and quartered	¼	cup granulated sugar
¾	cup firmly packed brown sugar	½	teaspoon cinnamon
1	cup flour	1	egg, beaten
		⅓	cup butter, melted

Arrange plums in a lightly buttered 10" x 6" x 2" baking dish. Sprinkle with the brown sugar. Combine the flour, sugar and cinnamon; add egg and stir with a fork until crumbly. Sprinkle flour mixture evenly over brown sugar; drizzle with the melted butter. Bake in a 375° oven for 45 minutes. Serve warm with plain cream or whipped cream.

Yield: 6 servings

Chambord Strawberry Parfait

A delicious way to end a special lunch or dinner. Chambord is a liqueur made of black raspberries, other fruits and honey.

1	tablespoon unflavored gelatin	1	teaspoon vanilla
1	tablespoon flour		Grated peel of one orange
¾	cup sugar	¼	cup Chambord
3	cups heavy cream	1	pint fresh strawberries
5	egg yolks (freeze whites for another recipe)	1	cup heavy cream, whipped
			Fresh strawberries for garnish

In a large heavy saucepan, mix the gelatin, flour and sugar. Beat egg yolks and heavy cream together and stir into gelatin mixture. Stirring constantly with a wire whisk, cook over medium heat for 10 minutes. Remove from heat and add vanilla. Pour into a large bowl and stir in orange peel and Chambord. Chill to thicken. Puree the strawberries in blender. Whip the heavy cream and fold into strawberries. Fold this into the thickened chilled cream mixture. Spoon into champagne glasses. Chill until firm. Garnish with fresh strawberries.

Yield: 6 servings

Apples Delicious

My childhood was spent in Pennsylvania. We loved the maple sugar molded into maple leaves and Xmas bells. I remember dropping maple syrup on the snow and then eating it. I used real maple syrup for this dessert. It takes very little and is so delicious.

5	tablespoons butter, divided	¼	cup milk
1	cup flour	6	medium Golden Delicious
2	teaspoons baking powder		apples, peeled, cored and cut
½	teaspoon salt		into ⅛" slices (6 to 6½ cups)
½	cup sugar	½	cup pure maple syrup
1	large egg		

Pre-heat oven to 400°. Spread 1 tablespoon softened butter on bottom and sides of a shallow 11"x 7"x 2" or 12"x 7"x 2" baking dish. Sift flour, baking powder and salt onto waxed paper. In a bowl, cream remaining 4 tablespoons butter and sugar until it is light and fluffy. Beat in the egg, then add ½ cup of the flour mixture, then 2 tablespoons of the milk. Then add the remaining flour and the remaining 2 tablespoons of the milk. Stir until the batter is smooth. Drop apple slices in a bowl, add the maple syrup and stir until apples are coated on all sides. Spread apple slices evenly in bottom of buttered dish and pour in batter, smoothing top with rubber spatula. Bake in the middle of the oven for 30 to 35 minutes, or until cake tester inserted in the middle of batter, comes out clean. Serve hot or at room temperature with a pitcher of light cream.

Yield: 6 to 8 servings

Baked "Fried" Apple or Peach Pies

These pies can be either baked or fried. Any dried fruit of your choice may be used. If using dried pears, add 1 teaspoon lemon juice.

Pastry:

2	cups flour
1	teaspoon salt

⅔   cup vegetable shortening or
      half butter and half shortening

In a large bowl, combine salt and flour, add shortening and mix with the tips of your fingers or with a pastry blender until mixture resembles coarse crumbs. Add water 3 tablespoons at a time, stirring with fork until mixture leaves sides of the bowl and forms a ball. Divide in half. Wrap one piece of dough and set aside. Roll out other half of dough on a lightly floured board to ⅛" thick. Cut out 5" rounds, reserving scraps. Top one side of each round with 2 level tablespoons filling. Moisten edges with water, fold in half; seal edges with tines of a fork. Proceed with rest of dough and filling, re-rolling scraps of dough. To bake, place on ungreased cookie sheet, brush with whole milk or cream and sprinkle with sugar. Bake in a 425° oven 15 minutes or until they just start to brown. To fry, heat 1½" of vegetable oil in a heavy saucepan to 375°. Fry until browned, 3 to 4 minutes. Sprinkle with powdered sugar.

Filling:

8   ounces dried apples or
     peaches
¾   cup sugar, divided

¼   teaspoon nutmeg or cinnamon
1¼   cups water

In a small heavy saucepan, combine peaches, ¼ cup of the sugar, nutmeg or cinnamon and water. Bring to a boil; reduce heat and simmer, stirring constantly, to prevent scorching, until fruit is tender and mixture is slightly thickened. Remove from heat, add the remaining ½ cup sugar and stir until dissolved. Cool.

Yield: 12 pies

These pies can be made ahead, wrapped tightly in plastic and place in a box and sealed or wrapped in foil and frozen for up to 3 weeks. Let thaw completely before cooking.

Biscuit Tortoni

This dessert can be either refrigerated or frozen. Number of servings depend on size of paper cups.

⅔ cup milk
½ cup sugar
6 egg yolks
1 cup finely crushed toasted
    almonds or almond macaroons

½ cup chopped almonds, toasted
2 cups whipping cream, whipped
1 teaspoon vanilla

Heat milk over hot, not boiling, water until small bubbles appear around edge of pan. Add sugar, stirring until dissolved. In a separate bowl, beat egg yolks. Then, stirring constantly, add a little of the hot milk. Then add the remaining milk and return to pot. Continue cooking over hot, not boiling water, for 5 minutes stirring constantly. Cool, stir in the crushed macaroons or almonds. Whip cream stiff, flavoring it with vanilla. Gently fold egg mixture in. Pour into paper cups or muffin cups placed in muffin tins. Sprinkle chopped toasted almonds on top. Refrigerate overnight to allow flavors to blend. Can be frozen, reserving chopped almonds to sprinkle on top when serving.

Yield: 8 to 10

Be sure to freeze the leftover egg whites. I usually freeze them two to a container or, if you have a recipe you want to use them for later, freeze all six in a freezer-proof glass jar. Thaw, bring to room temperature and whip like fresh ones.

Blintz Soufflé

As noted in the cheese blintz recipe, page 111, they can be frozen and then cooked. Hence this soufflé can be made with frozen blintzes, the soufflé prepared early, then baked at the last minute.

18 frozen blintzes
1 stick butter, melted
4 eggs
¾ cup orange juice

8 ounces sour cream
½ cup sugar
1 teaspoon vanilla

These proportions will fit in a 12" x 9" x 2" pan. Place blintzes in pan and pour melted butter over them. Beat eggs, add orange juice, sugar and vanilla. Fold in sour cream. Pour over blintzes. Bake 55 minutes at 325°. Serve warm and enjoy!

Yield: 18 servings

Carrot Pecan Pudding

This is not only a delicious pudding but also a healthy one.

Pudding:

1 pound carrots, scraped and sliced	¼ cup (½ stick) butter or margarine
½ cup brown sugar, packed	3 large eggs
2 tablespoons flour	1 cup whole milk
	1½ teaspoons cinnamon

Cook carrots in boiling salted water to cover until tender; drain. Put knife blade in food processor; add carrots. Process 10 seconds, then add sugar and next 5 ingredients and process until smooth, stopping once to push down sides. Pour mixture into 6 lightly buttered 8 ounce baking dishes or 8 lightly buttered 6 ounce baking dishes. Place on a cookie sheet, cover with foil and bake in a 350° oven for 15 minutes for the 8 ounce and 12 minutes for the 6 ounce. Remove from oven; uncover and sprinkle with pecan topping. Bake 20 minutes. Serve with whipped cream, if desired.

Pecan Topping:

½ cup chopped pecans	⅓ cup flour
½ cup firmly packed brown sugar	2 tablespoons butter

Combine first 3 ingredients in a small bowl; cut in the butter with the tips of your fingers or with a pastry blender until crumbly.

Yield: 6 servings

Frozen Ozark Pudding

Ozark Pudding is a very old recipe. Here is a somewhat glamorous way to serve it.

1 egg	½ cup chopped apple
¾ cup sugar	½ gallon coffee ice cream, divided
3 tablespoons flour	
1½ teaspoons baking powder	1 cup whipping cream, whipped
½ cup chopped pecans	Chopped pecans

Beat eggs at high speed until foamy, gradually add sugar and beat at high speed until mixture is thick and lemon colored. Combine flour and baking powder; fold into egg mixture. Fold in pecans and apple. Spoon into a buttered 9″ pie plate. Bake at 325° for 35 minutes. Cool. Crumble mixture into small pieces. Spread 1 quart of ice cream in a 9″ square pan. Sprinkle crumbled mixture evenly over ice cream. Top with remaining ice cream. Cover and freeze until firm. Cut into squares and garnish with whipped cream and pecans.

Yield: 9 servings

The plain Ozark Pudding was one of my mother's recipes.

Cheese Blintzes

This recipe was given to me by a dear friend. It is one of my favorites. Please do not substitute margarine for the butter.

Batter:

2	cups water	8	eggs
2	cups flour	3	tablespoons butter
2	teaspoons salt		

Add water to salt and eggs, beating well. Add melted butter and flour gradually. Put in container of a blender to mix. Let batter stand in refrigerator about an hour. Lightly grease a 6" skillet or crêpe pan with butter. Place skillet over moderately high heat. Pour about ¼ cup of the batter into skillet, making sure the batter completely covers the bottom of the skillet, barely. Fry until the blintze begins to blister and the edges begin to curl away from the sides of the skillet. Top will be slightly moist. Turn out on a kitchen towel, fried side up. Skillet must be buttered after each blintze is made unless skillet is the non-stick kind. In that case, grease only when necessary. Make up a number of these and then put 1 tablespoon of the filling in center of each blintze, on the browned side. Raise the bottom flap of dough to cover filling, then overlap with the top flap. Tuck both ends under so that they almost meet in back. Fry in a liberal amount of butter until brown on both sides or they can be browned in butter in the oven. Serve with applesauce and sour cream.

Filling:

2	pounds farmer's cheese (dry cottage cheese)	2	tablespoons sugar
1	pound cream cheese	1	teaspoon salt
4	egg yolks	2	teaspoons grated lemon rind (optional)

Have cheese at room temperature. Mash with a fork, then add egg yolks, salt, sugar and lemon rind, if desired. Blend well.

Yield: 50 Blintzes

May be prepared ahead of time and frozen uncooked as for Blintz Soufflé.

Helpful Hint: 1 pound cottage cheese — 2 cups.
Note: If cottage cheese is stored in the refrigerator upside-down, it will stay fresh longer.

Cheesecake Tarts with Cherries

This is simple to make using frozen puff pastry shells.

Pastry:

1   (10 ounce) package frozen puff
    pastry shells

Bake pastry shells according to package instructions.

Filling:

2   (3 ounce) packages cream
    cheese, room temperature
¼   cup powdered sugar

¼   teaspoon almond flavoring
Extra powdered sugar
Cherry pie filling

Beat cream cheese, sugar and flavoring together. Carefully remove top of each pastry shell. Remove any soft layers of pastry inside the shell and discard. Divide filling between shells. Place on cookie sheet and bake for 5 minutes at 350°. Cool. Just before serving, fill each shell with cherry pie filling. Top with reserved tops and dust with sifted powdered sugar.

Yield: 6 servings

Chocolate Almond Ice Cream

If you are ready for a rich ice cream — this is it!

1½ cups sugar
½   cup cocoa
¼   teaspoon salt
1   quart whole milk, divided
2   large eggs, beaten
3   cups whipping cream

¾   cup slivered almonds, toasted
    and chopped
½   teaspoon almond extract
Slivered, toasted almonds for
    garnish

Combine first 3 ingredients in a large, heavy saucepan. Combine 2 cups milk and eggs; stir into sugar mixture. Cook over medium heat, stirring constantly, until mixture thickens and coats the back of a metal spoon. Stir in remaining 2 cups milk; cool this chocolate mixture completely. Combine chocolate mixture, whipping cream, almonds and almond extract in freezer container of a 1 gallon freezer, Freeze according to manufacturer's instructions. Remove dasher and leave in freezer container if using right away or transfer to a covered container for storing.

Yield: About 2 quarts

Custard coats a spoon when your finger leaves a track when drawn across the back of the spoon.

Custard Ice Cream

This amount is perfect for the Donvier freezer.

6	eggs	4	cups scalded milk or
½	cup sugar		half-and-half
¼	teaspoon salt	1	teaspoon vanilla or flavoring to your taste

Beat eggs, sugar and salt. Gradually add scalded milk, stirring constantly. Cook in a double boiler over hot, not boiling water, until mixture coats a spoon. Add vanilla. Cool and freeze.

Yield: 1 quart

Cherry Crisp

This dessert is made with canned sour cherries with pastry on the bottom and crumbs on top.

Pastry:

¼	teaspoon salt	1	cup flour
½	cup brown sugar, packed	½	cup margarine or butter

Mix salt, brown sugar and flour. Cut in butter or margarine to fine crumbs. Press into a 11"x 7"x 2"baking dish. Bake at 350° for 15 minutes.

Filling:

1	cup sugar	4	cups pitted sour cherries
4	tablespoons cornstarch	½	teaspoon almond flavoring
1	cup cherry juice		

Mix sugar and cornstarch, add cherry juice. Cook over low heat, stirring constantly, until mixture begins to thicken. Add cherries and cook, stirring gently with a wooden spoon, until thickened. Add a few drops of red coloring and the almond flavoring. Mix, cool, then pour over the crust.

Topping:

1½	cups quick Quaker oats	5	tablespoons butter or
½	cup brown sugar, packed		margarine
¼	cup flour		

Mix topping ingredients to make crumbs. Spread over cherry mixture. Bake at 350° about 20 to 25 minutes. Serve warm.

Yield: 8 to 10 servings

Chocolate Almond Parfait

This is a delicious, pretty dessert that is easy to make. Since it is frozen, it can be made as much as two days ahead of time.

1 (6 ounce) package (1 cup) milk chocolate morsels or semi-sweet morsels	2 to 3 tablespoons Amaretto
2 tablespoons water	1½ cups whipping cream, whipped, or 3 cups whipped topping

Combine morsels and water in a small heavy saucepan. Cook over low heat, stirring constantly, until chocolate is melted. Cool. Add Amaretto, then fold in whipped cream.

Topping:

1 cup amaretti cookie crumbs	Toasted almonds for garnish

Layer mousse and amaretti crumbs into 6 (4 ounce) parfait glasses. Cover and freeze an hour or up to 2 days ahead. Garnish with additional whipped cream and almonds, if desired.

Yield: 6 servings

Either melt the chocolate and water in a heavy saucepan over low heat or in the microwave.

Double Chocolate Meringues

This recipe is strictly for chocolate lovers. Cocoa in the meringue and also chocolate chips.

¾ cup sugar	¼ teaspoon cream of tartar
6 tablespoons cocoa	1 teaspoon vanilla
3 egg whites, room temperature	1 cup (6 ounces) semi-sweet chocolate chips
⅛ teaspoon salt	

Line cookie sheets with parchment or brown paper. Mix sugar and cocoa in a small bowl. Beat egg whites with salt and cream tartar until they hold soft peaks. Gradually add sugar-cocoa mixture, then vanilla, and beat until stiff but not dry. Fold in chocolate chips. Drop meringue onto prepared pan by tablespoonfuls. Make an indentation in middle with bowl of spoon. Place in a cold oven. Turn temperature to 250°. Bake about 45 minutes, or until meringues can be lifted off the paper. Serve with a scoop of ice cream in the center, vanilla, chocolate, butter pecan or flavor of your choice.

Yield: 8 to 10 servings

Can be prepared ahead 1 day and stored in an airtight container. As with any meringue, do not make on a rainy day.

Chocolate Caramel Tart

This is a sinfully rich dessert so you should get at least 10 servings.

Sugar Cookie Crust:

1⅓ cups flour	1	large egg
⅓ cup sugar	1	teaspoon vanilla

With knife blade in food processor, process first 2 ingredients 1 minute or until mixture is crumbly. Add egg and vanilla through chute with processor running; process just until mixture forms a smooth dough. Roll out on a lightly floured board and fit into an 11″ tart pan, making sure you do not stretch the dough. Take a rolling pin and roll it over top of pan to cut off excess dough. Do not crimp. Prick bottom with a fork, then line with a circle of waxed paper. Place a layer of uncooked beans or rice in bottom. Bake at 375° for 7 minutes, then remove paper and beans and cook for about 5 minutes more or until light brown. Set aside to cool.

Chocolate Caramel Filling:

1½ cups semi-sweet chocolate morsels	1	(14 ounce) package Kraft vanilla caramels, unwrapped
¾ cup whipping cream, divided	3	cups toasted pecans or toasted almonds, chopped

Combine chocolate morsels and ¼ cup of the whipping cream in a small microwave-safe bowl; microwave on high for 1 to 1½ minutes or until chocolate melts, stirring once. Spread 1 cup of the mixture evenly in bottom of baked pastry, reserving remaining mixture. Chill pastry in refrigerator 30 minutes. Combine caramels and the remaining ½ cup whipping cream in a heavy saucepan; cook over low heat, stirring constantly, until caramels melt and mixture is smooth. Stir in pecans or almonds and spread over chocolate layer. Spoon the remaining chocolate mixture into a heavy-duty zip-top plastic bag. If chocolate has hardened, microwave on high until soft. Cut a small hole in corner of plastic bag; drizzle chocolate over top of tart. Chill at least 1 hour. Let stand at room temperature about 20 minutes before serving to raves.

Yield: 11″ tart pan

Tart pan should have a removable bottom to facilitate serving. The heavy-duty zip-top bag can be washed and reused. The beans or rice used can also be saved to use again. You can buy metal pellets at kitchen supply stores for this purpose also.

Chocolate Floating Island

This dessert is for chocolate lovers. You may flavor it with Amaretto instead of the vanilla, if you wish.

Meringues:

4½ cups milk
1½ teaspoons vanilla
1¼ cups sugar, divided

8   egg whites, room temperature
½   teaspoon cream of tartar
Dash salt

Combine milk, vanilla and ¼ cup sugar. Heat to simmer. Beat egg whites until foamy. Continue beating while adding remaining 1 cup sugar by tablespoonfuls until meringue holds its shape. With two spoons, drop egg-shaped balls of meringue on the simmering milk and simmer until they are firm, turning once. Carefully remove with a slotted spoon and place on a clean towel. Reserve the milk.

Chocolate Custard:

⅔ cup sugar
⅔ cup cocoa
8 egg yolks

1   teaspoon vanilla
4   cups hot milk from meringue

Measure the hot milk and add enough milk to make 4 cups. Mix sugar, cocoa, and egg yolks in a 6 cup saucepan. Slowly add the hot milk, stirring constantly with a wire whip. Cook over very low heat, stirring constantly, until mixture coats a metal spoon. Remove mixture from heat, add vanilla to taste and cool. Then transfer to your prettiest glass bowl. Place meringues on top and refrigerate until serving. You may garnish with toasted slivered almonds, if you wish.

Yield: 12 servings

As with the previous recipe for Floating Island, this dessert should also be made the day it is to be served.

Chocolate Soufflé, Sis Jackson

I like to bake individual soufflés when I can. Hope you like this recipe.

Soufflé:

4	tablespoons butter	⅛	teaspoon salt
2	(1 ounce) squares unsweetened chocolate	4	large eggs, separated
		½	cup sugar
4	tablespoons flour	1	teaspoon vanilla
1	cup milk		

Coat bottom and sides of 4 (8 or 10 ounce) soufflé dishes with butter then dust with granulated sugar. Set aside. Melt the butter and chocolate in a small saucepan over low heat; add flour, stirring until smooth. Cook 1 minute, stirring constantly, until thickened. Gradually add milk; cook over medium heat, stirring constantly, until thickened. Add salt and remove from heat. Beat yolks and sugar at medium speed until thick and lemon colored. Gradually add a little of the chocolate mixture to the yolk mixture; beat at medium speed until blended, gradually adding rest of chocolate mixture and vanilla. Beat egg whites until soft peaks form, then gently fold about ¼ into chocolate mixture. Then fold in rest of beaten whites. Spoon mixture into prepared dishes. With your thumb, make a indentation around edge of dish. This lets the soufflé have room to rise without falling over. Bake at 325° about 25 to 35 minutes or until puffed and set. Serve immediately with following Mocha Cream.

Mocha Cream:

¾	cup whipping cream	2¼	teaspoons cocoa
2	tablespoons sugar	¾	teaspoon instant coffee

Combine all ingredients in mixer bowl. Beat at high speed until stiff. Chill. About 1½ cups.

Yield: 4 servings

Can be baked in a 4 cup soufflé dish, if desired.

Chocolate Torte

A delicious dessert and one to be served at the table, if you like. You may either ice with the whipped cream or use a pastry tube to pipe the whipped cream. This freezes beautifully.

1	cup blanched almonds	¾	cup sugar
5	ounces sweet chocolate,	¼	teaspoon salt
	not semi-sweet	2	teaspoons vanilla
¼	cup cold coffee	½	pint whipping cream
5	eggs, separated		Chocolate curls (optional)

Toast almonds and finely chop. Place coffee and chocolate in heavy saucepan over very low heat and stir until chocolate is melted and smooth. Cool slightly. Beat egg yolks until light; add sugar gradually and continue beating until mixture is thick and pale in color. Add salt, vanilla and almonds and stir in chocolate. Beat egg whites until stiff but not dry and fold into chocolate mixture. Pour into 9"x 5" x 3" loaf pan that has been greased and bottom lined with waxed paper. Bake at 350° about 50 minutes or until wooden pick inserted in middle comes out clean. Cool for at least 20 minutes. Remove from pan to serving plate. Frost or decorate with whipped cream and chocolate curls.

Yield: 6 to 8 servings

To make chocolate curls, melt chocolate squares or morsels over hot water, then pour into a loaf tin until you have a piece at least 1" thick. Refrigerate until it hardens, remove from tin and let come to room temperature. Shave with a heavy knife.

Floating Island with Fruit

This dessert, as with other floating islands, should be made the day it is to be served.

Meringues:

2 egg whites	¼ cup sugar
Dash salt	3 cups milk

Beat the egg whites with the dash of salt to soft peaks. Gradually add sugar by tablespoonfuls and beat to stiff but not dry peaks. In skillet, heat the milk to simmer. Drop the meringues by spoonfuls onto the milk in 6 rounds. Cook slowly, uncovered, about 2 minutes, turn and cook about 3 minutes more or until meringues are firm to the touch. Lift out with a slotted spoon and drain on paper towels.

Custard:

3 eggs	Milk
2 egg yolks	1½ teaspoons vanilla
½ cup sugar	Strawberries for garnish
Dash salt	

Beat eggs and egg yolks slightly with the sugar and dash of salt. Stir in slightly cooled milk from meringues plus extra to make 3 cups. Cook in the top of a double boiler over hot, not boiling water, stirring constantly, until mixture coats the back of a metal spoon. Remove from heat; cool quickly by putting top of double boiler in ice water; add vanilla. Place whole hulled strawberries in a glass bowl or dish; pour custard over. Top with meringues. Chill in the refrigerator until serving.

Yield: 6 servings

Floating Island Robinson

I did not like the meringues when I was a child so my mother would give me some of the hot custard in a bowl. I have never forgotten how delicious it tasted.

Meringues:

2 cups milk	5 egg whites, room temperature
1 teaspoon vanilla	⅔ cup sugar

Pour milk into a 8" or 9" skillet. Heat over low heat until bubbles appear around edge of skillet. Beat egg whites until foamy, then very gradually add the sugar and then the vanilla. Continue to beat until egg whites are stiff. Remove skillet from heat and drop meringue on the milk in large, round tablespoonfuls, making 8 to 10 meringues. Return skillet to low heat; the surface of the milk should barely quiver. Cook the mounds of egg white for 2 minutes. Using a skimmer or slotted spoon, turn and cook 2 minutes longer on other side or until meringues are firm to the touch. Remove to a plate, reserving the milk.

Custard:

½ teaspoon vanilla	½ cup sugar
5 egg yolks	

Strain the reserved hot milk into a measure. Add enough extra milk to make 3 cups. Put in top of a double boiler; add the vanilla and, over boiling water, heat the milk until bubbles appear around edge of pan. Blend the egg yolks with the sugar using a fork or wire whisk. Add some of the hot milk gradually, stirring constantly. Then add egg mixture to the rest of the milk. Cook over the boiling water, stirring constantly, until mixture coats a metal spoon. Let cool to lukewarm, then pour into a crystal bowl, float meringues on top and chill until serving.

Yield: 8 to 10 servings

When this was served in a crystal bowl, Mother always placed a little dab of currant jelly in the middle of each meringue. This dessert should be made the day it is to be eaten as the meringues tend to deflate if made too far ahead.

Fruit with Cream

1 cup heavy cream	2 pints strawberries, pineapple
⅓ cup powdered sugar	cubes, orange sections or a
½ cup sour cream	combination of fresh fruit
1 teaspoon grated orange peel	Grated chocolate (optional)

Beat heavy cream with sugar until stiff. Fold in sour cream and grated orange peel. Spoon or pipe over fruit. Sprinkle with grated chocolate, if desired.

Yield: 6 to 8 servings

2 cups Cool Whip may be used if lower calories are desired.

Fresh Fruit with Amaretto

Peaches, raspberries or strawberries or a combination may be used for this dessert.

Fruit:

4   cups sliced peaches or 4 cups
     fruit of your choice

Place fruit in crystal dessert dishes and spoon chilled custard over.

Custard:

4	egg yolks, lightly beaten	1	tablespoon Amaretto or
½	cup sugar		liqueur of your choice
2	tablespoons flour	¼	teaspoon vanilla
1	cup whole milk		

Combine first 3 ingredients in a medium saucepan; gradually add milk, stirring until smooth. Cook over low heat, stirring constantly, about 6 or 7 minutes. Remove from heat and stir in Amaretto and vanilla. Cover and chill. Yield: 1½ cups.

Yield: 6 servings

Grand Marnier Bread Pudding

10	(½") slices homemade type	3	cups half-and-half
	bread, crusts removed, and	¾	cup sugar
	each slice cut into 4 triangles	1	tablespoon grated orange zest
¼	pound butter, melted	4	eggs
1⅓	cups Grand Marnier		

Dip one side of each bread triangle in melted butter, dip the other side in ⅓ cup Grand Marnier. Arrange these triangles in concentric circles, overlapping slightly, over the bottom and sides of a buttered 10"x 2"round baking dish; set aside. Bring half-and-half, sugar, orange zest and remaining Grand Marnier to simmer in a saucepan; remove from heat and let stand 15 minutes. Whisk eggs in a large bowl, then gradually whisk in the warm half-and-half mixture. Pour this over the bread slices. Let stand 15 minutes. Transfer baking dish to a pan that is just large enough to contain it. Add enough hot water to come halfway up the side of the baking dish. Bake on the middle shelf of a 325° oven for about 30 minutes or until custard is set. Adjust oven setting to broil. Broil until bread slices on top of pudding are golden brown, about 1 minute. Transfer pudding to a rack and let cool 10 minutes. Cut into wedges and serve.

Yield: 8 servings

Ice Cream

This is the ice cream my mother made most often. It is mixed in a freezer container — no pots to wash. Recipe can be increased to 1½ gallons by using 1½ times the recipe.

2	(12 ounce) cans evaporated milk, not condensed milk	1	quart whole milk
2	cups sugar	1	pint half-and-half or heavy cream
2	teaspoons vanilla		

Mix all ingredients in freezer container. Stir until sugar is dissolved, then freeze.

Yield: 1 gallon

Crushed fruit, nuts, etc., can be added midway of freezing.

Indian Puddings

I toured through the New England states several years ago and finally got my fill of Indian Pudding. In this recipe, single servings are baked in small casseroles, so they are cooked only 1½ hours instead of all day cooking.

½	cup firmly packed brown sugar	¼	cup light molasses
1	teaspoon cinnamon	¼	cup butter
¼	teaspoon ginger	4	cups milk
¼	teaspoon cloves	⅔	cup enriched cornmeal
¼	teaspoon salt	1	egg, beaten

Heat oven to 375°. Combine sugar, spices and salt in large saucepan. Add molasses, butter and 3 cups of the milk. Heat to boiling. Combine cornmeal and the remaining cup of milk. Pour all at once into hot mixture, stirring quickly. Cook until thickened, stirring constantly. Cover; simmer over low heat about 5 minutes. Stir a small amount of hot mixture into the beaten egg, then add mixture to rest of cornmeal mixture, stirring rapidly. Pour into 6 greased 8-ounce casseroles. Set in a large baking pan. Fill pan with hot water to within an inch of the top of casseroles. Bake, uncovered, at 275° for 1½ hours. Cool to lukewarm and serve with ice cream or a pitcher of plain cream.

Yield: 6 servings

Indian Apple Pudding

This is not as authentic recipe as the plain Indian Pudding recipe, but is very good.

5	cups milk	1	teaspoon cinnamon
⅔	cup cornmeal	½	teaspoon nutmeg
1	cup dark molasses	2	cups thinly sliced, peeled
1	teaspoon salt		cooking apples
1	teaspoon ginger		

Bring milk just to the boiling point. Remove from heat. Slowly stir in cornmeal. Cook 3 or 4 minutes over low heat just until mixture boils, stirring constantly. Remove from heat and add the molasses, salt, ginger, cinnamon and nutmeg. Place the sliced apples in a well-greased 2-quart casserole. Pour the hot cornmeal mixture over apples. Bake at 350° 60 minutes. Remove from oven, cool 20 minutes and serve warm with heavy cream, whipped, if desired.

Yield: 8 servings

Kahlúa Chocolate Velvet

This is a delicious recipe from a recipe pamphlet featuring Kahlúa.

⅓	cup Kahlúa	4	(1 ounce) squares semi-sweet
½	teaspoon instant coffee		chocolate
	granules	5	large eggs, separated
½	teaspoon vanilla	¼	teaspoon cream of tartar
2	(1 ounce) squares unsweetened	⅓	cup superfine sugar
	chocolate		

Measure Kahlúa, coffee granules, vanilla and chocolate into a 1-quart saucepan. Place directly over low heat or set pan in a shallow pan of hot water over low heat. Stir now and then until chocolate melts and mixture is smooth and thick. Meanwhile, beat egg yolks well in mixer bowl, then beat in chocolate mixture. Cool. When mixture is cool, beat egg whites with cream of tartar to soft peaks. Gradually beat in sugar to make a meringue. Add half of the meringue to chocolate mixture to lighten it, then fold in rest of meringue. Turn into a 1-quart serving dish or individual dessert dishes. Cover and chill until firm. Garnish with a dab of whipped cream and chocolate curls, if desired.

Yield: 6 or 8 servings

Chocolate Velvet is very rich. I like to serve it in small crystal glasses or demitasse cups garnished with candied violets.

Light Mexican Custard

This custard is only 105 calories per 6 ounce custard cup.

2 large eggs	¼ teaspoon almond extract
⅛ teaspoon salt	1 cup low-fat milk
2½ tablespoons sugar	1 cup evaporated skim milk
1 tablespoon flour	Ground cinnamon
1 teaspoon vanilla	

Combine all ingredients except cinnamon in container of electric blender; process at high speed 5 seconds. Pour mixture into 6 (6 ounce) custard cups; sprinkle with cinnamon. Place custard cups in a 13"x 9"x 2"baking pan. Pour boiling water to depth of 1"in pan. Bake at 325° until a knife inserted in center comes out clean. Cool and refrigerate.

Yield: 6 servings

Nectarine Pecan Crisp

This dessert can be prepared early in the day, nectarines do not turn brown as peaches do, and baked just before serving. Another plus, the nectarines do not have to be peeled.

4 nectarines, halved and pitted	2 tablespoons praline liqueur

Arrange nectarines, cut side up, in a buttered shallow baking dish and sprinkle with liqueur.

Topping:

1 cup chopped pecans	4 teaspoons butter
4 tablespoon dark brown sugar, packed	4 teaspoons flour

Mix pecans, sugar, butter and flour in a small bowl with your fingertips until crumbly. Spoon pecan topping on tops of nectarines, pressing gently to fill hollows and then smooth top. Bake in a 350° oven about 20 minutes or until topping is brown and bubbly. Let cool just to room temperature before serving.

Yield: 8 servings

Meringues with Lemon Brandy Filling

These meringues also have a penuche topping which makes them divine.

Meringues:

3 egg whites, room temperature	¾ cup sugar
¼ teaspoon cream of tartar	½ cup finely chopped pecans
¼ teaspoon salt	

Beat egg whites with cream of tartar and salt until frothy. Add sugar, one tablespoonful at a time, beating after each addition. Continue beating until egg whites are stiff but not dry. Fold in pecans. Cover a baking sheet with foil or brown paper. Pile meringue in 6 mounds about 3" in diameter. Make a depression in the center of each with the bowl of the spoon. Bake at 275° about an hour or until they turn loose of the foil or paper. Cool.

Brandy Filling:

3 egg yolks	¼ cup lemon juice
¼ cup sugar	2 tablespoons brandy
1 teaspoon grated lemon rind	1 cup heavy cream, whipped

Beat egg yolks with sugar, lemon rind, lemon juice and brandy in top of a double boiler. Cook over simmering water, stirring constantly, until thickened. Remove from heat and cool, covered, in the refrigerator. Then fold in the whipped cream and chill overnight. When ready to serve, spoon filling in the meringues and top with penuche topping.

Penuche Topping:

¼ stick butter	½ cup chopped pecans
¼ cup sugar	

Melt butter in small heavy skillet. Stir in sugar and pecans. Cook over low heat, stirring, for 5 to 7 minutes or until sugar begins to turn golden. Turn out on foil, cool and crumble into small pieces.

Yield: 6 servings

As with other meringues, these should not be made on a rainy day.

Peach Custard

This dessert has to be made with fresh peaches. The combination of custard and peaches is delicious. Can be made a day ahead and refrigerated after cooking. The half peach has to be a size that will fit in a 6 ounce custard cup.

3	medium-size firm but ripe peaches	4	eggs
1	cup heavy cream and 1 cup whole milk, or 2 cups half-and-half	¼	cup sugar
		1	teaspoon vanilla
		¼	teaspoon ground nutmeg

Pre-heat oven to 325°. Drop peaches into enough boiling water to cover them completely. Let set about 5 to 7 minutes or until they can be skinned easily. Peel the peaches, halve them and remove pits. Place each half, cut-side down in a 6 ounce custard cup and set aside. In a medium bowl, beat eggs, vanilla and sugar together with a wire whisk. In a small heavy saucepan, warm cream and milk over moderate heat until small bubbles form around sides of pan. Pour slowly over egg mixture, beating constantly with a wire whisk. Pour custard over peaches, sprinkle with nutmeg. Place in a rectangular baking pan. Pour enough boiling water into the pan to come halfway up the sides of the custard cups. Bake for 30 to 40 minutes or just until custard is set. Do not overbake or custard will be watery. Remove from pan and cool before serving. If not serving within an hour, refrigerate. If you prefer, you may refrigerate them before serving or serve them at room temperature.

Yield: 6 servings

I have also made the custard with undiluted evaporated milk (not condensed milk).

Peach Dumplings

Fresh peaches are washed, but not pitted or peeled in this dessert. Hard to believe, but true!

Filling:

8 medium fresh peaches	½ cup brown sugar, packed
1 cup water	

Wash and dry peaches, but do not remove skin or pits.

Place water and sugar in a small saucepan, bring to a boil and cook until a thin syrup is formed.

Crust:

3 cups flour	1 tablespoon fresh lemon juice
1½ teaspoons salt	10 to 12 tablespoons ice water
1¼ cups shortening	

Mix flour and salt. Cut in shortening with tips of fingers or with a pastry blender until mixture looks like cornmeal. Add lemon juice mixed with 10 tablespoons water. Mix with a fork until mixture makes a ball. If mixture is dry, add the remaining 2 tablespoons water. Roll out on a lightly floured board until about a scant ¼" thick. Cut into 6" squares and wrap around a peach, leaving stone in and skin on. Peach should be placed stem-end down with pastry wrapped over the top and joined at bottom. Bake in a 2" deep pan at 425° about 15 minutes. Lower heat to 350° and bake about 35 to 45 minutes, basting several times with the water and brown sugar syrup. Cool, make a hole in the top of pastry with an ice tea spoon and slip out the stone. Skin will have disintegrated. Before serving, place back in a 350° oven to warm. Serve with a pitcher of heavy or light cream.

Yield: 8 servings

Peach Pudding Brûlée

I sometimes frown on shortcut recipes, but this one is too good to miss. It is made with canned peaches.

1   (1 pound, 13-ounce) can sliced peaches, drained
1   cup milk
8   ounces dairy sour cream
1   (3¾ ounce) package instant vanilla pudding mix

4   tablespoons brown sugar, packed
3   tablespoons broken toasted pecans or almonds

Divide peaches among 6 dessert dishes. Blend milk into sour cream in medium-size mixing bowl; add pudding mix and beat until smooth and thickened, about 1 minute.

Spoon over peaches. Chill. While pudding chills; press brown sugar through a sieve onto a small cookie sheet in a ¼" layer. Broil, 3" from the heat until sugar has melted in a lacy pattern. Cool on cookie sheet, then break into pieces and place on top of puddings. Sprinkle with pecans.

Yield: 6 servings

Do not put broiled sugar on puddings until ready to serve.

Pumpkin Pudding

This is a change from the traditional pumpkin pie.

1   stick butter (½ cup), softened
¾   cup firmly packed dark brown sugar
¼   cup granulated sugar
2   large eggs
2   cups flour
1½ teaspoons baking powder
1¼ teaspoons cinnamon

¾   teaspoon ground cloves
¾   teaspoon ginger
¾   teaspoon nutmeg
¼   teaspoon baking soda
¾   cup canned pumpkin
¼   cup unsulphured molasses
½   cup finely chopped pecans

Cream the butter with brown and granulated sugars, then beat until fluffy. Add eggs, one at a time, beating well after each addition. Sift together the dry ingredients. In a small bowl, mix the pumpkin and molasses and add to the butter mixture alternately with the flour mixture. Stir in the pecans. Turn the batter into a well-buttered 1-quart pudding mold and cover it tightly with the lid or a double piece of foil tied tightly with string. Set the mold in a kettle with a lid, add enough hot water to come two thirds of the way up the sides of the mold. Steam the pudding over moderate heat for 2 hours and 30 minutes. Let the mold stand on a rack, uncovered, for 15 minutes, then invert on a serving plate. Serve the pudding warm with sauce of your choice.

Yield: 8 servings

Quaker Apple Crisp

This dessert can be frozen after preparation and cooked when you need it.

Filling:

8	large cooking apples, peeled and sliced	1	teaspoon cinnamon
		1	cup brown sugar, packed

Place sliced apples in a 9" x 13" x 2" buttered pan. Combine brown sugar and cinnamon. Spread half over the apples.

Topping:

1	cup granulated sugar	½	teaspoon salt
1	cup flour	1	teaspoon baking powder
1	egg, beaten	½	cup melted butter or margarine

Combine granulated sugar, flour, salt and baking powder in a bowl, Mix well, then add egg and mix with a fork until a dough forms. Spread over apple slices. Sprinkle remaining brown sugar mixture over, then drizzle melted butter over top. Bake in a 350° oven for 40 to 45 minutes or until apples are tender and juice has thickened.

Yield: 10 servings

I have also made this with fresh peaches. However, reduce brown sugar to ¾ cup.

Raspberries with Sabayon

Strawberries may be substituted if raspberries are not available.

4	egg yolks, room temperature	1	tablespoon Framboise (raspberry) brandy
¼	cup sugar		
¼	cup dry white wine	1	pint raspberries

Beat egg yolks and sugar in bowl with a wire whisk or in mixer at high speed until mixture is light colored and forms a ribbon when beater is lifted. Gradually beat in wine and brandy 1 tablespoon at a time. Place bowl over a saucepan of simmering water. Cook over low heat, beating constantly, until mixture thickens to a fluffy custard, about 5 minutes. (Be sure to stop cooking before eggs curdle). Remove immediately from heat. Divide raspberries in 4 dessert dishes. Spoon over sabayon and serve immediately.

Yield: 4 servings

Remember to save the egg whites. If you do not need them right away, freeze in a glass or plastic jar. When thawed and brought to room temperature, they can be used and whipped the same as fresh.

Rio Grande Meringues

This was our favorite dessert when we dined at The Snack Shop in Houston many years ago. The tartness of the sauce contrasts deliciously with the sweetness of the meringues.

Meringues:

3	egg whites, room temperature	1	cup sugar
¼	teaspoon cream of tartar	½	teaspoon vanilla

Beat egg whites until frothy, add cream of tartar and vanilla. Beat until soft peaks form. Add sugar by tablespoonfuls, beating after each addition, until whites are stiff but not dry. Cut 8 circles of foil or brown paper 3½" in diameter. Place a rounding tablespoon (⅓ cup) of the meringue on each of the circles, which have been placed on a cookie sheet. Make a depression in center of each meringue with the bowl of the spoon. Bake about 40 minutes in a 250° oven, or until meringues can be lifted off the paper. If they do not turn loose, bake a little longer. Do not try to make these on a rainy day. If not using that day, place meringues in a tightly covered container.

Sauce:

1	level tablespoon flour	1½	cups water
2	level tablespoons cornstarch	¼	cup lemon juice
1	cup sugar	1	tablespoon butter
¼	teaspoon salt	1	teaspoon grated lemon rind
⅓	cup frozen orange juice, undiluted		

Mix dry ingredients in a heavy saucepan. Stir in juices and water and cook over medium heat until mixture boils. Boil, stirring constantly, about 3 minutes or until mixture thickens and is clear. Remove from heat and add the butter and lemon rind. Let cool covered with waxed paper, then refrigerate in a covered container.

To assemble; Put a scoop of vanilla ice cream in well of each meringue and spoon sauce over.

Yield: 8 meringues

To make a variation of this recipe, fold in ½ cup chopped nuts of your choice and use different sauces.

Steamed Plum Pudding

This recipe is exceptionally good, with less calories and the extra flavor of whole wheat bread.

Pudding:

5   (½") slices whole wheat bread, torn into small pieces
⅔   cup evaporated skim milk
2   slightly beaten egg whites
½   cup firmly packed dark brown sugar
¼   cup cooking oil
2   tablespoons frozen orange juice mixed with 2 tablespoons water
½   teaspoon vanilla
1   (12 ounce) package pitted prunes cut into small pieces
¾   cup chopped pecans or walnuts
¾   cup whole wheat flour
2   teaspoons cinnamon
¼   teaspoon nutmeg
¼   teaspoon cloves
½   teaspoon baking soda
¼   teaspoon salt

In a large bowl, soak the bread pieces in the skim milk until bread is softened. Stir until bread is broken up. Add egg whites, brown sugar, oil, orange juice and vanilla. Add prunes and nuts. Mix whole wheat flour, spices, baking soda and salt and add to bread mixture. Spray a 6½ cup tower pudding mold with vegetable coating. Pour pudding mixture in mold. Cover mold with cover or cover tightly with a double thickness of foil tied with string. Put in kettle with a lid and pour hot water to two-thirds of the depth of the mold. Cover the kettle, bring water to a boil and steam for 2 or 3 hours or until a tester placed in deepest part of mold comes out clean. Cool pudding about 20 minutes, then unmold and serve with orange sauce.

Orange Sauce:

¼   cup sugar
1   tablespoon cornstarch
⅓   cup frozen orange juice
⅔   cup water
Dash salt
2   teaspoons lemon juice

Mix sugar, cornstarch, orange juice and water in a small saucepan. Cook over medium heat, stirring constantly, until thickened. Remove from heat, add the salt and lemon juice and serve warm over pudding.

Yield: 8 to 10 servings

Strawberries with Kirsch

This is a dessert that requires a minimum of preparation.

2	quarts strawberries	¼	cup Kirsch
1	(12 ounce) jar of strawberry jam		

Wash and hull strawberries, drain well and place in a pretty crystal bowl. Chill. Place strawberry jam in a small bowl with Kirsch and stir to soften. When ready to serve, be sure there is no water in the bottom of the bowl. Pour softened jam over berries. This makes them shiny with a delightful taste. Serve with white custard sauce.

White Custard Sauce:

3	eggs, separated	1	cup heavy cream
1½	cups powdered sugar	1	teaspoon vanilla

Beat egg yolks until thick and lemon-colored, Add powdered sugar and vanilla to egg yolks and blend. Beat egg whites until stiff but not dry. Fold in egg yolk mixture. Whip cream until stiff, fold into egg mixture and add. Spoon over fruit.

Yield: 6 servings

Strawberry Cassis Sherbet

This is another dessert that can be made in a Donvier freezer. So easy and so good!

2	pints strawberries or raspberries	1	cup water
		½	cup crème de cassis
1	tablespoon sugar	2	tablespoons fresh lemon juice
¼	cup sugar		

Lightly mash strawberries or raspberries together with the 1 tablespoon sugar in a large bowl. Let stand at room temperature 1 hour. Place the ¼ cup sugar and water in small saucepan. Cook over low heat until sugar dissolves, stirring constantly. Bring to boiling then lower heat to simmer and cook 5 minutes. Place syrup in a bowl, cool, then refrigerate about 1 hour. Press strawberries and their juice through a sieve, discard seeds. There should be 3½ cups. Mix puree with crème de cassis, lemon juice and cold syrup. Freeze, then remove dasher and let ripen 2 hours before serving.

Yield: 1 quart

I sometimes serve this as an intermezzo. It is also a light dessert after a rich meal.

Strawberry Shortcake

Mother always served this warm. After baking the shortcake, she split it and spread it generously with butter, then put slightly sweetened crushed strawberries between the layers and also on top. It was served with a pitcher of heavy cream.

2	cups sifted flour	⅔	cup half-and-half
2	tablespoons sugar	3 to 4	cups lightly sugared sliced
3	teaspoons baking powder		strawberries
½	teaspoon salt	1	cup whipping cream, whipped,
½	cup butter or margarine		or plain cream
1	beaten egg		

Sift together dry ingredients; cut in butter until mixture resembles coarse crumbs. Combine egg and half-and-half; add all at once, stirring with a fork just enough to moisten. Spread dough in greased 8"x 1½"round pan, building up edges slightly. Bake at 450° for 15 to 18 minutes. Remove from pan; cool on rack 5 minutes. Split in two layers; lift top off carefully. Butter bottom layer. Spoon berries between layers and then replace top and spoon rest of berries over. Serve with cream and enjoy!

Yield: 6 to 8 servings

Three-Crust Peach Cobbler

This cobbler recipe is an old-fashioned one with three portions of crust.

Pastry for a double crust pie		3	tablespoons flour
5	cups sliced fresh peaches or	¼	cup sugar
	nectarines	⅛	teaspoon salt
1	cup sugar	½	teaspoon almond flavoring
¼	cup water	Butter	

Roll half of the pastry very thin and line a 11"x 7"x 2"deep baking dish with it. Roll the other half of pastry and cut into strips. Bake half the strips in a 375° oven until light brown. Put fruit, sugar and water in a saucepan and cook until fruit is soft. Mix flour, the ¼ cup sugar and salt and add to the fruit. Cook, stirring, until slightly thickened. Add flavoring and cooked pastry strips. Spoon in crust-lined dish, dot with butter and cover with uncooked pastry strips. Bake at 400° about 40 minutes or until fruit is tender and cobbler is brown and bubbly. Serve warm. I like it served with a pitcher of cream.

Yield: 6 to 8 servings

For those who do not like to make pastry, prepared pastry sheets may be used for this recipe.

Tortilla Apple Dessert

This is a different, easy dessert to serve after a Mexican supper. It can be prepared early in the day and then warmed to lukewarm before serving.

1	cup light brown sugar, packed	2	teaspoons cinnamon
2	cups water	10	(6") corn tortillas or 12 (5")
1	cup butter or margarine		Whipped cream or ice cream
4	cups peeled and chopped		Ground cinnamon for garnish
	Golden Delicious apples		(optional)

Combine sugar and water in a small saucepan; cook over medium heat, stirring constantly, just until sugar melts. Set aside. Place butter in a 13"x 9"x 2"baking dish. Place in a 350° oven to melt. Combine apples and 2 teaspoons cinnamon, stirring to coat. Dip tortillas in melted butter to soften. Place about ⅓ cup apple mixture down center of each tortilla. Roll up and place, seam side down, in baking dish in remainder of melted butter. Pour sugar mixture over tortillas. Cover with aluminum foil and bake at 350° for 25 minutes. Uncover and bake 5 minutes. Let stand 10 minutes before serving warm with whipped cream. Sprinkle with cinnamon, if desired.

Yield: 10 to 12 servings

I like it served with a scoop of vanilla ice cream dribbled with Praline liqueur. Recipe can be halved and baked in a 7" x 10" x 2" pan.

Walnut-Apple Steamed Pudding

Pudding:

¾   cup chopped walnuts
2¼ cups flour
1   teaspoon salt
1   teaspoon baking powder
½   teaspoon baking soda
½   teaspoon cinnamon
¼   teaspoon each nutmeg and
     ginger

¼   cup butter or margarine,
     softened
½   cup brown sugar, packed
1   large egg
⅓   cup honey
½   cup milk
1   cup shredded apple
½   cup raisins

Remove 2 tablespoons of the walnuts and chop fine, then sprinkle in a well-greased 6 cup pudding mold. Sift dry ingredients together. Cream butter, sugar, egg and honey until light and fluffy. Add dry ingredients alternately with milk. Fold in apples, nuts and raisins. Turn into prepared mold. Cover tightly and steam in deep kettle with a lid, with hot water coming two thirds up side of mold, for 1½ hours. Let stand 10 minutes, then unmold on serving plate. Serve warm with Fluffy Hard Sauce.

Fluffy Hard Sauce:

½   cup butter or margarine
1   cup powdered sugar

½   teaspoon vanilla or brandy to
     taste
¼   cup heavy cream

Beat butter with sugar until fluffy; add extract or brandy. Fold in whipped cream. Refrigerate.

Yield: 10 servings

Zucchini and Carrot Pudding

In the fall I always get hungry for steamed puddings. They are handy to have in the freezer for unexpected company as they can be sliced and warmed in the top of a double boiler over boiling water. This one is both delicious and healthful.

¾ cup raisins	¼ cup grated carrot
¼ cup apple juice	1½ cups flour
1 stick butter, softened	1½ teaspoons cinnamon
¾ cup dark brown sugar, firmly packed	1 teaspoon baking powder
	1 teaspoon baking soda
2 large eggs	½ teaspoon freshly grated nutmeg
¾ cup grated zucchini, squeezed dry	

Let the raisins and apple juice soak in a dish for 30 minutes. In mixer bowl, cream the butter and brown sugar until it is fluffy. Add eggs, one at a time, beating well after each addition. Stir in zucchini and carrots. Sift dry ingredients together and add half to the zucchini mixture, stir in the raisin mixture, then stir in the remaining flour mixture. Turn the batter into a well-buttered 1-quart steamed pudding mold. Cover it tightly with the lid or a double layer of foil secured with string. Set the mold on a rack in a kettle with a tight-fitting lid, add enough hot water to come two-thirds of the way up the sides of the mold. Steam the pudding over moderate heat for 1 hour and 30 minutes. Let the mold stand on a rack, uncovered, for 15 minutes, then invert the pudding onto a serving plate. Serve warm with hard sauce or sauce of your choice.

Yield: 8 servings

A variety of sauces is in the sauce section of this book. This pudding can be made with ½ cup grated potato and ½ cup carrots, if you prefer.

Eggs &
Cheese

Mindy, Katie and John Wooldridge

Baked Eggs and Cheese

Another good breakfast or brunch casserole.

½	cup soft style cream cheese with chives	12	eggs, beaten
3	tablespoons whole milk	6	slices bacon, cooked crisp and crumbled
2	tablespoons margarine	1	cup grated Cheddar cheese

Beat cream cheese and milk together in a bowl. Set aside. Melt margarine in a large skillet over medium heat. Add eggs and cook, without stirring, until eggs begin to set around the edges, then gently lift and fold eggs so that uncooked portion flows underneath. Continue cooking until eggs are barely cooked. They should be moist and glossy. Place half of eggs in a lightly buttered 2-quart square or rectangular casserole. Spread with half the bacon, then half of the cream cheese mixture and half the Cheddar cheese. Repeat layers. Bake in a 350° oven, uncovered, about 20 minutes or until lightly browned.

Yield: 6 servings

Broiled Cream Cheese Sandwiches

Delicious filling of cream cheese and strawberry preserves.

1	(8 ounce) package cream cheese, room temperature	½	cup whole milk
12	slices firm-type sandwich bread	½	teaspoon vanilla
½	cup strawberry preserves	¼	teaspoon nutmeg
3	eggs	¼	cup margarine or butter

Divide cheese between 6 slices of bread. Spread jam over cheese. Top with remaining slices of bread. Beat eggs, vanilla, milk and nutmeg in a shallow bowl. Place margarine in a 15″ x 10″ x 1″ pan and place in a 300° oven to melt. Dip sandwiches in egg mixture and place in melted margarine. Broil 5 inches from the heat for 2 to 3 minutes. Turn and brown on other side. You may also cook the sandwiches on a well buttered griddle, if you prefer.

Serve with fresh fruit of your choice.

Yield: 6 sandwiches

Ham and Egg Crêpes

*This recipe is great to have for a party or for breakfast on special occasions.
The crêpes can be prepared the day before and baked the next day. The onions
and mushrooms can be sautéed and refrigerated leaving only the final
preparation of the sauce.*

Crêpes:

3 eggs	½ teaspoon salt
1½ cups milk	1½ tablespoons vegetable oil
1⅓ cups flour	

Combine ingredients in container of electric blender; process 1 minute. Scrape
down sides of blender with rubber spatula; process an additional 15 seconds.
Refrigerate 1 hour. This makes crêpes light in texture. Brush bottom of a 10″
crêpe pan with vegetable oil; place pan over medium heat until oil is just hot. I hold
my hand over the pan until I can feel the heat. Pour about 3 tablespoons batter
into pan, swirling it so batter covers the pan in a thin film. Cook about 1 minute
until underside is light brown. Flip crêpe out on a towel, browned side up, to cool.
Then stack between layers of waxed paper to keep them from sticking together.
You should have about 12 crêpes when finished with batter.

Filling:

2 tablespoons butter	½ cup milk
1¼ cups finely chopped cooked ham	¼ cup water
8 eggs	¼ teaspoon pepper

Melt butter in large skillet; sauté ham in butter about 5 minutes or until it is lightly
browned. Combine eggs, milk, water and pepper and beat well. Add egg mixture
to ham. Cook, stirring occasionally, until eggs are firm but still moist. Spoon ¼
cup egg mixture in center of each crêpe; fold sides of crêpe over filling. Place
crêpes, seam side down, in a lightly buttered 13″x 9″x 2″baking pan, folding ends
under. Cover and bake at 350° for 10 to 15 minutes or until crêpes are thoroughly
heated.

Mushroom Sauce:

3 tablespoons butter or margarine	1 teaspoon dry mustard
½ pound fresh mushrooms	½ teaspoon salt
2 tablespoons finely minced onion	⅛ teaspoon pepper
1 tablespoon flour	1 (8 ounce) carton sour cream
⅓ cup milk	2 tablespoons chopped parsley leaves for garnish

Melt butter in large skillet; sauté mushrooms and onion 3 to 5 minutes. Do not
overcook or mushrooms will shrink. Add flour and stir until vegetables are coated.

Continued on next page

Cook, stirring, 1 minute; then add milk gradually. Cook over medium heat, stirring constantly, until thickened and bubbly. Stir in mustard, salt and pepper. Add sour cream and parsley. Cook over medium heat, stirring constantly, just until heated. Do not let boil. Serve over crêpes.

Yield: 6 servings

Ham Crustless Quiche

Crust:

½ cup water

¼ teaspoon salt

⅓ cup quick-cooking yellow grits

Bring water and salt to a boil in a small saucepan; stir in grits. Remove from heat; let stand 5 minutes, then put in a buttered 10" Pyrex pie plate, making a crust.

Filling:

1 (12 ounce) can evaporated milk

1½ cups chopped cooked ham

1 cup (4 ounces) shredded sharp Cheddar cheese

3 large eggs, lightly beaten

1 tablespoon chopped fresh parsley

½ teaspoon dry mustard

Dash hot sauce or to taste

Mix milk, ham, cheese, eggs, parsley, dry mustard and hot sauce. Pour into grits crust. Bake at 350° until custard is set. Serve warm.

Yield: 6 servings

Oven-baked French Bread

This is similar to a cheese strata only with cream cheese. The use of evaporated milk instead of the whipping cream results in a good product and cuts calories considerably. Do as your conscience dictates.

6 (1") slices French bread, cut into 1" cubes

1 (8 ounce) package cream cheese, softened

12 large eggs

2 cups whipping cream or evaporated milk

½ cup pure maple syrup

Place bread cubes in a lightly buttered 13" x 9" x 2" baking dish. Set aside. Beat cream cheese at medium speed in mixer until smooth. Add eggs and next 2 ingredients, beating until blended. Pour over bread cubes; cover and refrigerate 8 hours or overnight. Remove from refrigerator; let come to room temperature; let stand at room temperature 30 minutes. Bake at 375° for 40 to 50 minutes or until set, covering with foil after 25 minutes . Serve with additional pure maple syrup.

Yield: 15 servings

Sausage Crêpes

This casserole can be completely assembled without sauce the day before and refrigerated. Remove from refrigerator next day and bring to room temperature before baking in a 325° oven until hot.

Filling:
1	pound bulk pork sausage	¼	teaspoon ground thyme
¼	cup minced onion	1	(4½ ounce) jar sliced
½	cup grated sharp Cheddar		mushrooms, drained
	cheese	¼	teaspoon garlic salt
1	(3 ounce) package cream		
	cheese, softened		

Cook sausage and onion in heavy skillet until sausage is brown, stirring to crumble; drain. Add next 5 ingredients. Make crêpes according to recipe in Ham and Egg Crêpes except make 16 (6") crêpes instead of 12 (10") crêpes. Fill each crêpe with about 2 tablespoons sausage mixture. Roll up and place, seam side down in two lightly greased 12" x 8" x 2" baking dishes. Cover and bake for 25 minutes in a 350° oven.

Sour Cream Sauce:
1	cup sour cream	½	cup butter

Combine sour cream and butter, mixing well; spoon over crêpes. Bake, uncovered, 5 minutes.

Yield: 6 servings

Helpful Hint: 8 ounces Cheddar cheese — 2 cups grated.

Spiced Pancakes

Pancakes:

3	cups flour	¼	teaspoon cloves
2	tablespoons baking powder	¾	cup raisins
2	tablespoons brown sugar, packed	2¼	cups milk
1	teaspoon salt	½	cup oil
3	teaspoons cinnamon	3	large eggs

Into a bowl, sift together the flour, baking powder, salt, cinnamon and cloves. Stir in the raisins and brown sugar. Make a well in dry ingredients and add the milk, oil and eggs. Stir batter with a fork until it is just combined. Batter will be lumpy. Fold over batter with a rubber spatula to be sure flour is all incorporated. Put ⅓ cup of batter on a lightly greased griddle for each pancake. Cook over medium heat until bubbles start to come on the surface, then turn and bake until underside is lightly brown. Serve with Chocolate Pecan Syrup.

Chocolate Pecan Syrup:

¾	cup maple syrup (I like to use the pure maple syrup)	¾	cup butter
3	tablespoons cocoa	⅓	cup chopped pecans

In a small saucepan, heat the syrup until it is hot. Remove pan from heat and whisk in the cocoa and butter until mixture is smooth. Add pecans and serve warm.

Yield: 6 servings

Helpful Hint: *Heating your pan before adding the oil prevents even eggs from sticking.*

Two-Cheese Polenta

This makes a satisfying brunch or lunch with the addition of sautéed fresh spinach and grilled tomatoes.

⅔ cup finely chopped onion	⅔ cup freshly grated Parmesan cheese
3 tablespoons olive oil	2⅓ cups grated mozzarella
2 cups yellow cornmeal	½ cup freshly grated Parmesan cheese
5 cups water	
1½ cups half-and-half	

In a kettle, cook the onion in the oil over moderately low heat, stirring, until it is softened. Add water, bring to a boil and add 1 cup of the cornmeal, a little at a time, stirring constantly. Reduce heat to low, add the remaining 1 cup cornmeal in a thin stream, stirring constantly. Add the half-and-half, ⅔ cup of the Parmesan and salt to taste. Pour half of the mixture into a buttered 13″ x 9″ baking dish, spread it evenly and sprinkle it with ¼ cup of the remaining Parmesan and half of the mozzarella. Smooth the remaining cornmeal mixture evenly over the mozzarella and sprinkle the top with the remaining ¼ cup of Parmesan and the remaining mozzarella. Bake on the middle shelf of a pre-heated 350° oven for 30 to 40 minutes, or until the cheese topping is melted and golden. Let cool slightly before cutting.

Yield: 8 servings

Entrées

Carter, Bin and Lacy Johnson

Basil Chicken

4	(6 ounce) boneless, skinless chicken breasts	1	tablespoon grated Parmesan cheese
½	cup butter or margarine, softened	¼	teaspoon garlic powder, not garlic salt
3	teaspoons dried basil, crushed or 2 tablespoons fresh, minced	⅛	teaspoon salt
		⅛	teaspoon pepper

Lightly salt breasts on both sides. Mix rest of ingredients at low speed of mixer until blended and smooth or mix with a fork. Place breasts in a shallow, rectangular casserole just large enough to hold them. Spread with butter mixture. Cover and bake in a pre-heated 325° oven about 20 minutes or until breasts are firm to the touch. Place on a mound of cooked rice and spoon pan juices over.

Yield: 4 servings

If you prefer to grill the chicken instead of baking, mix ⅓ cup butter or margarine with ¼ cup chopped fresh basil for a basting sauce. Serve with the basil butter.

Chicken Almond

1½	pounds skinned and boned chicken breasts	¼	pound frozen sugar peas or snow peas, thawed and drained
⅓	cup peanut oil		
2	cups celery cut diagonally	1	teaspoon cornstarch
2	cups onion, coarsely chopped	2	tablespoons water
1	cup canned bamboo shoots, sliced	2	ounces blanched, slivered, toasted almonds
1	cup canned water chestnuts, sliced		

Cut chicken in about ¾" cubes. Brown quickly in hot oil in wok or large skillet. Add next 4 ingredients. Cover and cook about 7 minutes. Scatter sugar peas on top, cover, and cook 2 minutes more. Mix cornstarch and water, add and cook, stirring, until slightly thickened. Sprinkle with part of the almonds. Pass the rest of almonds and soy sauce at the table.

Yield: 6 servings

Breast of Chicken Olé

Amount of crumbs needed depends on size of breasts, in other words, whether they are thick or thin. Reserve part of the crumbs, adding crumbs when they are needed. In that way, the reserved crumbs can be refrigerated and saved for another time.

Chicken:

1	cup cracker crumbs	8	(4 to 6 ounce) boneless,
2	tablespoons taco mix		skinless chicken breasts

In a shallow dish combine crumbs and taco mix. Mix well. Dip chicken in crumbs and place in a greased 13"x 9"x 2"baking dish.

Sauce:

4	green onions, white only, chopped	1	cup (4 ounces) Monterey Jack cheese, grated
2	tablespoons margarine	1	cup (4 ounces) Velveeta
2	cups whipping cream or evaporated milk, undiluted		cheese, cut into small dice
		1	(4 ounce) can green chilies, drained

Place margarine in saucepan over low heat until melted, add onions and sauté until tender. Add cream and remaining ingredients; pour over chicken making sure that cheese is well distributed. Bake at 350° about 15 to 20 minutes or until chicken is just firm to the touch.

Yield: 8 servings

If you are substituting evaporated milk for the heavy cream, one 12 ounce can of evaporated milk contains 1½ cups. A 5 ounce can contains 2 tablespoons more than a half cup. Also, there are 5 tablespoons of taco mix in a package.

Chicken with Artichokes

This entrée is prepared in about 30 minutes.

4	(6 ounce) skinless, boneless chicken breasts	1	(10½ ounce) can chicken broth or equivalent homemade
3	tablespoons flour	¼	cup sliced ripe olives
½	teaspoon salt	2	tablespoons capers
¼	teaspoon pepper	1	(14 ounce) can artichoke
2	tablespoons olive oil		hearts, rinsed and halved

Mix flour, salt and pepper and dredge chicken in it. Heat olive oil in a skillet over medium heat. Add chicken and cook 3 minutes on each side or until lightly browned. Add chicken broth and next 2 ingredients. Bring to a boil and then simmer 20 minutes or until thickened and bubbly. Add artichokes, heat and serve.

Yield: 4 servings

Chicken Angel

Angel hair pasta bundles are usually available at your super markets. This is a pretty dish to serve for guests. Also, it provides an entrée plus a green vegetable and a starch.

Chicken:

8   nested-style angel hair pasta bundles

8   (6 to 8 ounce) boneless, skinless chicken breast halves

1   teaspoon salt

½   teaspoon pepper

1   (6 ounce) can sliced mushrooms, drained; juice reserved

1   (10 ounce) package frozen chopped spinach, thawed and drained

Cook angel hair pasta according to directions. Drain well, keeping nests in shape. Sprinkle chicken with salt and pepper; arrange in a lightly buttered 13"x 9"x 2" casserole. Mix mushrooms and spinach together and spread over chicken. Place cooked pasta nests over spinach mixture.

Sauce:

1   (10¾ ounce) can cream of chicken soup, undiluted

⅔   cup mushroom juice combined with water

4   ounces Monterey Jack cheese, cut into small dice

4   ounces Cheddar cheese, cut into small dice

Combine soup and mushroom juice-water mixture in a small saucepan. Bring to a boil, stirring with a wire whisk until smooth. Pour sauce over pasta nests. Bake in a pre-heated 350° oven about 20 to 30 minutes until chicken is tender. Mix cheeses together and spread over chicken. Return to oven and bake until cheese melts.

Yield: 8 servings

The spinach does not have to be precooked.

Chicken with Bleu Cheese Sauce

Chicken:

1	cup fresh soft bread crumbs	3	tablespoons olive oil
½	cup grated Parmesan cheese	¼	cup whole milk
¼	teaspoon salt	1	tablespoon white wine
¼	teaspoon pepper		Worcestershire sauce
1¼	teaspoons dried whole thyme, crushed	8	(6 ounce) skinless, boneless chicken breast halves
3	tablespoons butter or margarine, melted		

Combine first 5 ingredients in a pie plate. Mix butter, oil, milk and Worcestershire sauce in shallow bowl. Dip chicken in mixture, then in crumb mixture. Arrange chicken on a lightly greased cookie sheet or in a greased shallow casserole. This can be done the day before and refrigerated, covered. Next day, let come to room temperature before placing in a 350° oven. Bake about 15 minutes or until breasts are just firm to the touch. Do not overbake. Serve with Bleu cheese sauce.

Bleu Cheese Sauce:

1	green onion, chopped	1	(10¾ ounce) can condensed chicken broth, undiluted
1	stalk celery with leaves, chopped	1	cup whipping cream
2	tablespoons butter, melted	2	tablespoons Bleu cheese, crumbled
½	cup dry white wine		

Sauté onion and celery in butter until tender. Add wine and broth. Bring to a boil and cook over medium heat, stirring, until liquid is reduced to about 1 cup. Strain, then return to saucepan. Add whipping cream and bring to a boil. Reduce heat and simmer, stirring, about 15 minutes or until the mixture is reduced to a cup. The sauce may be made a day ahead and refrigerated, then reheated. Finish as directed. Remove from heat; add cheese and stir until cheese is melted.

Yield: 8 servings

For those who do not like Bleu cheese, Swiss cheese may be substituted.

Helpful Hint: *Bottled Italian salad dressing makes a great marinade for meat or chicken.*

Chicken Breasts Sauté

Red wine is used in this recipe. Remember, do not cook with a wine you would not drink. A number of California wines as well as those of other states are good and moderately priced.

Chicken:

6	(6 ounce) boned and skinless chicken breasts	2	tablespoons olive oil
		¼	cup finely chopped onion
2	tablespoons butter	1	clove garlic, minced

Pre-heat oven to 325°. Brown chicken in olive oil and butter. Add onion and garlic, cook 5 minutes. Place chicken breasts, with onion and garlic, in a baking dish just large enough to hold them comfortably.

Sauce:

2	tablespoons flour	1	cup hot chicken broth
½	teaspoon salt	½	cup red wine
¼	teaspoon pepper		Chopped parsley as garnish

In a small bowl, combine salt, pepper and flour. Slowly add hot chicken broth. Mix well, bring just to a boil, stirring, add wine then pour over chicken. Bake in oven, uncovered, until tender. Garnish with chopped parsley.

Yield: 6 servings

Chicken Chili Bake

This is a low calorie dish, 263 calories per serving.

½	cup brown rice, uncooked	1	(10¾ ounce) can fat-free cream of chicken soup, undiluted
1¾	cups homemade chicken broth, cooked and fat removed or equivalent in ready-to-serve fat-free chicken broth	1	cup frozen whole kernel corn, thawed
2	cups chopped cooked chicken breast (skinned before cooking)	½	cup finely chopped onion
		1	tablespoon Worcestershire sauce
1	(12 ounce) jar medium salsa	2	teaspoons chili powder
		1	teaspoon oregano, crushed
		¼	teaspoon pepper

Combine rice and chicken broth in a saucepan; bring to a boil. Cover, reduce heat and simmer for about 40 minutes or until rice is tender and water is absorbed. Combine chicken and remaining ingredients in a large bowl; stir in rice. Spoon mixture into a 2-quart casserole coated with vegetable spray. Bake at 350° for 30 minutes or until bubbly.

Yield: 5 servings

Chicken Breasts in Vermouth

This is a recipe for larger groups.

24	(4 to 6 ounce) boneless, skinless chicken breasts
1	cup butter or margarine, divided
½	cup olive oil, divided
2	cups thinly sliced onion
2	pounds small fresh mushrooms, stems removed
1½	teaspoons salt
1	tablespoon thyme, crumbled
1	teaspoon pepper
2	bay leaves
1½	cups dry vermouth
2	cups chicken broth

Sauté chicken breasts in ¼ cup olive oil and ¾ cup butter until golden, about 10 minutes. Place in a large baking pan 17"x 12"x 2½", overlapping them slightly. Heat oven to 350°. Put remaining butter and oil in skillet and sauté onions until limp, then add mushrooms and cook about 3 minutes, until onions are golden. Spread mixture over chicken. Combine drippings in skillet with salt, pepper, thyme and bay leaves. Add vermouth and chicken broth; bring to a boil, stirring, then pour over chicken. Cover pan tightly with foil. Bake, basting twice, about 20 minutes or until breasts are tender. Remove breasts to a platter to keep warm. Strain pan juices and set aside.

Sauce:

¼	cup vermouth
2	tablespoons flour

Pan drippings

Bring pan juices to a boil and reduce to 2 cups. Combine vermouth and flour, add to pan juices. Bring to boiling and simmer 2 minutes until slightly thickened. Spoon sauce over chicken.

Yield: 24 servings

Helpful Hint: Mushrooms stay fresh longer refrigerated in a paper bag.

Chicken and Cheese Strata

Recipe may be halved to serve 8.

22 slices white bread (homemade type), cubed
8   large eggs, beaten
2   pounds Cheddar cheese, grated
4 to 6 cups cubed cooked chicken
1   (8 ounce) can sliced mushrooms, drained

2   jiggers sherry
2   (10¾ ounce) cans cream of mushroom soup
2   soup cans full of whole milk
1   teaspoon salt
Dash white pepper
1   stick butter or margarine, melted

Butter 2 (7" x 11") casseroles. In a large bowl, thoroughly mix the soup, milk, eggs, sherry, salt, pepper and butter. Place a layer of bread cubes in each of the casseroles, then layers of chicken, mushrooms and cheese. Repeat layers. Divide soup-milk mixture between casseroles. Refrigerate overnight. Bake at 350° 1 hour. Cut into squares to serve. May be topped with mushroom sauce, if desired.

Mushroom Sauce:

4   tablespoons butter or margarine
3   tablespoons flour
    salt and pepper to taste

2   cups light cream or whole milk
1   (4 ounce) can sliced mushrooms, drained
¼   cup grated Parmesan cheese

Melt butter in saucepan; stir in flour, salt and pepper. Add cream or milk slowly, stirring constantly with a wire whisk. Cook 2 minutes or until thickened. Add Parmesan cheese and mushrooms. Makes about 3½ cups sauce.

Yield: 16 servings

Chicken Chinese

This recipe contains several vegetables, but is only 325 calories per serving.

1	pound skinless, boneless chicken breasts	¾	pound small new potatoes
1	tablespoon cornstarch	½	pound medium mushrooms
2	tablespoons soy sauce	3	teaspoons peanut oil, divided
2	tablespoons dry sherry	¼	teaspoon salt, divided
2	teaspoons minced peeled ginger root	1	cup frozen peas, thawed and drained well
2	small onions	¼	teaspoon dried rosemary, crushed
1	(12 ounce) zucchini		

Cut chicken into 1″ chunks. In a medium bowl, mix cornstarch, soy sauce, sherry and ginger. Dip chicken in this mixture until well coated; set aside. Cut each onion into quarters. Cut zucchini and potatoes into bite-sized chunks. Cut stems from mushrooms, rinse and pat dry.

In a non-stick wok or skillet, heat 1 teaspoon oil over medium heat. Add potatoes and onions and ⅛ teaspoon salt. Cover and heat, turning potatoes and onions occasionally, until brown and tender. Spoon into a large bowl. In same skillet or wok, over high heat, add 1 teaspoon oil. Cook zucchini and ⅛ teaspoon salt until tender-crisp, stirring frequently. Remove to same bowl. In same skillet over high heat, add 1 teaspoon oil, add chicken with the marinade and cook until tender, stirring constantly. This will take only about 4 or 5 minutes. Return all vegetables to the skillet and add peas and rosemary. Heat and serve.

Yield: 4 servings

Chicken Italian

This is an easy recipe to prepare for a crowd as recipe can be doubled or tripled as needed.

6-7	slices bread, dried in the oven and made into crumbs	1	clove garlic, crushed
2	(3 pound) fryers cut into serving pieces	2	teaspoons salt
		1	teaspoon pepper
½	cup grated Parmesan cheese		Dash nutmeg
¼	cup fresh parsley leaves, chopped		Dash cayenne pepper
			Pinch of oregano, crushed
		2	sticks margarine, melted

Measure 2 cups of the crumbs, mix with cheese and next 7 ingredients. Dip chicken into melted margarine, then into crumbs. Place close together in a shallow roasting pan lined with foil. Pour remaining margarine over. Bake at 350° for 1 hour. Do not turn.

Yield: 10 servings

Chicken Fricassee

Chicken Fricassee is a combination of a sauté and a stew. No liquid is included in a sauté. In a stew, the meat is simmered in liquid from the beginning of its cooking. This entrée may be prepared ahead and reheated without losing any of its qualities.

1 (3 pounds or more) fryer, cut up	2 cups chicken stock
16 small white onions or ½ medium onion, minced	1½ cups white vermouth
	½ cup heavy cream
	Fresh lemon juice to taste
2 tablespoons butter	1 quart fresh mushrooms, quartered
2 tablespoons olive oil	
½ teaspoon salt	½ teaspoon tarragon, crushed between palms of your hands
¼ teaspoon white pepper	
3 tablespoons flour	

Over moderate heat in a heavy large sauté pan or electric skillet, heat olive oil and butter to foaming. Turn down heat to medium-low and add chicken. Turn the chicken several times so that chicken cooks without browning. When it stiffens slightly, season with salt and pepper and tarragon. Add onions around chicken. Cover and cook over low heat only 10 minutes, turning once. Uncover the pan and sprinkle the flour over, turning the chicken and onions so the flour is absorbed. Cook 3 minutes more turning once. Remove from heat and gradually add the vermouth and enough chicken stock to almost cover chicken. Cover and simmer until chicken is tender. Remove smaller pieces of chicken when tender and continue cooking the rest. Return all chicken to pan, add mushrooms and simmer only 4 minutes. Add the cream and simmer until sauce coats chicken lightly. Add more cream, if sauce is too thick. Taste and correct seasoning and add drops of lemon juice to taste. Place in serving casserole arranging mushrooms around chicken. Surround with rice or noodles.

Yield: 4 to 6 servings

Roasting chickens, young stewing hens or fryers may be used. However, fryers should weigh 3 pounds or more. Fricassees may be served with rice or noodles.

Chicken Marinara

This sauce may also be used with fish or meat.

Chicken:
6   (5 ounce) boneless, skinless
     chicken breasts

Place chicken in an oblong baking dish just large enough to hold it comfortably. Bake, covered, in a 375° oven for 10 minutes or until it is just firm to the touch; drain. Lower heat to 350°. Pour heated sauce over chicken; top with grated cheese. Return to oven and bake 5 minutes, uncovered. Serve with sauce.

Marinara Sauce:
¼   cup chopped onion
1   clove garlic, minced
2   tablespoons olive oil
2   (14½ ounce) cans diced
     tomatoes

Salt and pepper
1   tablespoon lemon juice
1½   teaspoons Italian seasoning
1   bay leaf
¼   cup grated Parmesan cheese

Sauté garlic and onion in olive oil in a heavy saucepan or skillet, stirring constantly, until onion is limp but not brown. Add rest of sauce ingredients; bring to a boil, then simmer, stirring occasionally, about 20 minutes or until mixture has thickened. Remove from heat and discard bay leaf. Taste for seasoning with salt and pepper.

Yield: 6 servings

Working Woman's Chicken

This recipe calls for a 3½ pound chicken. However, you may use unboned chicken breasts or unboned thighs, if you prefer. The wine caramelizes the onions and gives a rich taste to the chicken.

2   tablespoons olive oil
1   medium onion, chopped
1   (3½ pound) fryer, cut up

1   cup white wine
1   cup chicken broth
Salt and pepper

Sauté onion in oil over medium heat until light brown. Remove from skillet. Season chicken with salt and pepper and place in skillet. Sauté about 5 minutes on each side or until light brown. Add wine, chicken broth and onion. Simmer, covered, about 30 minutes or until chicken is done. If chicken gets too dry, add a little more chicken broth.

Yield: 4 to 6 servings

Serve with Rice and Almonds in the vegetable section of this cookbook, along with a green salad and a good domestic Chardonnay.

Chicken Moutarde

This entrée can be made on top of the stove. It is delicious served with a green vegetable and Pecan Rice.

Chicken:

6	(6 ounce) boneless, skinless chicken breasts	2	tablespoons butter
		2	tablespoons olive oil

Lightly brown chicken breasts in the butter and olive oil. Remove from skillet. Remove skillet from heat.

Sauce:

1	cup whipping cream or evaporated milk	1½ to 2 tablespoons Dijon mustard or to taste
1	level tablespoon cornstarch	Salt and pepper to taste
1	cup chicken broth	

Add cornstarch to cream, mix until smooth. Add to skillet and stir to scrape up brown bits. Add chicken broth and mustard. Simmer for 10 minutes. If sauce gets too thick, add more broth. Return chicken to skillet and cook, covered, about 15 minutes or until firm to the touch. Add salt and pepper to taste to the sauce. Place a little sauce on a heated dinner plate and place chicken on top. Pass any remaining sauce.

Yield: 6 servings

If you prefer, the browned chicken breasts can be placed in a casserole and finished in a 325° oven for 20 minutes, or until breasts are just firm to the touch.

Chicken with Mushrooms

This is an easy way to fix smothered chicken.

1 (3½ pound) chicken, cut into pieces, or equivalent of chicken parts	Freshly ground pepper
	3 tablespoons butter
	2 tablespoons vegetable oil
Salt	

Pre-heat oven to 350°. Wash chicken under cold running water and pat dry with paper towels. If chicken is wet, it will not brown. Season with salt and a little pepper. In a heavy 12" skillet, melt the butter and oil over medium heat. Lightly brown the chicken pieces, a few pieces at a time, skin side down, then turn them. Lightly brown other side. Transfer the pieces to a shallow casserole just large enough to hold them in one layer.

Gravy:

4 tablespoons minced onion	½ cup whipping cream or evaporated milk, undiluted
3 tablespoons flour	
1½ cups chicken stock, fresh or canned	½ pound fresh mushrooms, sliced

To the fat remaining in the skillet, add the onions and cook them over medium-low heat until they are soft. Stir in the flour, mix well with a spoon and pour in the chicken stock. Bring the stock to a boil, stirring constantly with a whisk, then cook at simmer 2 or 3 minutes. Pour sauce over chicken in the casserole, cover tightly and cook in the center of the oven about 20 minutes. Then scatter mushrooms around chicken, basting them with the pan gravy. Cook, covered, another 10 minutes until chicken is tender but not falling apart. To serve, place chicken on a deep platter. Skim the gravy of as much fat as possible, then stir in cream or evaporated milk. Simmer a minute or two until sauce thickens, stirring constantly. Taste for seasoning and pour over chicken.

Yield: 4 to 6 servings

As I have mentioned before, evaporated milk thickens the same as heavy cream does and is lower in calories. Use either one you prefer.

Chicken Nicole

Olive oil added to butter for sautéing keeps the butter from burning.

Chicken:

6	(5 or 6 ounce) boneless, skinless chicken breasts	2	tablespoons butter
		1	tablespoon olive oil

Salt and pepper

Season chicken breasts with salt and pepper. Heat butter and olive oil in heavy skillet. Roll chicken breasts in the butter-oil mixture. Over low heat, let meat whiten slowly on both sides. Using tongs, start turning breasts from side to side every second minute. When you touch the meat with your index finger, you will feel it becoming stiffer. It is done when your finger does not sink into the meat, between 6 to 8 minutes depending on the thickness. Remove breasts and keep warm between two plates.

Sauce:

1	tablespoon olive oil	4	slices lean bacon, cooked and crumbled
½	pound fresh mushrooms, sliced		
½	cup chicken broth	2	tablespoons thinly sliced green onion tops (no white)
⅔	cup heavy cream		

Increase heat and add sliced mushrooms to the skillet. Sauté quickly in olive oil only a few minutes until juices are released. Remove from skillet with a slotted spoon. Add chicken broth to the skillet and simmer for about 5 minutes. Add cream and cook, stirring, until sauce coats the back of a spoon. In other words, when you draw your finger over the back of the spoon, it leaves a track. Return chicken and mushrooms to the skillet to heat. Taste for seasoning, then place on dinner plates or serving platter and garnish with green onion tops and the crumbled bacon.

Yield: 6 servings

If you wish to have less calories in this dish, substitute undiluted evaporated, not condensed, milk in this entrée for the heavy cream.

Chicken with Rosemary

Rosemary and white wine make this dish special.

Chicken:

12	(6 ounce) boneless, skinless chicken breasts	1	teaspoon salt
2	tablespoons olive oil	½	teaspoon pepper
2	tablespoons butter	2	teaspoons rosemary, finely crushed
¾	cup flour		

Combine flour, salt, pepper and rosemary in a shallow dish. Dust chicken lightly with flour mixture. Melt the olive oil and butter in a skillet and brown chicken on both sides. Remove from skillet and keep warm by covering them with a dish.

Sauce:

2¼	cups dry white wine	1	cup chopped green onions
1	pound fresh mushrooms, sliced	1	clove garlic, minced

In same skillet, sauté mushrooms, green onions and garlic in butter and olive oil until soft. Add wine, heat and stir to deglaze. Return chicken breasts to skillet. Cover and cook about 10 minutes or until they are just firm to the touch. Serve with sauce.

Yield: 12 servings

I like to serve this entrée with wild rice and fresh asparagus dressed with lemon juice and Parmesan cheese. In index: Asparagus Supreme.

Grilled Chicken, Raleigh House

This is how we made our grilled chicken breasts. It is one recipe I did not share as it was so very simple to make. I did not want to give away my secret.

Boneless, skinless chicken breasts   Light Italian or French Wishbone
    (as many as you need)   salad dressing

Roll or pound chicken breasts to make them of equal thickness. Pour a little of the dressing into a stainless or ceramic pan deep enough to hold the amount of breasts you wish to cook. Place a layer of chicken in pan, then pour over a little more of the dressing. Continue layering until all chicken is in the marinade. Cover and refrigerate at least 2 or 3 hours or overnight. Drain well and cook on grill about 5 minutes on one side, then turn and cook until firm when touched with your index finger.

Yield: As many servings as you need

We always served this with steamed fresh vegetables and almond rice.

Chicken and Sausage Jambalaya

This recipe uses light Italian dressing instead of oil for sautéing. Turkey sausage is used instead of pork which all adds up to less calories. The uncooked rice is cooked along with other ingredients.

1	pound boned and skinned chicken breasts	2½	cups chopped onion
¼	teaspoon pepper	1½	cups sliced green onions
Dash red pepper		2	cloves garlic, minced
6	tablespoons light Italian dressing, divided	3	cups chicken broth
12	ounces turkey sausage	1½	cups Uncle Ben's rice, uncooked
2½	cups chopped celery	1	teaspoon salt

Cut chicken into bite-sized pieces; season with pepper and red pepper. Add 3 tablespoons Italian dressing to an electric skillet. Set heat at 325° and add chicken. Cook, stirring, for 3 minutes only. Remove from skillet and set aside. Cook sausage in skillet over medium heat until meat is light brown and crumbly. Remove and set aside. Add the remaining 3 tablespoons Italian dressing to skillet and sauté the celery, onion, green onions and garlic about 5 minutes or until crisp tender. Add the chicken broth, rice and salt. Bring to a boil and simmer, covered, until rice is tender. Return all ingredients to the skillet. Set heat at medium and cook until heated through. Taste for seasoning and serve.

Yield: 6 servings

Fettuccine, Chicken and Artichokes

This is a delicious dish for special guests.

4	(4 ounce) skinless, boneless chicken breasts	1	cup coarsely chopped walnuts
8	ounces spinach or plain fettuccine, cooked according to directions and kept warm	½	cup minced onion
		1	teaspoon dried sweet basil, crushed
1	(6½ ounce) jar marinated artichoke hearts	½	teaspoon dried tarragon, crushed
1	clove garlic, minced	4	tablespoons grated Parmesan cheese

Pat chicken dry, then cut into bite-sized strips. Set aside. Drain artichoke hearts, reserving marinade. Put 2 tablespoons of the marinade in a large skillet or sauté pan. Add garlic, walnuts, onion, basil and tarragon. Stir-fry until onion is crisp-tender. Remove from skillet. Set aside. Add the chicken to the skillet and stir-fry just until chicken becomes opaque. Add walnut mixture and artichoke hearts. Cook, stirring, until heated through. Place warm pasta on heated plates, spoon chicken mixture over and sprinkle with grated Parmesan cheese.

Yield: 4 servings

Chicken and Shrimp Casserole

All white or all dark chicken parts may be used instead of whole chicken.

1	(3 or 3½ pound) fryer, cut into 8 pieces	¼	teaspoon freshly ground pepper
½	teaspoon salt	½	cup olive oil

Sprinkle chicken with salt and pepper. In a heavy 12″ skillet, heat the olive oil over moderate heat. Add the chicken and cook for 4 or 5 minutes on each side until golden brown. Transfer to a 3-quart casserole and set aside.

Sauce:

¾	cup minced onions	1	cup dry white wine
1½	teaspoons minced garlic	1	pound medium shrimp
3	tablespoons all-purpose flour	2	tablespoons finely chopped fresh parsley leaves
¼	teaspoon paprika		

Drop onions and garlic into the skillet and cook over low heat, stirring, until golden but not brown. Mix in the flour; cook, stirring constantly, just 2 minutes. Add the paprika, pour in the wine and bring to a boil over high heat scraping up any brown bits in the skillet. Pour over chicken in casserole. Cover with lid or foil. Place in a pre-heated 350° oven and cook for 30 minutes or until juices of chicken are a clear yellow. If juices are tinged with pink, cook additional time. Shell shrimp and devein them. Wash and set aside. When chicken is done, arrange shrimp on top of chicken, cover casserole and cook only 5 minutes longer or until shrimp are pink. Arrange chicken and shrimp on heated platter. Taste the sauce for seasoning and then ladle sauce over them. Sprinkle with the parsley and serve at once.

Yield: 8 servings

Sweet-Sour Chicken

4	(4 or 5 ounce) boneless, skinless chicken breasts	3	tablespoons raspberry or strawberry jelly
Salt		3	tablespoons white wine vinegar
2	tablespoons unsalted butter or margarine	¼	cup whipping cream or undiluted evaporated milk
¼	cup finely minced onion		

Sprinkle chicken lightly with salt. Melt butter in a skillet, add chicken and cook over medium heat for 5 minutes. Turn chicken, arrange onions around edge of skillet and continue cooking 5 or 10 minutes more or until chicken is golden and onion is tender. Remove chicken from skillet and keep warm. Add jelly and vinegar to skillet and scrape up brown bits in pan. Bring to a boil, stir in cream. Heat and pour over chicken.

Yield: 4 servings

Chicken Tetrazzini

This is a great dish for buffet dinners. It has enough chicken in it to satisfy the male guests.

1	(8 ounce) package spaghetti	1	(4 ounce) can sliced
6	tablespoons margarine or		mushrooms, undrained
	butter, divided	½	teaspoon salt
1	small onion, diced	½	cup grated Parmesan cheese
¼	cup flour	4	slices white bread, torn into
1¾	cups whole milk		small pieces (3 cups crumbs)
1	cup chicken broth, preferably	1¾	cups frozen small peas, thawed
	homemade	3	cups diced cooked chicken

In saucepot, cook spaghetti as label directs, drain, and return to saucepot. Meanwhile, in a 2-quart saucepan over medium heat, cook onion in 3 tablespoons butter until tender. Stir in flour until blended. Remove from heat and gradually add milk, chicken broth, mushrooms with their liquid and salt. Cook, stirring constantly, until mixture is slightly thickened. Remove from heat and stir in cheese. In a small saucepan, melt remaining 3 tablespoons butter. Remove from heat and stir in bread crumbs. Pre-heat oven to 350°. Gently toss spaghetti with sauce mixture, chicken and peas. Spoon into a 12"x 9"baking dish. Top with buttered crumbs. Bake 20 minutes or until heated through and bubbly.

Yield: 6 servings

I served this accompanied with a tangy slaw, hot rolls and strawberry tarts for dessert.

Teriyaki Chicken

This is a low calorie dish, only 158 calories per serving.

Marinade:

¼	cup water	2	tablespoons sugar
¼	cup reduced-sodium soy sauce	1	tablespoon grated fresh ginger
¼	cup molasses	2	cloves garlic, chopped
¼	cup cider vinegar	2	pounds boneless, skinless
			chicken thighs or breasts

Combine water, soy sauce, molasses, vinegar, sugar, ginger and garlic in plastic bag. Reserve a little of marinade. Add chicken. Seal tightly. Refrigerate several hours or overnight. Pre-heat grill or broiler. Remove chicken from marinade. Grill or broil 5"from heat. Turn and brush with marinade. Broil for another 5 minutes or until chicken is firm to the touch.

Yield: 8 servings

This can be grilled or broiled.

Chicken with Vegetable Sauce

This is almost a complete meal. It only needs the addition of brown or white rice to complete it.

Vegetables and Chicken:

2	tablespoons olive oil	¾	teaspoon salt
3	medium carrots	¼	teaspoon sweet basil, crumbled
4	medium zucchini, about 8 ounces each	⅛	teaspoon pepper
6	green onions, divided	6	(5 or 6 ounce) boneless, skinless chicken breast halves
2	tablespoons olive oil	2	tablespoons olive oil

Cut carrots and zucchini in half crosswise; cut each half lengthwise into thin strips. Cut each onion in half lengthwise, then cut into 1″pieces. In a 5-quart Dutch oven, heat the olive oil. Over medium heat, cook carrots 2 minutes, stirring. Add zucchini, ½ of onions, salt, pepper and basil. Cook about 3 minutes longer or until vegetables are tender-crisp. Remove vegetables to a large bowl with a slotted spoon. In the same Dutch oven, heat 2 tablespoons olive oil. Add chicken breasts and lightly brown on both sides. Set aside.

Sauce:

1¼	cups water or chicken broth	⅛	teaspoon pepper
¼	cup dry white wine	½	cup half-and-half
1	teaspoon salt	1	tablespoon flour
¼	teaspoon sweet basil, crumbled		

In Dutch oven, add water or broth, wine, salt, basil and pepper and remaining green onions. Add chicken. Heat to boiling, cover and simmer about 15 minutes or until chicken is tender. Mix half-and-half and flour together; gradually add to liquid. Cook until slightly thickened. Add reserved vegetables. Taste for seasoning, then heat and serve.

Yield: 6 servings

Overnight Chicken Italian

1	(2½ or 3 pound) fryer cut into serving pieces		Juice of ½ lemon
⅓	cup oil (half olive oil and half corn oil)	1	teaspoon garlic salt
		½	cup grated Romano cheese
¼	cup cider vinegar	½	cup dry bread crumbs
			Salt and pepper

Marinate chicken overnight in mixture of oil, vinegar, lemon and garlic salt. Next day place chicken in baking pan and sprinkle lightly with mixture of bread crumbs, cheese, salt and pepper. Cover pan loosely with foil and bake at 350° about 45 minutes or until tender. Serve with cooked spaghetti or pasta of your choice flavored only with butter and garlic.

Yield: 4 servings

Chicken Wild Rice Casserole

I recommend using a food processor for the preparation of this dish, as the cheeses and vegetables have to be finely minced, however, it can be done with a sharp knife.

½	cup fresh parsley leaves	3	cups cooked chicken or turkey cut into ½" dice
4	green onions		
1	medium stalk celery, cut into 1" pieces	2	cups cooked wild rice
		1	teaspoon dried oregano, crushed
1	medium tomato, seeded and quartered	1	teaspoon salt
¼	stick unsalted butter		Dash pepper

Grease a 9" x 13" baking dish, set aside. Pre-heat oven to 350°. Finely mince parsley in food processor. Set aside. Then, with processor running, drop in green onions and celery through feed tube and mince finely. Coarsely chop tomato by hand and set aside. Melt butter in heavy skillet over low heat, add onion mixture and sauté until soft. Add minced parsley, chicken or turkey, tomato, rice, oregano, salt and pepper. Stir just until heated through, about 2 minutes. Remove from heat and add 1 cup of mornay sauce; reserve remainder. Place mixture in prepared dish. Bake 20 minutes, then spread remainder of sauce over casserole and broil 6" from the heat until hot and bubbly.

Mornay Sauce:

1	ounce piece Parmesan cheese, room temperature	3	tablespoons flour
		1½	cups whole milk
1	ounce mozzarella cheese	¼	teaspoon salt
3	tablespoons butter or margarine		Dash nutmeg
		¼	teaspoon pepper

Finely mince cheeses. Set aside. Melt butter in a heavy 1 quart saucepan over low heat. Add flour and stir about 2 minutes. Remove from heat and add milk, salt, nutmeg and pepper. Return to medium heat, and cook, stirring constantly, until mixture thickens. Cool slightly and add cheeses. Taste for seasoning. Set aside.

Yield: 6 servings

I always use the quick soak method for cooking wild rice. The recipe is in the vegetable category of this cookbook.

Helpful Hint: 1 pound spaghetti — 4 to 5 cups.

Coq au Vin

This entrée can be prepared the day before, placed in a casserole and refrigerated. Next day, bring to room temperature and heat at 325° about 30 or 40 minutes or until heated through.

6	slices lean bacon, cooked crisp and broken up	1	cup beef or chicken broth
8	chicken thighs or a 3½ pound fryer cut into 8 pieces	1	tablespoon tomato paste
2	cups dry red wine	1	teaspoon salt
12	small white onions	1	teaspoon minced garlic
2	medium carrots, cut in half crosswise, then cut into thin sticks	½	teaspoon thyme leaves, crushed
3	tablespoons flour	1	(1½") bay leaf
		8	ounces small fresh mushrooms, halved

Cook bacon in large deep skillet over medium heat until crisp. Remove and set aside, saving bacon drippings. Place chicken in drippings, skin-side down. Cook 10 to 12 minutes or until brown. Remove chicken. Pour off fat and discard. Pour ½ cup wine into skillet and cook over medium heat scraping up brown bits from bottom of pan. Return chicken to skillet, skin-side up, add carrots and onions. Cook, covered, over medium heat 8 to 10 minutes. Mix flour, remainder of wine, broth and tomato paste. Add to skillet and cook until thickened, then add salt, garlic, thyme, bay leaf and mushrooms. Bring to a boil, reduce heat. Cover and simmer 25 to 30 minutes, stirring occasionally, until chicken and vegetables are tender. Discard bay leaf. Sprinkle bacon over top and serve.

Yield: 4 servings

Crusty Chicken

6	(5 or 6 ounce) boneless skinless chicken breasts	2	tablespoons chopped fresh parsley
¾	cup cracker crumbs		Salt and pepper
¾	cup chopped roasted peanuts	1	stick margarine, melted

Season chicken breasts lightly with salt and pepper. Mix cracker crumbs, peanuts and parsley in a shallow bowl. Dip chicken in the melted margarine, then in the crumbs. Place fairly close together, but not touching, in a shallow baking dish. Pour the rest of the margarine around the chicken. Bake in a 325° oven for about 20 minutes or until chicken is just tender.

Yield: 6 servings

Turkey and Ham Casserole

I have always liked the combination of poultry with smoked meats. This is one of my favorites.

½	cup finely chopped onion	3	tablespoons dry vermouth
7	tablespoons butter, divided	2	cups cubed cooked turkey
3	tablespoons flour	1	cup cubed cooked ham
½	teaspoon salt	1	(8 ounce) can sliced water
¼	teaspoon pepper		chestnuts, drained
1	(5 or 6 ounce) can sliced	½	cup coarsely grated Gruyère or
	mushrooms, undrained		Swiss cheese
1	cup half-and-half	1½	cups fresh bread crumbs

Pre-heat oven to 375°. In a heavy 2-quart saucepan or skillet, sauté chopped onion in 4 tablespoons of the butter until onion is soft, not brown. Remove pan from heat and blend in the flour, salt and pepper. Add mushrooms and liquid, half-and-half and vermouth. Cook, over medium heat, stirring, until thickened. Add turkey, ham and water chestnuts. Place in a shallow 2-quart casserole. Top with the cheese. Melt the remaining 3 tablespoons butter, toss with the crumbs, and sprinkle around the edge of the casserole. Bake in a 350° oven about 25 minutes or until bubbly.

Yield: 6 servings

This casserole can be made ahead of time and refrigerated until the next day.

Turkey and Sausage Casserole

This casserole would be appropriate for serving for a brunch as well as other meals.

½	pound bulk sausage	1	cup Uncle Ben's rice,
1	cup chopped celery		uncooked
2	cups chopped onion	4	ounces medium noodles or
1	tart green apple, peeled, cored		small macaroni, uncooked
	and chopped	4	cups cubed cooked turkey or
3	cups chicken stock, flavored		chicken
	with salt and pepper	1	cup sliced blanched almonds

Pre-heat oven to 350°. Sauté sausage, onion and celery until meat is lightly browned. Add apple, chicken stock, rice, turkey or chicken and almonds. Place uncooked noodles in bottom of a lightly buttered 13"x 9"x 2" casserole. Spoon turkey mixture over making sure that noodles are covered. Cover tightly with foil and bake for 1 hour. Uncover and fluff mixture with a fork to mix noodles in, then sprinkle 1 cup grated Parmesan cheese over and serve.

Yield: 8 to 10 servings

Turkey Meat Loaf

This recipe can also be made with lean ground pork.

2	pounds ground raw turkey or chicken
½	cup soft bread crumbs
⅓	cup finely chopped green pepper
¼	cup whole milk
3	large eggs
1½	teaspoons salt
¼	teaspoon finely chopped fresh thyme or ⅛ teaspoon dried thyme, crushed
⅛	teaspoon dried rosemary, crushed
¼	teaspoon pepper
4	ounces sliced fresh mushrooms, sliced
	Vegetable cooking spray

Combine turkey and next 8 ingredients in a large bowl; stir in mushrooms. Divide mixture into 6 portions; place each portion into a vegetable sprayed 4" x 2½" x 1½" loaf pan or individual casseroles. Place pans or casseroles in a shallow baking pan. Bake at 350° for 25 to 30 minutes or until done. Let stand 5 minutes before turning out onto dinner plates or platter.

Yield: 6 servings

This recipe may be made in 1 large loaf. Place mixture in a 7½" x 3" x 2" loaf pan coated with vegetable spray. Bake at 350° for 1 hour and 5 minutes.

Turkey, Tomato Sauce with Pasta

1	pound ground raw turkey
2	tablespoons olive oil
1	cup chopped onion
3	cloves garlic, minced
2	(15 or 16 ounce) cans tomatoes with juice, broken up
1	teaspoon leaf oregano, broken up
1	teaspoon salt
¼	teaspoon pepper
½	teaspoon leaf basil, crumbled
1	bay leaf

Cook turkey in oil in large skillet about 5 minutes. Add onion and garlic; cook about 5 minutes until turkey is no longer pink. Stir in tomatoes, oregano, salt, pepper, basil and bay leaf. Simmer, uncovered, for 30 minutes or until thickened. Remove bay leaf and taste for seasoning. Cook pasta according to directions. Drain and toss with sauce. Serve grated Parmesan cheese in a bowl for guests to help themselves.

Yield: 4 servings

Helpful Hint: 8 ounces macaroni — 2 to 2½ cups.

Beef and Bean Casserole

This is a satisfying complete meal dish. I usually serve a green salad with it.

⅓	cup salad oil or olive oil	1	(15½ to 20 ounce) can
3	medium red or green peppers		garbanzo beans, drained
	cut into bite-size pieces	1	(10 ounce package) frozen
2	medium onions, chopped		baby lima beans, thawed
2	medium zucchini, cut into	1	(6 ounce) can tomato paste
	½ inch slices	½	cup water
2	pounds lean ground beef	2	teaspoons salt or to taste
1	(16 ounce) can tomatoes,	2½	teaspoons brown sugar,
	undrained		packed
		¼	teaspoon pepper

In a 12″ skillet, heat salad oil over medium heat. Cook onion and peppers until limp, stirring constantly. Remove to a 4½-quart casserole. In drippings remaining in skillet, cook ground beef over medium heat until lightly browned. Add remaining ingredients and heat to boiling. Spoon into casserole; mix well. Taste for seasoning adding salt, if necessary.

Bake, covered, in a 350° oven for 1 hour or until vegetables are fork tender.

Yield: 8 servings

I always buy lean ground meat. The cheaper ground meat contains fat and sometimes water, so you end up with less product after cooking, and also less protein.

Grits Italian

This entrée could be served at a brunch or luncheon with just a salad to complete the meal. It can easily be increased to accommodate a crowd.

1	pound bulk sausage, mild or	1	clove garlic, minced
	hot according to your taste	1	(8 ounce) zucchini, washed and
1½	pounds lean ground beef		sliced in ¼″ slices
¾	cup regular grits	1	medium onion, minced
1	(14 ounce) jar pizza sauce	2½	cups (10 ounces) Monterey
⅛	teaspoon salt		Jack cheese, grated
⅛	teaspoon pepper		

Brown sausage and ground beef in a large skillet, stirring until it crumbles. Drain well. Cook grits according to directions; spoon into a lightly greased 13″x 9″x 2″ casserole. Combine pizza sauce and next 3 ingredients. Layer half each of pizza sauce, meat, zucchini, onion and cheese over grits. Repeat layers, omitting cheese. Cover and bake at 325° for 25 minutes. Add remaining cheese and bake, uncovered, an additional 5 minutes.

Yield: 8 servings

Beef and Cabbage Casserole

The rice does not have to be pre-cooked in this layered ground beef casserole. It cooks in the broth along with the other ingredients. Chicken broth may be substituted for the beef broth, if necessary.

1½	pounds lean ground beef	¼	teaspoon pepper
2	medium onions, diced	¾	cup Uncle Ben's rice, uncooked
1	(2 pound) head of green cabbage, coarsely shredded	1	(13¾ ounce) can beef broth, undiluted
2	medium carrots, thinly sliced	½	cup water
2½	teaspoons salt		

In a 5-quart saucepot or Dutch oven, cook onion and ground beef until beef is lightly browned, stirring until meat is broken up. Remove saucepot from heat and add cabbage, carrots, salt and pepper. Mix well. Place rice in bottom of a 3 quart casserole, spoon ground beef mixture on top; pour broth and water over mixture. Bake, covered, in a 350° oven for 1 hour. To serve: Toss beef mixture and rice with a fork to mix well.

Yield: 6 servings

Homemade broth is always preferable. I save and freeze any extra broth from cooking chicken, etc.

Ground Beef Florentine

An easy, delicious casserole.

2	tablespoons olive oil	1	can cream of celery soup, undiluted
1	pound lean ground beef or turkey	1	cup sour cream
1	medium onion, chopped	1	tablespoon uncooked rice
1	(8 ounce) can sliced mushrooms, drained	1	teaspoon salt
2	cloves garlic, crushed	¼	teaspoon pepper
1	teaspoon oregano, crushed	6	ounces sliced mozzarella cheese, cut into strips
2	(10 ounce) packages frozen chopped spinach, thawed and drained well		

Cook the meat, onion, mushrooms, garlic and oregano in the olive oil, stirring, until meat crumbles. Mix spinach, soup, sour cream, rice, salt and pepper in a large bowl, add meat mixture and mix well with a fork. Place in a 2-quart casserole, cover and bake at 350° for 35 minutes. Uncover and place strips of cheese on top. Return to oven and bake an additional 5 minutes or until cheese is melted.

Yield: 4 servings

Easy Lasagna

This is a delicious casserole and a shortcut to most lasagnas. Another plus is that it can be prepared the day before or in the morning of the day you are going to serve it. It can also be frozen before baking.

2 pounds lean ground beef	½ teaspoon dried basil, crumbled
1 teaspoon salt	Grated Parmesan cheese
1 envelope spaghetti sauce mix	12 ounces sliced mozzarella
2 (1 pound) cans tomatoes	cheese
1 (15 ounce) can tomato sauce	9 lasagna noodles

In a large skillet or saucepan, cook meat over medium heat, stirring, until it crumbles. Add salt, spaghetti sauce mix, tomatoes, tomato sauce, basil and a generous sprinkling of grated Parmesan cheese. Simmer 30 minutes, stirring occasionally. Cook lasagna noodles until barely tender, drain and then cover with cold water. Drain again and set aside. In a 12" x 9" x 2" casserole, place a thin layer of meat sauce, then a layer of noodles, then a layer of mozzarella cheese. Sprinkle with Parmesan cheese. Repeat layers, saving enough meat sauce to pour over top layer. Bake at 325° for about 30 minutes or until sauce has thickened and casserole is bubbly.

Yield: 8 servings

I recently discovered that any pasta dish can be made without precooking the pasta. Just fix it the day before you want to cook it. Place it, covered, in the refrigerator and cook next day.

Helpful Hint: *When sautéing meat, sprinkle a small amount of salt into a pan before adding oil to prevent spatters. This also helps vegetables retain their color during stir-frying.*

Italian Casserole

This is a pretty dish to serve on a buffet with its green and white topping. It may be prepared ahead and refrigerated, covered, for a day. Do not be dismayed at the number of ingredients, it is well worth the trouble.

2	pounds lean ground beef	¼	teaspoon pepper
2	tablespoons olive oil	1	(6 ounce) can sliced mushrooms, undrained
½	cup finely minced onion		
1	clove garlic, minced	3	(10 ounce) packages frozen chopped spinach, thawed and drained well
1	(6 ounce) can tomato paste plus ½ can water		
2	(8 ounce) cans tomato sauce	1	pound creamed cottage cheese
2	teaspoons dried basil, crumbled	Dash of salt	
		1	(8 ounce) package mozzarella cheese
2	teaspoons dried parsley		
1	teaspoon salt	½	cup grated Parmesan cheese
1	teaspoon oregano, crumbled		

Put olive oil in a large skillet and sauté beef, onion and garlic over medium heat until beef is crumbly and onion is transparent. Add tomato paste, water, tomato sauce, basil, parsley, salt, oregano and pepper. Add mushrooms with their juice, reserving 16 slices. Simmer over low heat until thickened, stirring occasionally. Divide meat into 5 equal portions. In a medium bowl, combine spinach and cottage cheese with a dash of salt. Mark off spinach mixture into 5 equal portions. Cut twelve 2½" x ½" x ½" slices from mozzarella cheese. Dice remaining mozzarella cheese. In a 13"x 9"x 2"baking dish, arrange alternately in lengthwise strips 3 portions of spinach mixture and 2 portions meat mixture, covering bottom of baking dish. Sprinkle with diced mozzarella and Parmesan cheese. Make a second layer, alternating in lengthwise strips 3 portions meat mixture and 2 portions spinach mixture. Using mozzarella cheese strips, make 4 crosswise rows over meat and spinach mixtures, using 3 strips, placed end to end, for each row. Garnish meat portion with the mushroom slices. Bake in a 350° oven about 25 minutes or until bubbly.

Yield: 8 to 10 servings

Lasagna, Ann's

This is my granddaughter, Ann's, recipe. I like it because the noodles do not have to be pre-cooked and it makes two casseroles, enough for a crowd. Need I say it is also delicious?

2	tablespoons olive oil	2	(10 ounce) packages frozen chopped spinach, thawed and drained
1	cup chopped onion		
1	large clove garlic or two medium size, minced	3	cups (24 ounces) creamed cottage cheese
1½	pounds lean ground beef		
2	packages dried spaghetti mix	½	teaspoon salt
2	(6 ounce) cans tomato paste	½	cup grated Parmesan cheese, divided
2	(8 ounce) cans tomato sauce		
3½	cups water	1	pound mozzarella cheese, grated
3	large eggs, beaten		
		12	lasagna noodles, uncooked

Add olive oil to a deep heavy skillet or stock pot. Sauté onion, garlic and meat, stirring to break meat up. Add spaghetti mix, tomato paste, tomato sauce and water. Bring to a boil, then simmer 3 minutes. Combine spinach, eggs, cottage cheese, salt and ¼ cup Parmesan cheese in a large bowl. Lightly grease two 13"x 9" x 2" casseroles and set side by side. In each pan, place a thin layer of sauce, then 3 of the noodles, then ¼ of the spinach mixture. Then sprinkle with part of the grated mozzarella cheese. Repeat layers leaving enough of the sauce to cover last layer of mozzarella cheese. Sprinkle with rest of grated Parmesan cheese. Cover with foil and bake for 1 hour in a 350° oven.

Yield: 24 servings

This can also be frozen before cooking. Take it out of the freezer the day before it is to be cooked and place in the refrigerator to be sure that it is thawed before baking per directions.

Helpful Hint: *For speed and size-consistency when making meat balls, roll handfuls of the meat mixture into logs. Cut each log into 1" sections, then roll sections into balls and cook.*

Meat Loaf Olé

I have always been conscious of nutrition so I like this recipe for meat loaf as it calls for whole wheat bread instead of the usual white bread or cracker crumbs.

4	slices whole wheat bread	2	large eggs, lightly beaten
1	large onion, chopped	1	(10 ounce) can tomatoes with
½	green pepper, chopped		green chilies
1	pound lean ground beef	¾	teaspoon salt
½	pound ground pork		

Make crumbs of the whole wheat bread in food processor. Remove and set aside. Cook onion and green pepper in a non-stick skillet, stirring constantly, until tender. Stir onion and green pepper into bread crumbs; add ground beef and remaining ingredients, mixing well. This is a soft mixture. Shape into a 12″ loaf and place on rack in broiler pan. Cover loosely with foil and bake at 350° for 1 hour, then remove foil and bake about 20 minutes longer to brown. Cool about 5 minutes before cutting.

Yield: 6 servings

The oil in the skin of green pepper disagrees with some people. Roast pepper in the oven until skin blisters and partly blackens. Remove from the oven, put in a pot and cover tightly. Let set for 5 minutes, then wrap in a towel and rub off skin.

Mexican Rice

7	tablespoons olive or salad oil	5	tomatoes, skinned and sliced
1½	cups Uncle Ben's rice	1	tablespoon chili powder
2	pounds lean ground beef	1¾	cups water
2	medium onions, finely chopped	2	teaspoons salt
1½	cloves garlic, minced	¾	cup raisins
1	(4 ounce) can green chilies, undrained	8	strips lean bacon

Warm 4 tablespoons oil in a skillet and fry rice until pale gold. Remove and reserve rice. Put remaining oil in skillet and sauté beef, onions and garlic. Cook, stirring, until beef is broken up and onions are limp. Add tomatoes, chili powder and green chilies. Heat for 1 minute then add water and salt. Boil briskly for 3 minutes, then add rice, then raisins that have been scalded in boiling water. Place in a baking dish, arrange bacon on top. Bake at 300° for about 1 hour.

Yield: 6 servings

2 tablespoons chopped hot green chili pepper may be used instead of the green chilies if a highly seasoned dish is preferred.

Mexican Tamale Pie

This is a recipe given to me by a dear friend over fifty years ago. It is the only one I have ever found with the addition of eggs.

4	tablespoons olive oil	3	tablespoons chili powder
2	pounds lean ground beef	1½	cups yellow cornmeal
2	cloves garlic, minced	3	large eggs, beaten
2	large onions, chopped fine	1	cup milk
2	cans yellow niblet corn, drained	2½	teaspoons salt
		½	teaspoon pepper
1	(14½ ounce) can diced tomatoes	1	tablespoon Worcestershire sauce
¾	cup tomato juice	1	cup Fritos, crumbled

Heat olive oil in heavy skillet, add meat, garlic and onions. Cook, stirring, over medium heat until meat is crumbly. Add corn, tomatoes, tomato juice and chili powder which has been dissolved in a little water. Cook, stirring constantly, about 15 minutes. Add the yellow cornmeal. Beat eggs with milk. Add some of the hot mixture to the eggs and then stir into the cornmeal mixture. Add the seasonings and cook 10 minutes longer. Pour into 5-quart casserole. Bake 25 minutes in a 350° oven, then place cheese over top. Bake another 10 minutes, then sprinkle Fritos over and heat another 5 minutes. This can be prepared a day ahead of time, but do not add cheese or Fritos until ready for the oven.

Yield: 10 to 12 servings

Marinated Steak

Top sirloin steak is a flavorful piece of meat, but not as tender as a sirloin steak. The marinade in this recipe results in a tender, flavorful entrée.

8	(6 ounce) boneless top sirloin steaks	½	teaspoon whole dried basil
		½	teaspoon chili powder
¼	cup vegetable oil	½	teaspoon pepper
1	large clove garlic, halved		Vegetable cooking spray

Place meat in a shallow stainless steel or ceramic dish. Pierce meat every ½ inch with a fork. Heat oil in a small skillet over medium heat. Add garlic and rest of ingredients; stir well. Warm, then pour over meat. Cover and let stand at room temperature 1 hour, turning twice, or refrigerate several hours. Remove meat from marinade; place on a rack in a shallow roasting pan coated with vegetable spray. Discard the marinade. Broil steak 5 inches from the heat 5 minutes per side or until desired degree of doneness. Serve with salsa, if desired.

Yield: 8 servings

Beef Filet with Brandy

This is a classic main course that is a universal favorite.

4	pounds center-cut beef filet	½	teaspoon summer savory
1	medium clove of garlic, minced		leaves, crumbled
2	medium shallots, minced	¼	teaspoon salt
½	teaspoon dried thyme leaves,	⅛	teaspoon pepper
	crumbled	3	tablespoons brandy
		⅓	cup olive oil, divided

Combine garlic, shallots, thyme, summer savory, salt, pepper, brandy and ¼ cup olive oil in a large stainless steel or glass baking dish. Turn meat in marinade, cover, and refrigerate at least 12 hours or as long as 2 days, turning occasionally. Adjust oven rack to the lowest position and heat oven to 450°. Remove meat from marinade, pat dry with paper towels and rub with remaining olive oil. Transfer meat to a heavy roasting pan. Roast 15 minutes turning to sear on both sides. Roast 15 to 20 minutes longer for rare (125°). Let stand 5 minutes, remove strings, slice and serve immediately. Spoon any meat juices, that result from slicing, over the meat before serving.

Yield: 8 servings

Ask butcher to remove sinew and fat from filet and tie with string. The pieces remaining after trimming the filet to 4 pounds can be used for Beef Stroganoff or other dishes. Be sure to ask for them.

Roast Brisket

I like this recipe as the vegetables are cooked with the meat. The pan juices make a tasty gravy.

10 to 12 pound brisket		6 or 8 medium carrots scraped	
Garlic salt			and cut into 1″ pieces
1	bottle Heinz chili sauce	16	medium size new potatoes,
¾	cup Lipton's onion soup mix		washed and peeled around
			once

Remove most of the fat from the top of the brisket and all that you can from the underside of the brisket. Rub all over with garlic salt. Place fat-side up in baking pan. Pour the bottle of chili sauce over, then sprinkle with the onion soup mix. Add 1″ water to the pan. Cover tightly (I usually use foil), and bake at 275° for 6 or 7 hours or until fork tender. Add carrots and potatoes 1 hour before brisket is done.

Yield: 16 servings

Spanish Beef Stew

This stew improves in flavor if cooled, then placed, covered, in the refrigerator overnight. To serve next day, discard bay leaf and season stew with salt and pepper to taste. Garnish with parsley. Recipe can be halved.

6	slices lean bacon cooked crisp, then crumbled, reserving bacon grease	1	cup water
		¼	cup tomato paste
		1	bay leaf
4	pounds lean beef chuck, cut into 1½" cubes	6	carrots, halved lengthwise and cut crosswise into 2" pieces
½	cup flour seasoned with salt and pepper	½	pound small fresh mushrooms, cut in half
2	tablespoons olive oil	½	cup canned chopped pimientos, drained
1	cup chopped onion		
2	cups chopped celery	¾	cup black olives, quartered
2	cups dry red wine	½	cup minced fresh parsley for garnish
2	(14 or 15 ounce) cans plum tomatoes with juice		

In a kettle cook the bacon over moderate heat until it is crisp, transfer it to paper towels to drain, then crumble it. Heat the fat remaining in the kettle over moderate heat and in it brown the chuck cubes, tossed with the flour, in batches, transferring it as it is browned to a bowl. Add the oil to the kettle and cook the onion and celery over moderate heat until vegetables are tender. Stir in the wine, tomatoes with their juice, tomato paste, 1 cup water, bay leaf and meat along with any juices that are in the bowl. Bring the liquid to a boil and place in a deep casserole. Cook, covered, in a pre-heated 325° oven for 1½ hours. Stir in the carrots and mushrooms and bake for one hour. Stir in pimiento and black olives and bake, covered, another 30 minutes or until meat and vegetables are tender.

Yield: 10 to 12 servings

Note: I sometimes cook the stew for the first 1½ hours, cool to lukewarm and place in refrigerator overnight. The next day I add the carrots and mushrooms, cook the additional hour, then proceed with the rest of the cooking and seasoning.

Sauerbraten with Spaetzle, Roberta

A friend of mine in the Hill Country served this with boiled potatoes. However, the spaetzle are traditionally served with sauerbraten, so I am including this recipe. It is also sometimes served with boiled red cabbage.

Marinade:

1	cup red wine vinegar	2	medium onions, very thinly
½	cup cider vinegar		sliced
1	cup Burgundy	1	stalk celery, chopped
1	bay leaf	Few	sprigs parsley
2	whole allspice	1	tablespoon salt
4	whole cloves	1	tablespoon pepper
1	large carrot, cut into strips		

In large glass or ceramic bowl, combine vinegars, Burgundy, onion, carrot, celery, parsley, bay leaf, allspice, cloves, salt and pepper.

Roast:

4	pound beef roast, rump or round	⅓	cup oil

Wipe meat with a damp cloth. Add meat to marinade; refrigerate, covered, 3 days. Turn several times to marinate evenly. Remove meat from marinade; wipe dry. Reserve marinade in small saucepan. Heat Dutch oven or large, heavy kettle very slowly. Dredge meat with 2 tablespoons of the flour and brown well on all sides in the oil. Pour in marinade; simmer meat, covered, 2½ to 3 hours, or until tender. Then strain liquid from meat into a 1-quart bowl or measure.

Gravy:

3½	cups cooking liquid	1	tablespoon brown sugar,
6	tablespoons flour, divided		packed
		½	cup crushed gingersnaps

In small bowl, make a paste of the cold water, the remaining 4 tablespoons flour and sugar. Stir into liquid with a wire whisk. Bring to a boil, stirring constantly, add gingersnaps. Pour over meat; simmer, covered, 20 minutes. Remove meat to heated platter. Slice in ¼" slices. Pour some of the gravy over and serve the rest in a bowl. Serve with spaetzle, if desired.

Spaetzle:

3	cups flour	4	eggs, beaten
¾	cup water	1	stick butter
1	teaspoon salt	1	cup bread crumbs

Heat 4 quarts water to boiling in a 6 quart saucepot. Place all the above ingredients in a bowl and beat until smooth. Reduce heat to medium. Set a colander,

Continued on next page

preferably one with large holes, over the simmering water. With a spoon, press a few tablespoons of the dough at a time through the colander directly into the simmering water. Stir the spaetzle gently to prevent them from sticking together, then boil briskly about 4 to 6 minutes or until tender. Taste to make sure. Drain the spaetzle thoroughly in a sieve and keep warm while cooking rest of dough. To serve: Melt the butter over moderate heat. When foam subsides, add the bread crumbs. Cook, stirring, constantly, until crumbs are golden brown. Place spaetzle in a serving dish and sprinkle crumbs over. Keep warm until serving.

Yield: 8 servings

The sauerbraten may be baked in the oven rather than on top of the stove, if you prefer. Bring the casserole to a boil over high heat. Cover tightly and cook in a pre-heated 350° oven the same amount of time or until meat is tender.

Rump Roast

One cup of beef broth may be substituted for the Burgundy.

1	**(5 pound) boneless beef rump roast**	1	**cup dry red wine, Burgundy preferred**
1	**(1 ounce) envelope onion soup mix (⅓ cup)**		

Place roast in a Dutch oven or heavy baking pan. Sprinkle with the soup mix and pour wine over. Cover tightly and bake at 300° for 2 to 2½ hours or until tender. Serve with pan juices skimmed of fat.

Yield: 8 to 10 servings

Peachy Pork Picante

1	**pound boneless lean pork, cut in ¾" chunks**	1	**(8 ounce) bottle chunky-style salsa**
1	**tablespoon taco mix**	⅓	**cup peach preserves**
1	**tablespoon vegetable oil**		

Coat pork with taco mix. Heat oil in non-stick skillet over medium-low heat; add pork and cook until light brown, stirring occasionally. Add preserves and salsa to pan, lower heat to simmer. Cover and cook for 15 minutes or until tender. Do not overcook or meat will be dry. Serve over rice or noodles.

Yield: 4 servings

Baked Pork Shoulder

A pork shoulder is fatter than a pork loin. However, in this recipe, the roast is seared for 20 minutes and is then drained of the fat. It is then cooked in milk, which makes it very tender and delicious.

1	(3½ pound) pork shoulder	1	tablespoon olive oil
1	teaspoon salt	8	cloves garlic, peeled
½	teaspoon pepper	1	quart milk

Sprinkle entire surface of pork with the salt and pepper. Heat oil in a Dutch oven or casserole that can be used on top of the stove. Cook pork over medium-high heat, turning to sear all sides, about 20 minutes. Remove and discard all but 2 tablespoons drippings. Add garlic cloves; sauté until golden brown, about 4 minutes. Place pork back in Dutch oven and add enough milk to come two-thirds up the sides of the meat. Bring to a boil; partially cover and simmer, turning pork occasionally, about 1½ hours, or until tender. Transfer pork to a warm platter; cover and keep warm. Bring milk to a boil, then simmer, stirring occasionally, until reduced to 1½ cups, about 15 minutes. Sauce should be golden brown and look curdled. Season sauce with salt and pepper to taste. To serve: Cut pork across the grain into ¼" slices. Spoon some of the sauce over and serve.

Yield: 6 servings

Cooked rice with raw chopped, unpeeled apple and toasted slivered almonds is a good addition.

Pork and Apple Casserole

Another casserole with an Oriental touch.

6	pork chops, rib or loin, cut ¾" thick	2	tablespoons soy sauce
½	teaspoon salt	2	tablespoons Heinz ketchup
¼	teaspoon pepper	2	teaspoons cornstarch
1½	cups apple juice	¼	teaspoon ground ginger
2	tablespoons light brown sugar, packed	1	large red skinned baking apple

Trim most of fat from chops. Arrange them in an oblong baking dish large enough to hold them in one layer; sprinkle with salt and pepper. Bake at 325° about 30 minutes. Turn chops once during baking. Combine apple juice and next 5 ingredients in a saucepan. Heat mixture to boiling over medium heat and cook until slightly thickened. Remove from heat. Core apple and cut into 6 rings. Remove baking dish from oven. Skim off any fat from baking dish. Place an apple ring on top of each pork chop, Pour apple juice mixture over chops. Bake 15 minutes or until chops are tender, basting occasionally with sauce in baking dish.

Yield: 6 servings

Pork Chops with Rice Almondine

This recipe is for pork chops with an Oriental touch.

4 large or 8 small pork chops	1 tablespoon brown sugar, packed
2 tablespoons olive oil	1 tablespoon soy sauce
1 medium onion, sliced very thin	Salt and pepper to taste
¼ cup water	¼ cup sherry

Heat oil in large skillet and brown chops on both sides over medium-low heat. Add the onion, water, sugar, soy sauce, salt and pepper. Reduce heat to low, cover and simmer about 20 minutes or until almost done. Add sherry and simmer, uncovered, 5 minutes longer.

Rice Almondine:

2 cups cooked rice	Salt and pepper to taste
½ cup sour cream	4 tablespoons (½ stick) butter
½ cup frozen peas, thawed and drained	½ cup soft bread crumbs
	6 tablespoons slivered almonds

Pre-heat oven to 400°. Grease a casserole dish. Combine rice, sour cream, peas, salt and pepper. Spoon into casserole and dot with butter. Combine bread crumbs and almonds and sprinkle over rice. Bake about 5 minutes or until heated through.

Yield: 4 servings

Helpful Hint: 1 pound rice — 2¼ to 2½ cups.

Roast Pork with Cherries

The spicy sweet sour sauce makes this entrée a little different.

1 (4 or 5 pound) boneless pork loin roast	1 teaspoon pepper
1 teaspoon salt	1 teaspoon rubbed sage

Sprinkle salt, pepper and sage over roast. Place roast, fat side up, on a rack in shallow roasting pan. Insert a meat thermometer into the thickest part of the meat. Bake in a 325° oven for about 2 hours or more until thermometer registers 160°.

Cherry Sauce:

1 (16 ounce) can pitted sour red cherries	1 tablespoon lemon juice
12 whole cloves	¼ cup white vinegar
1 (3″) piece stick cinnamon	2 tablespoons butter, room temperature
1½ cups sugar	3 or 4 drops red food coloring
¼ cup cornstarch	

Drain cherries, reserve liquid and add water enough to make ¾ cup. Tie cloves and cinnamon in a cheesecloth bag. Combine ½ cup of the cherry liquid, sugar, vinegar and spice bag in saucepan. Bring to a boil; reduce heat and simmer, uncovered, 10 minutes. Remove spice bag. Combine cornstarch and remaining ¼ cup of cherry liquid; add to hot liquid slowly, stirring constantly, with a wire whisk. Cook over medium heat, stirring constantly, until thickened and clear. Add cherries, lemon juice, butter and red food coloring. Heat and serve with roast pork.

Yield: 8 to 10 servings

South of the Border Stew

Do not be dismayed at the long list of ingredients as most are prepared foods. This is a flavorful and nourishing dish. Recipe can be doubled.

2	pounds boneless pork loin, cut in 1" cubes	3	cloves garlic, pressed
¼	cup flour	2	teaspoons ground cumin
2	tablespoons vegetable oil	2	teaspoons cocoa
2	(4 ounce) chorizo sausages, cut into ½" slices	1	teaspoon dried oregano, crushed
3	(14½ ounce) cans chicken broth or equivalent homemade broth	¼	teaspoon salt
		1	(2") piece stick cinnamon
1	(14½ ounce) can diced tomatoes	2	(15 ounce) cans black beans, rinsed and drained
3	(4 ounce) cans diced green chilies, undrained	1	(15½ ounce) can white hominy, rinsed and drained
1	large white or purple onion, sliced into thin rings	1	(10 ounce) package frozen whole kernel yellow corn
		½	cup beer or tequila
			Flour tortillas

Dredge pork in flour; set aside. Heat oil in a large skillet over medium heat; add pork and cook until browned, stirring often. Add sausage and cook 2 minutes, stirring. Add next 10 ingredients. Bring to a boil, then simmer for 1 hour, stirring occasionally. Stir in beans, hominy, corn and beer or tequila; simmer slowly for 30 minutes. Remove cinnamon stick. Serve with hot buttered tortillas.

Yield: 3 quarts, 6 servings

Stir-Fried Pork with Broccoli

This recipe can be used as a guide for other stir-fries using poultry or shellfish with snow peas, cabbage, mushrooms or green beans as vegetables. Almonds can be substituted for the cashews.

Sauce:

4	teaspoons soy sauce	2	teaspoons dry sherry
2	teaspoons sugar	2	teaspoons sesame oil or
2	teaspoons cornstarch		peanut oil
2	teaspoons red or white wine vinegar	¼	teaspoon salt

Mix the soy sauce, sugar, cornstarch, vinegar, wine, oil, and salt in a small bowl and set aside.

Pork and vegetables:

2½	teaspoons cornstarch, divided	4	green onions
2	tablespoons chicken stock or water	1	medium clove garlic, minced
1	pound boneless pork tenderloin or pork loin	1	piece fresh ginger (1½ teaspoons, minced)
1	bunch broccoli (about 12 ounces)	4	tablespoons sesame or peanut oil
1	large red bell pepper	½	cup cashews

Dissolve 1½ teaspoons of the cornstarch in the chicken stock. Set aside. Slice the pork thinly against the grain and rub with the remaining teaspoon cornstarch. Cut broccoli into small florets and blanch in a kettle of boiling water until almost tender, about 3 minutes. Drain well and pat dry. Cut the red pepper into ¼" strips and set aside. Thinly slice the onions, set aside. In a wok or deep skillet, heat 2 tablespoons oil until hot but not smoking. Stir-fry the red peppers and cashews until peppers soften slightly and cashews start to brown, about 30 seconds; remove and set aside. Add pork and stir-fry until seared on both sides, about 1 minute; remove and set aside with the peppers. Heat the remaining 2 tablespoons oil, add the garlic, onions and ginger and stir-fry about 15 seconds. Return the red peppers, cashews and pork to the wok. Immediately stir in broccoli, sauce, and cornstarch-chicken stock mixture. Toss until sauce coats ingredients and thickens slightly, about 45 seconds. Serve immediately with steamed rice.

Yield: 4 servings

Lamb Stew with Popovers, Cynthia

If this stew is served in the popovers, it will make 6 servings. If served by itself, 4 servings. As with all stews, flavor is improved if made, cooled, refrigerated and reheated the next day.

3	tablespoons olive oil	¼	teaspoon dried rosemary, crushed
2	pounds boneless lamb, cut into 1" cubes	¼	teaspoon dried marjoram, crushed
1	medium onion, chopped	⅛	teaspoon pepper
1	clove garlic, minced	1	bay leaf
2	tablespoons flour	6 to 8	small new potatoes, peeled once around, then sliced ¼" thick
1½	cups chicken broth		
½	cup dry white wine		
2	tablespoons lemon juice	3	carrots, scraped and sliced diagonally into ½" slices
1½	teaspoons salt		

Heat olive oil in a Dutch oven over medium heat; add lamb and cook until lightly browned, stirring. Remove lamb and reserve 2 tablespoons of the drippings. Add onion and garlic to drippings; cook over medium heat, stirring constantly, until vegetables are tender. Return lamb to Dutch oven and sprinkle with flour, stirring well. Add broth, white wine, lemon juice, salt and next 4 ingredients. Bring to a boil; cover, reduce heat and simmer for 30 minutes. Add potatoes and carrots; simmer 20 to 30 minutes or until vegetables are tender. Discard bay leaf. Serve in popovers or plain.

Popovers:

2	large eggs	½	teaspoon salt
1	cup milk	1	tablespoon vegetable oil
1	cup sifted flour		

Place eggs in mixing bowl; add milk, flour and salt. Beat 1½ minutes with electric beater. Add oil; beat only 30 seconds more, do not overbeat. Fill a well greased popover pan or custard cups ½ full. This batter makes 6 to 8 popovers depending on depth of pans. Bake in a 475° oven for 15 minutes. Reduce oven to 350° and bake about 25 minutes longer or until browned and firm. A few minutes before removing from the oven, prick with a fork to let steam escape. If you like popovers dry and crisp, turn off oven and leave popovers in the oven with the door open an additional 30 minutes.

Yield: 4 to 6 servings (7 cups)

I like to mince garlic rather than press it. When garlic is pressed, it sometimes becomes bitter. An addition of ¼ cup finely chopped pecans to the popovers is tasty for serving at a luncheon.

Baked Catfish

This is a low calorie way to cook fish in the oven.

¼   cup yellow cornmeal
¼   cup flour
¼   cup grated Parmesan cheese
½   teaspoon paprika
½   teaspoon salt

⅛   teaspoon red pepper
1   egg white
2   tablespoons skim milk
4   (4 or 5 ounce) catfish fillets
Butter-flavored cooking spray

Combine first 6 ingredients in a shallow bowl and set aside. Whisk together the egg white and milk. Dip fillets in milk mixture, then dredge in cornmeal mixture.

Place on a foil-lined baking sheet coated with cooking spray. Coat each fillet with cooking spray. Bake at 350° about 30 minutes, until fish flakes easily with a fork. Serve immediately with lemon or lime wedges.

Yield: 4 servings

Baked Flounder

4   flounder fillets (4 to 6 ounces each)
2   tablespoons minced onion
½   teaspoon salt

⅛   teaspoon pepper
⅓   cup apple juice
2   tablespoons dry white wine
2   tablespoons lemon juice

Arrange fillets in a lightly greased 12"x 8"x 2"baking dish. Sprinkle with onion, salt and pepper. Combine apple juice, wine and lemon juice; pour over fish. Cover and bake at 350° for 25 minutes or until fish flakes easily when tested with a fork. Transfer fish to a heated platter. Strain and reserve ⅔ cup liquid.

Sauce:
⅔   cup liquid from fish
2   tablespoons butter
2   tablespoons flour

¼   cup whipping cream or evaporated milk
⅓   cup grated Parmesan cheese
Minced fresh parsley leaves

Melt butter in a heavy skillet over low heat; add flour, stirring constantly. Remove from heat and add cream and reserved ⅔ cup liquid. Mix with a wire whisk, return to heat and cook, stirring constantly, until mixture thickens. Taste for seasoning and pour over fish. Sprinkle with cheese and parsley.

Yield: 4 servings

Baked Red Snapper Fillets

Cod or any firm-fleshed fish may be used.

2	pounds red snapper fillets	2	tablespoons dry white wine
¾	teaspoon salt	2	tablespoons water
⅜	teaspoon freshly ground pepper		

Wipe fish with a damp cloth and season both sides with salt and pepper. Arrange close together in a single layer in a shallow baking pan. Mix wine and water and pour over fish. Bake in a pre-heated 350° oven until thickest part of fish barely separates when tested with a dinner knife, about 20 minutes, basting often with pan drippings. With a slotted spatula, lift onto paper towels to drain just a moment, then place on warm plates. Pour on preferred butter sauce and serve.

White or Red Butter Sauce:

⅓	cup minced shallots	¾ to 1 cup unsalted butter,
⅓	cup red wine or dry white wine	softened
⅓	cup mild red wine vinegar	Freshly ground pepper to taste
¼	teaspoon salt or to taste	

In a heavy saucepan bring to boil shallots, vinegar, wine and salt. Boil, uncovered, until liquid has been reduced to a thick syrup, about 10 minutes. Remove from heat and let saucepan cool until just warm. Place over very low heat and begin adding butter, (be sure to use unsalted butter, a heavy saucepan and very low heat to make this sauce.) You might have a problem with the sauce separating if regular salted butter is used. Begin adding the butter about 1½ tablespoons at a time, whisking constantly until each addition is incorporated. Taste for seasoning.

Yield: 4 servings

You can use a lesser or the larger amount of butter in the sauce. Less butter makes a tangier sauce; the greater amount of butter, a richer, mellower sauce. The sauce made with the white wine is beurre blanc, the sauce with the red wine, beurre rouge.

Baked Red Snapper Olé

This is an easy way to cook fish and delicious, too.

Fish:

6	(4 ounce) skinless red snapper fillets

½   cup lime juice
½   teaspoon salt

Arrange fillets in a shallow dish; drizzle lime juice over and sprinkle with salt. Cover and chill 2 hours.

Sauce:

1   cup thinly sliced onion
1   teaspoon vegetable oil
1   (4 ounce) jar diced pimiento, drained
2   cups chopped fresh tomatoes

1   teaspoon canned chopped green chilies
½   teaspoon capers
Salt and pepper to taste

Sauté onion in oil in large skillet over medium heat. Add pimiento and next 4 ingredients. Cover and cook about 6 minutes or until onion is transparent. Remove fillets from marinade; discard marinade. Arrange fillets on tomato mixture. Cover and cook 6 minutes on each side or until fish flakes when tested with a fork. Remove fillets to serving plate; keep warm. Continue cooking tomato mixture over medium heat, uncovered, until thickened — about 10 minutes. Season with salt and pepper. Spoon ¼ cup tomato mixture over each fillet. Serve immediately.

Yield: 6 servings

You may garnish with parsley and lime slices, if you wish.

Fish Almondine

This is easy to prepare. The sauce is made while the fish is baking.

1   pound fresh or frozen fish fillets
4   tablespoons soft butter or margarine

3   tablespoons chopped toasted almonds
1   tablespoon grated lemon rind
½   teaspoon salt
⅛   teaspoon pepper

Defrost fillets, if frozen. Wipe dry with a paper towel. Arrange in a greased shallow baking pan. Combine remaining ingredients in a bowl. Spread on fillets. Bake, uncovered, in a 350° oven for 10 to 12 minutes. Serve with lemon wedges dipped in paprika.

Yield: 4 servings

Orange Roughy with Broccoli Sauce

I think you will like this different sauce for fish.

Broccoli Sauce:

1½	cups fresh broccoli, trimmed, peeled and chopped	1	small red bell pepper, minced
¼	cup small broccoli flowerets for garnish	2	tablespoons unsalted butter, divided
			Salt and pepper to taste

Cook the chopped broccoli in salted water until it is tender. Drain it, reserving 3 cups of the cooking liquid, then rinse in ice water and set aside. In a saucepan, cook the bell pepper in 1 tablespoon butter, over low heat, covered, stirring occasionally, until it is softened. Set aside and cover to keep warm.

Fish:

4	(6 ounce) pieces of orange roughy	1	cup vermouth
½	cup minced onion	¼	cup heavy cream

In a skillet large enough to hold the orange roughy in one layer, combine the onion, vermouth and reserved broccoli liquid. Bring mixture to a boil and then simmer for 10 minutes. Add the fish and poach it, covered, at a low simmer, turning it once, until it just flakes. Transfer to a plate with a slotted spatula and cover to keep warm. Strain ½ cup of the cooking liquid into a blender and puree it with the cooked broccoli, cream and salt and pepper to taste. Transfer the sauce to a small saucepan and cook over low heat until it is heated through. Blanch the broccoli flowerets in boiling salted water for 1 minute and drain, then toss them in a bowl with 1 tablespoon butter, salt and pepper to taste. Cover the bottom of a heated platter with a layer of the sauce and arrange the fish on top. Garnish with the broccoli flowerets and 2 tablespoons of bell pepper. Add rest of red bell pepper to the remaining sauce and serve it with the fish.

Yield: 4 servings

Honeyed Shrimp

This recipe calls for large shrimp. However, if they are unavailable or too expensive, medium shrimp can be substituted.

1½	pounds unpeeled large fresh shrimp	2	tablespoons honey
3	tablespoons peanut oil	2	tablespoons Heinz catsup
2	teaspoons minced garlic	1	tablespoon white vinegar
1	teaspoon peeled, minced ginger root	1	tablespoon dry sherry or rice wine
1	(10½ ounce) can chicken broth or equivalent homemade	1	tablespoon soy sauce
1	tablespoon cornstarch	2	green onions, cut into 1" lengths and shredded

Remove shell from shrimp leaving tail intact. Take out black vein and wash under running water. Drain on paper towels. Pour peanut oil around top of a pre-heated wok, coating sides. Add shrimp, garlic and ginger root and cook over medium heat, until shrimp turn pink. Combine broth and next 6 ingredients, stirring until smooth. Add to shrimp mixture, stirring constantly. Bring to a boil; cook 1 minute, add onions and cook until heated. Serve immediately.

Yield: 3 to 4 servings

Sautéed Sea Scallops

There are two kinds of scallops — bay scallops and sea scallops. I prefer the sea scallops which average 10 to 20 per pound.

1½	pounds sea scallops, sliced in half, crosswise	2	tablespoons olive oil
½	cup flour	1	large clove garlic, minced
½	teaspoon salt	1	green onion (white part only) minced
⅛	teaspoon pepper	¾	cup dry white wine
3	tablespoons butter		Minced parsley for garnish

In a large non-stick skillet, melt 2 tablespoons of the butter. Sauté the onions and garlic until tender but not brown. Remove from pan. Mix the flour, salt and pepper together in a shallow bowl. Lightly dredge the scallops, which have been well rinsed and dried, into the seasoned flour. Add the remaining tablespoon butter and the olive oil to the skillet and sauté the scallops in two batches, turning them as they become golden brown. Remove scallops to six buttered scallop shells and keep warm. Return the garlic and onions to the skillet and deglaze the pan with the white wine. Bring to a boil, scraping up brown crust from pan. Boil for 2 minutes or until wine becomes syrupy. Pour over scallops and sprinkle with parsley.

Yield: 6 servings

Scallop or Shrimp Jambalaya

The name jambalaya is believed to come from the French for ham, "jambon", and an African word for rice, "ya". If you wish a fiery Creole/Cajun taste, increase the quantity of cayenne pepper.

2	slices (2 ounces) of bacon or pre-cooked ham	¾	cup Uncle Ben's rice
1	medium onion, chopped	1½	cups chicken broth
1	medium clove garlic, minced	⅛	teaspoon cayenne pepper
1	small green pepper in ¼" dice	1	teaspoon salt
1	celery stalk in ¼" dice	½	teaspoon pepper
2	green onions (white part only) cut into thin rings	1	pound sea or bay scallops or medium shrimp

If using sea scallops, cut in half crosswise after washing well to remove sand. In a 3-quart saucepan, sauté the bacon until crisp, drained, then broken up. (Ham just needs to be in ¼" dice.) Add the onions and sauté over low heat until softened. Add the garlic and sauté for 30 seconds. Stir in the green pepper, celery and rice; sauté, stirring constantly, until rice is golden and the vegetables soften slightly, about 3 minutes. Add the broth, cayenne pepper, salt and pepper. Bring to a boil, reduce heat, cover, and simmer until liquid is fully absorbed, about 18 minutes. Add scallops or shrimp, cover and simmer until they just turn opaque. Stir in green onion rings and serve immediately.

Yield: 4 servings

Shrimp and Angel Hair Pasta

Recipe can be doubled.

1	pound unpeeled medium-size shrimp	1	cup half-and-half
4	ounces angel hair pasta, uncooked	¼	cup chopped parsley leaves
		1	teaspoon fresh dillweed or ½ teaspoon dried
½	cup butter	¼	teaspoon salt
2	cloves garlic, minced	⅛	teaspoon pepper

Peel and devein shrimp; set aside. Cook pasta according to package directions. Drain and set aside; cover to keep warm. Melt butter in a heavy skillet over medium-high heat; add shrimp and garlic. Cook until shrimp are opaque, stirring constantly. Remove shrimp, and set aside, reserving garlic and butter in skillet. Add half-and-half to skillet; bring to a boil, stirring constantly. Reduce heat to low and simmer about 15 minutes or until thickened, stirring occasionally. Add shrimp, parsley and seasonings; stir until blended. Serve over angel hair pasta. Garnish with sautéed red or green pepper strips, if desired.

Yield: 2 or 3 servings

Shrimp and Scallop Sauté

The shrimp and scallops in this entrée are cooked in butter instead of boiled which I prefer for richer flavor.

3	tablespoons butter	1	pound sea scallops, washed
⅓	cup chopped fresh parsley leaves		well and drained
1	large clove garlic, minced	3	tablespoons whipping cream
Pinch of dried thyme, crumbled		1	tablespoon lemon juice
Salt and freshly ground pepper		Chopped parsley	
1	pound medium shrimp, shelled and deveined	Paprika	
		Freshly cooked rice	

Melt butter in large skillet over medium heat. Add parsley, garlic, thyme, salt and pepper; heat, stirring, for 2 minutes. Add shrimp and scallops and sauté until shrimp and scallops are opaque, about 5 minutes. Reduce heat to medium-low; add cream and lemon juice. Stir until sauce thickens slightly, 2 to 3 minutes. Garnish with chopped parsley and paprika. Serve with rice.

Yield: 4 to 6 servings

Be sure to wash the scallops as they sometimes have sand in them.

Shrimp with Vermouth

A delicious way to serve shrimp for a first course, a light supper, or a luncheon.

20	unpeeled large shrimp	2	cloves garlic, minced
¼	cup butter or margarine	2	tablespoons minced fresh
¾	cup fresh crabmeat, drained and flaked		parsley
		1½	tablespoons lemon juice
¼	cup dry vermouth		

Peel shrimp, leaving tails on; devein and set aside. Melt butter in a large skillet; add shrimp, crabmeat and next 4 ingredients. Bring to a boil; reduce heat, and simmer until shrimp is opaque. Do not overcook. Spoon mixture into 4 individual serving dishes; crabmeat in center and shrimp arranged around it. Garnish with parsley sprigs and lemon wedges, if desired.

Yield: 4 servings

Pies

Kristen Calame and Bradley Graves

Almond Macaroon Tart

Tart Pastry:

6	tablespoons butter or margarine	1	egg yolk
3	tablespoons sugar	1	cup sifted flour

Cream butter in a small bowl until soft; add sugar, creaming until mixture is light and fluffy. Add egg yolk, then flour; blend until smooth. Chill 1 hour, then turn chilled dough out on lightly floured board; shape into a roll. Pinch or cut off small pieces of dough. With floured hands, pat dough into a thin layer to fill lightly buttered 3" tart tins. Fill ¾ full of almond filling; place on cookie sheet. Roll out remaining dough and cut into ½" wide strips. Arrange 2 strips in cross on top of each tart; crimp ends. Bake at 350° 25 minutes or until golden brown. Cool in tins, then remove carefully.

Filling:

⅔	cup blanched almonds, finely ground	2 egg whites
¾	cup sifted powdered sugar	¼ teaspoon almond extract

Combine almonds, powdered sugar, egg whites and almond extract in a small bowl; beat until fluffy. Fill tarts.

Yield: 8 to 10 tarts

Frozen Raspberry Pie

This pie is flavored with Chambord, a liqueur created in the time of King Louis XIV of France. It is a magnificent liqueur made of small black raspberries, other fruits and honey.

1	quart vanilla ice cream	1 chocolate cookie crumb crust
1	pint raspberry sherbet	Fresh raspberries or chocolate curls
¼	cup Chambord (raspberry liqueur)	for garnish

Soften ice cream and sherbet slightly, then fold together with the liqueur until blended. Spoon into pie crust and freeze at least an hour. Garnish with either raspberries or chocolate curls, if desired.

Yield: 6 servings

If raspberry sherbet is not obtainable, strawberry may be substituted. The raspberry liqueur will flavor it satisfactorily.

Amaretto Chocolate Pie

This is a "company dessert" and should be served at the table.

Crust:

1	ounce unsweetened chocolate
6	tablespoons unsalted butter
2	tablespoons sugar

30   amaretti (small Italian almond macaroons), crushed

In the top of a double boiler, melt 1 ounce of the chocolate with 6 tablespoons of butter, then let the mixture cool. In a 9" x 3" springform pan, combine 2 tablespoons of the sugar with the amaretti, stir in the chocolate mixture and combine well. Press crumb mixture onto bottom and one third up side of the pan and chill the crust.

Filling:

3	ounces chocolate	3	tablespoons light corn syrup
8	tablespoons butter	¼	cup heavy cream
4	large eggs, room temperature	1	teaspoon vanilla
¼	teaspoon salt	2	tablespoons Amaretto
1½	cups sugar		Whipped cream for garnish

In the top of a double boiler, melt the chocolate and butter and let the mixture cool. In a mixing bowl, beat together the eggs and salt, then add the 1½ cups sugar a little at a time. Beat the mixture until it is thick and pale. Beat in the corn syrup, the heavy cream, the Amaretto, the vanilla, and the chocolate mixture. Pour the filling into the crust. Bake in the middle of a pre-heated 350° oven for 45 minutes. Let it cool on a rack. Run a thin knife around the edge of the pan, remove the side of the pan. Slide the pie onto a crystal serving plate. Pipe the whipped cream on top and serve.

Yield: 9" springform pan

Chocolate Caramel Pecan Pie

This pie can be made the day before, if you like. Chocolate Cookie Crumb Crust is in index of this cookbook.

Filling:

1   (14 ounce) package Kraft vanilla caramels
½   cup butter or margarine
½   cup whipping cream or evaporated milk

2   cups toasted pecans, chopped coarsely
Chocolate cookie crumb crust

Melt caramels with butter and cream in a heavy saucepan, stirring constantly. Remove from heat and whisk until smooth. Stir in pecans. Pour into chocolate cookie crumb crust and chill until firm.

Topping:

⅓   cup semi-sweet chocolate chips
2   tablespoons butter or margarine
2   tablespoons whipping cream or evaporated milk

2   tablespoons white corn syrup
½   teaspoon vanilla
1   cup whipping cream for garnish, optional

Melt chocolate chips and butter over low heat. Remove from heat and add cream, corn syrup and vanilla. Mix and pour over chilled pie. Chill at least 1 hour before serving with or without whipped cream.

Yield: 6 to 8 servings

Cranberry Cherry Pie, Graves

I like this slightly tart pie. It may be made with a top crust or with a crumb topping. The cherry pie filling simplifies the preparation.

2   cups fresh or frozen cranberries
¾   cup sugar
2   tablespoons cornstarch

1   (21 ounce) can cherry pie filling
½   teaspoon almond extract
1   (15 ounce) package prepared pie crust or homemade

Prepare pie crust according to directions for two-crust pie. In large bowl, combine cranberries, sugar and cornstarch; mix well. Fold in cherry pie filling and almond extract. Spoon into pie crust. Cut remaining crust into ½" wide strips. Arrange in a lattice design over top and crimp edges. Brush pastry strips with milk or half-and-half and sprinkle sugar over top. Bake at 400° for 35 to 45 minutes or until crust is brown and filling is thick and bubbly.

Yield: 9" double crust pie

Cranberry Apple Pie

This is a double crust pie — delicious with a wedge of cheese.

Pastry for a double-crust pie
1   cup sugar, divided
1½   tablespoons cornstarch
1   teaspoon cinnamon
3   large Golden Delicious apples, peeled, cored, quartered, then cut crosswise in ¼" slices
½   cup fresh cranberries, picked over and rinsed
½   cup white raisins
½   cup walnuts or pecans, chopped
4   tablespoons butter or margarine, cut into bits
1   egg beaten with 1 tablespoon water for egg wash

Divide pastry dough into 2 pieces, one a little larger than the other. Chill the larger piece while proceeding with pie. Roll the smaller piece of dough ⅛" thick to fit a 9" pie tin. Leave a ½" overhang. Combine ¾ cup sugar, cornstarch, cinnamon, then add the cranberries, apples, raisins and pecans. Toss mixture to mix well. Place filling in pie shell and dot it with the butter. Roll out the remaining piece of dough into a 14" round and drape it over the filling taking care not to stretch it. Trim the top crust leaving a 1" overhang, fold the overhang under the bottom crust and press it to seal it, then crimp the edge. Cut a few vents in top crust to let steam escape. Brush the top crust with the egg wash, then sprinkle with the remaining ¼ cup sugar. Bake on middle shelf of a pre-heated 400° oven for 20 minutes, then reduce temperature to 350° and bake for 30 minutes more until crust is brown and apples tender. Serve warm or at room temperature.

Yield: 6 to 8 servings

Fresh Peach Glazed Pie

This recipes dates back over fifty years. It was given to me by Aunt Pearl.

Filling:
4   large peaches, peeled and sliced
1   cup sugar
1   cup water
¼   cup cornstarch
⅛   teaspoon salt
¼   teaspoon almond extract
1   tablespoon butter or margarine
1   cooked 9" pie shell

Mix cornstarch with sugar in a saucepan, add water. Mix well, then cook over medium heat, stirring constantly, until thickened and clear. Add butter, salt and extract. Cool to lukewarm, then pour over peaches. Mix gently with a spatula and spoon into cooked 9" pie shell. Place in refrigerator until ready to serve.

Yield: 9" pie

This should be eaten the day it is made.

Dried Apple Pie, Eastman

Dried apples are handy to have on hand. They make delicious apple sauce and can also be used in some cake recipes. Apple cider was a kitchen staple in Pennsylvania where I grew up. Apple juice may be substituted, if necessary.

Pastry for 2-crust pie:

2	cups flour	1	teaspoon salt
¾	cup Crisco	5	tablespoons cold water

Cut Crisco into flour and salt with two knives or pastry blender until it forms pea-sized chunks. Sprinkle water over 1 tablespoon at a time. Toss lightly with a fork until dough forms a ball. Divide into slightly unequal portions. Roll the larger portion into a round ⅛" thick and fit into a 9" pie plate. Roll the remaining dough into a round ⅛" thick and transfer to a foil-lined baking sheet. Chill the pastry.

Filling:

¾	pound dried apples	2	tablespoons butter or
4	cups apple cider		margarine, cut into bits
¼	cup plus 1 tablespoon sugar	1	tablespoon whole milk
3	tablespoons cornstarch	3	tablespoons heavy cream
½	teaspoon cinnamon		Ice cream or Cheddar cheese as an
¼	teaspoon freshly grated nutmeg		accompaniment

In a kettle, combine the apples and the cider, adding water if necessary to just cover apples. Bring to a boil and simmer the apples, partially covered, stirring occasionally, for 20 to 30 minutes or until they are softened but not mushy. Drain the apples, reserving ¼ cup of the cider and let them cool. Into a bowl, sift together ¼ cup sugar, the cornstarch, cinnamon and nutmeg. Add the apples and toss together, then add the cider and toss until it is combined well. Spoon the apple mixture into the shell and dot it with the butter. Lay the reserved pastry loosely over the filling and crimp edges together decoratively. Brush pastry lightly with milk, sprinkle it with the remaining 1 tablespoon sugar and cut several long vents in top crust. Bake the pie on a baking sheet in the lower third of a pre-heated 425° oven for 15 minutes, reduce heat to 400° and bake 30 minutes more. For old-fashioned pour-through pie, drizzle the cream into steam vents 5 minutes before pie has finished baking. Serve the pie warm with ice cream or cheese.

Yield: 6 to 8 servings

At one of our church suppers, a small hole was made in the tops of frozen apple pies then 2 or 3 tablespoons of cream were drizzled in. The tops were sprinkled with sugar and then baked according to directions. Everyone thought they were homemade!

Fresh Peach Pie with Cream Cheese Crust

I like to serve this directly from the dish at the table.

Cream Cheese Crust:

8 tablespoons butter, softened	2 tablespoons sugar
8 tablespoons cream cheese, softened	¼ teaspoon salt
1¼ cups flour	2 tablespoons heavy cream or evaporated milk

In a large mixing bowl, cream butter and cheese by beating them together with a spoon until smooth and fluffy. Sift the sugar, flour and salt into the cheese mixture, then add the cream. With a large spoon or your hands, mix thoroughly until dough can be gathered into a ball. Dust lightly with flour, wrap in waxed paper and refrigerate while you prepare the filling. Then roll the pastry into an 11″ square. Lift it up on the rolling pin and gently drape it over the top of the dish containing the peach filling. Crimp the edges well around the outside of the dish. Brush with the egg beaten with the water, then sprinkle with the sugar. Cut 2 small vents in the top of the crust to allow steam to escape. Bake in the middle of the oven for 35 to 40 minutes or until crust is golden brown. Serve warm with a pitcher of cream.

Filling:

1½ pounds fresh peaches	1 teaspoon vanilla
1 tablespoon flour	½ teaspoon almond extract
2 tablespoons brown sugar, packed	1 egg yolk beaten with 2 teaspoons water
3 tablespoons melted butter	1 teaspoon sugar

Pre-heat oven to 350°. Drop peaches into a pan of boiling water. Scoop out after about 30 seconds and, while they are still warm, remove the skins with a small knife. Cut the peaches in half, remove the pits and slice thinly. Combine the peaches, flour, brown sugar, melted butter, vanilla and almond extract in a large bowl. Mix them together gently, but thoroughly. With a spatula, scrape the contents of the bowl into an 8″ x 8″ x 2½″ baking dish. Spread the peaches evenly. Top with crust. Brush with egg mixed with water. Sprinkle with sugar. Cut 2 slits in top of crust to allow steam to escape. Bake on middle shelf of oven for 35 to 40 minutes until crust is golden brown. Serve warm with a pitcher of cream.

Yield: 6 servings

Frozen Chocolate Pecan Pie

The crust of this pie has no flour, just chopped pecans.

Pecan Crust:

2   cups coarsely chopped pecans
1/3 cup brown sugar, packed
3   tablespoons butter or
    margarine, melted

2   teaspoons Kahlúa or liqueur
    of your choice

Combine all ingredients, mixing well. Press mixture evenly over bottom and sides of a buttered 9" pie plate. Bake at 350° for 10 to 12 minutes. Press sides of crust up with the back of a spoon. Cool before filling.

Filling:

6   (1 ounce) squares semi-sweet
    chocolate or 1 cup semi-sweet
    chocolate morsels
1/2 teaspoon instant coffee
    granules

2   eggs, beaten
2   tablespoons Kahlúa
1/4 cup powdered sugar
3/4 cup whipping cream
1   teaspoon vanilla

Place chocolate morsels and coffee granules in top of a lightly buttered double boiler over simmering water. Do not let water touch bottom of boiler inset. Cook until chocolate melts. Gradually add about 1/4 of the chocolate to beaten eggs, then add to remaining chocolate in double boiler. Gradually stir in Kahlúa and powdered sugar. Cook, stirring constantly, until mixture thickens slightly. Cool to room temperature. Beat whipping cream until soft peaks form; fold into chocolate mixture, add vanilla and spoon into pecan crust. Cover and freeze. Transfer from freezer to refrigerator 1 hour before serving. To serve; spread with topping.

Topping:

3/4 cup whipping cream
1   tablespoon Kahlúa or liqueur
    of your choice

Grated sweet chocolate

Beat cream in mixing bowl until frothy; gradually add Kahlúa, beating until stiff peaks form. Pipe or dollop whipped cream around edge of pie. Sprinkle with grated sweet chocolate.

Yield: 6 to 8 servings

Fudge Pie Supreme

This is a super rich chocolate pie. If you garnish it with whipped cream, please do not sweeten it.

Filling:

½ cup (1 stick) butter or margarine, softened
3 large eggs
¾ cup firmly packed light brown sugar
1 (12 ounce) package semi-sweet morsels, melted
2 teaspoons instant coffee granules
1 teaspoon rum extract or flavoring of your choice
½ cup flour
1 cup coarsely chopped walnuts
1 unbaked 9″ pastry shell
Whipped cream and walnuts for garnish

Cream butter; gradually add brown sugar, beating at medium speed until light and fluffy. Add eggs, one at a time, beating well after each addition. Add melted chocolate, coffee granules and rum extract. Add flour and nuts. Pour into unbaked pie shell. Bake at 350° for 25 minutes. Cool completely. Chill. Serve with whipped cream or ice cream.

Yield: 6 to 8 servings

Orange Raspberry Tarts

This recipe is another recipe that uses frozen orange juice, undiluted.

Filling:

½ cup (1 stick) butter or margarine
½ cup sugar
1 egg yolk (freeze egg white for future use)
3 large eggs
1 (6 ounce) can frozen orange juice, thawed and undiluted
12 baked (3″) tart shells
1 (12 ounce) jar raspberry jam
Whipped cream for garnish, if desired

Combine butter and sugar in top of a double boiler over hot water and let butter melt. In a small bowl, beat egg yolk, eggs and orange juice together, then add to butter slowly, beating constantly. Cook, stirring, about 10 minutes or until thickened. Cool and spoon into shells. Melt jam in a small heavy saucepan over low heat; spread on orange filling. Refrigerate until serving.

Yield: 12 (3″) tarts

The jam topping can be replaced with 4 ounces semi-sweet chocolate morsels in a heavy zip-top bag, microwaved for 1 to 2 minutes on high or until chocolate melts. Snip a tiny corner from the bag, squeeze and drizzle chocolate over orange filling.

Holiday Mince Pie

A friend of mine in the Hill Country always put a half orange ground up in her mince pie. I use a shortcut by putting in undiluted frozen orange juice. It gives the same flavor as the orange and rind.

Filling:

¾	cup raisins	1	(27 ounce) jar mincemeat
3	tablespoons brandy	1	large cooking apple, cored and finely chopped (does not have to be peeled)
3	tablespoons frozen orange juice, undiluted		
1	(15 ounce) package refrigerated pie crusts or homemade	1	cup chopped nuts of your choice
			Pie crust sheets

Combine raisins and brandy in a large bowl; let stand 2 hours. Unfold 1 pie crust and press out fold lines; sprinkle with flour, spreading over surface. Place flour-side down in a 9" pie plate; fold edges under and flute. Set aside. Combine raisin mixture with rest of ingredients; spoon into pastry shell. Roll remaining crust on a lightly floured surface to press out fold lines. Cut out with a leaf-shaped cutter, mark veins with a pastry wheel or knife. Dip in granulated sugar and lay on top of filling. Bake at 375° for 10 minutes; cover edges with aluminum foil to keep them from getting too brown and bake for 25 minutes more. Serve warm or cold.

Yield: 9" pie

I have given directions for using pie crust sheets in this recipe. You may make your own, if you like. You may like this pie served warm with a hard sauce spiked with brandy. However, it is delicious as is.

Kahlúa Black Russian Pie

This is similar to Grasshopper Pie, but flavored with Kahlúa. It is frozen so can be made days ahead. Make chocolate curls with any semi-sweet chocolate. You can make them in advance and store in freezer or refrigerator. Make curls with a thin knife.

Chocolate Cookie Crust:

1	cup cream-filled chocolate sandwich cookie crumbs	2	tablespoons melted butter

Combine cookie crumbs and butter in an 8" pie tin. Mix well and press firmly in an even layer over bottom and sides of pan to form a crust. Place in freezer until firm.

Filling:

24	large marshmallows	⅓	cup Kahlúa
½	cup cold whole milk	1	cup heavy cream, whipped
⅛	teaspoon salt		Semi-sweet chocolate for curls

Melt marshmallows with milk and salt in top of a double boiler over hot water. Cool until mixture will mound on a spoon. Stir in Kahlúa. Beat cream stiff and fold into marshmallow mixture. Chill about 30 minutes, until mixture holds ripples when stirred lightly. Turn into chilled cookie shell and freeze firm. Before serving, arrange a circle of chocolate curls in the center (optional) and cut into wedges.

Yield: 8" pie

Make chocolate curls in a cool dry place. For 16 to 20 1½-inch curls, melt 3 ounces chocolate. Pour into a small bread tin, buttered. Smooth top. When it is solid, unmold. Let come to room temperature. A potato peeler can also be used.

Lemon Cream Pie

This filling could also be used as a filling for cream puffs or tarts.

Lemon Filling:

1	cup sugar	3	egg yolks
3	tablespoons cornstarch	1	cup milk
¼	cup butter (do not substitute)	1	cup dairy sour cream
¼	cup fresh lemon juice	1	(9″) pie shell, baked
	Grated rind of 1 lemon	¼	cup heavy cream, whipped

Combine sugar, cornstarch, butter and milk in a heavy saucepan. Mix well, then cook over medium heat, stirring constantly, until mixture thickens. Remove from heat. Beat egg yolks, lemon juice and lemon rind together. Add a little of the hot mixture to them, then slowly add to the rest of the hot mixture, beating constantly. Return to heat and cook just a few minutes more. Remove to a bowl, cool and chill. Fold sour cream into lemon mixture and spoon into pie shell. Refrigerate until serving with a garnish of unsweetened whipped cream.

Yield: 6 to 8 servings

Lemon Pecan Pie

This makes a large pie and requires either a 10″ pastry shell or a 9″ deep-dish pastry shell.

Pastry shell:
1   9″ deep-dish pastry shell
or 10″ shell

Bake pastry shell at 400° 5 to 7 minutes. Remove from oven and cool completely.

Filling:

4	large eggs	2	teaspoons grated lemon rind
6	tablespoons butter or margarine, softened	¼	cup lemon juice
		3	level tablespoons flour
1	cup light corn syrup	1¼	cups coarsely chopped pecans
½	cup firmly packed brown sugar		Whipped cream

Combine eggs and next 6 ingredients; stir in pecans and pour into prepared crust. Bake at 350° for 40 minutes. Cool on a wire rack and serve with whipped cream, if desired.

Yield: 8 servings

This pie freezes well after baking. Thaw at room temperature and serve or pieces may be warmed in the microwave and served.

Maple Custard Pie

I mentioned before that I always had pure maple syrup on pancakes and waffles when a child in Pennsylvania. Perhaps that is why I am so fond of this pie.

Pastry:

6 tablespoons unsalted butter, cut into ¼" dice	1 tablespoon sugar
2 tablespoons shortening	¼ teaspoon salt
1½ cups flour	3 or 4 tablespoons ice water

In a large bowl, combine the butter, shortening flour, sugar and salt. With your fingertips, lightly rub the flour and fat together until mixture is like coarse meal. Add 3 tablespoons ice water all at once. Mix together with a fork until it forms a ball. If dough does not hold together, add the remaining tablespoon water. Dust dough with a little flour, wrap in waxed paper and refrigerate for at least an hour before rolling out. Pat dough into a circle about 1" thick. Dust a little flour over board and roll the circle until it is ⅛" thick and 13" in diameter. Gently press dough into a 9" pie tin. Cut the edge with scissors leaving a 1" overhang. Tuck edge in and crimp.

Filling:

1 cup heavy cream	1 teaspoon vanilla
1 cup milk	4 large eggs
½ cup pure maple syrup	

Pre-heat oven to 325°. In a small heavy saucepan, warm cream, milk, maple syrup and vanilla over moderate heat, stirring occasionally, until small bubbles appear around the edges of pan. Remove from the heat and cover to keep warm. In mixer bowl, beat eggs for 2 or 3 minutes until they begin to thicken and cling to beater. Beating constantly, pour the maple syrup mixture in a slow, thin stream. Pour filling in pie shell. Bake in the middle of the oven about 40 minutes or until a knife inserted in the middle comes out clean. Remove pie from oven and let it cool to room temperature. Chill if not using within 1 hour. Garnish with whipped cream and chopped walnuts, if desired.

Yield: 6 to 8 servings

Simplified Fruit Tart

This recipe can be made in a flash in case of unexpected company. Particularly if you have a pie crust in the freezer, as I usually have, or use a refrigerated ready made crust.

Pastry:

1¼ cups flour
⅛ teaspoon salt

½ cup unsalted butter,
cut into bits
3 tablespoons ice water

Combine salt and flour, cut in butter with pastry blender or tips of the fingers until mixture resembles coarse meal. Add water by tablespoonfuls and form dough into a ball. Roll out on lightly floured board into a circle that will fit a 9" tart pan with a removable bottom. Line crust with parchment paper or waxed paper and place a layer of uncooked beans or rice or the metal pellets made for that purpose. Bake at 375° about 10 minutes, remove paper and beans and bake until crust is a light brown. Let cool slightly, then remove to a serving plate.

Filling:

1½ cups prepared fresh fruit of
your choice

¼ cup preserves or apple jelly

About an hour before serving, place well drained fruit in pie shell. Heat preserves or jelly to lukewarm and pour over fruit. Place in refrigerator until serving. Garnish with whipped cream, if desired.

Yield: 6 to 8 servings

The variety of fruit used dictates the flavor of preserves or jelly. Apple jelly goes with nearly every fruit.

Peach Pecan Pie

This pie can be made with either fresh or frozen sliced peaches.

Filling:

4 cups fresh or frozen sliced
peaches, thawed
½ cup sugar
2 tablespoons tapioca
1 teaspoon lemon juice

½ cup flour
¼ cup firmly packed brown sugar
¼ cup butter or margarine
½ cup chopped pecans
1 9" unbaked pie shell

Combine first 4 ingredients in a large bowl; let stand 15 minutes. Combine flour and brown sugar; cut in butter with a pastry blender or tips of your fingers until mixture resembles coarse meal. Stir in pecans. Sprinkle ⅓ of flour mixture in the bottom of pastry shell. Add peaches and top with remaining flour mixture. Bake at 425° for 10 minutes. Reduce temperature to 350° and bake an additional 20 to 30 minutes or until golden brown. Serve warm or cold.

Yield: 6 to 8 servings

Pecan Meringue Pie

This is a frozen dessert with a butterscotch sauce.

Pie:

1 egg white, room temperature	1 quart vanilla ice cream,
¼ cup sugar	softened
1½ cups chopped pecans	Extra pecan halves for garnish

Beat egg white at high speed in electric mixer; gradually add sugar, beating until stiff peaks form and sugar is dissolved. Fold in chopped pecans. Spread meringue on bottom and sides of a buttered 9" pie plate. Bake at 400° for 12 minutes or until lightly browned. Cool. Spread ice cream evenly over crust; cover and freeze until ice cream is firm. Serve with butterscotch sauce.

Butterscotch Sauce:

2 cups brown sugar, packed	4 tablespoons white corn syrup
½ cup half-and half	½ stick butter

In saucepan, combine all ingredients. Cook over medium heat, stirring, until mixture boils. Continue to cook, stirring, about 3 minutes or until thickened. Cool and serve over wedges of pie.

Yield: 9" pie

Southern Pecan Pie

I once had some guests from Australia who liked pecan pie, but needed a recipe that did not require corn syrup. As in England, corn syrup is not available. This is the recipe I gave them.

1 unbaked 8" pastry shell	1 teaspoon vanilla
1 cup brown sugar, packed	½ cup butter, melted (do not
½ cup granulated sugar	substitute)
1 tablespoon flour	1 cup pecans, chopped
2 large eggs	Whipped cream or ice cream
3 tablespoons milk	(optional)

Mix brown sugar, white sugar and flour. Add eggs, milk, vanilla and melted butter; beat well. Fold in pecans. Pour into unbaked pastry shell. Bake in a 375° oven for 40 to 50 minutes or until knife inserted near the edge comes out clean. Center will firm up when pie is cooled. Serve slightly warm with whipped cream or ice cream.

Yield: 8 servings

If you prefer a stronger brown sugar taste, use dark brown sugar.

Super Sweet Potato Pie

Please indulge in this pie even though it is loaded with calories.

Pastry:

1 cup unbleached flour	½ cup frozen butter,
Pinch salt	cut into 1″ pieces
	3 tablespoons ice water

Mix flour and salt in food processor, using 3 or 4 on/off turns. Blend in butter using on/off turns until mixture resembles coarse meal. With machine running, pour water through feed tube until dough just starts to hold together; do not let it form a ball. Turn out on a lightly floured board and shape into a patty. Wrap in plastic and chill at least 1 hour. Then roll into an 11″circle and fit into a 9″pie tin.

Filling:

1 tablespoon butter, softened	¼ teaspoon nutmeg
1 cup cooked mashed sweet potatoes	½ teaspoon salt
	1½ cups coarsely chopped pecans
2 large eggs, beaten	or walnuts
1 cup evaporated milk	1 cup whipping cream, whipped
¾ cup light brown sugar, packed	for garnish
½ cup dark corn syrup	¼ cup Frangelico or praline
1 teaspoon vanilla	liqueur
½ teaspoon ginger	3 tablespoons powdered sugar
½ teaspoon cinnamon	

Whisk butter into mashed sweet potatoes in a large mixing bowl, add beaten eggs, then add next 8 ingredients. Place in prepared pie shell and sprinkle pecans on top. Bake at 375° about 45 to 50 minutes or until a knife inserted around edge of pie comes out clean. Pie will firm up as it cools. Serve warm or cold topped with whipped cream mixed with sugar and liqueur of your choice.

Yield: 6 to 8 servings

Since I am fond of both liqueurs, I alternate to suit my fancy.

Plum Pie

Do not pare the plums. It is the contrast of the sweet fruit and tart skin that makes this pie so special.

Filling:

1 cup sugar	6 cups (2¼ pounds) thinly sliced
⅓ cup flour	plums
¼ teaspoon ginger	Pastry for a double-crust 9″ pie
¼ teaspoon cinnamon	

Combine sugar, flour, ginger and cinnamon in a large bowl. Add plums and toss to mix. Pre-heat oven to 425°. Divide pastry into 2 balls, one slightly larger than the other. Roll larger ball into an 11″ circle to fit a 9″ pie tin. Spoon in filling. Roll second ball into an 9½″ circle and cut into ½″ wide strips. Arrange in lattice pattern over pie and flute edges. Brush lattice crust with a little whole milk or half-and-half and sprinkle with sugar. Bake on cookie sheet 15 minutes. Reduce heat to 375° and bake about 1 hour more or until bubbly near the center.

Yield: 8 servings

You may either make the crust using one of the recipes in the pastry section of this book or buy the pie crust sheets.

Butter Pastry Crust

This amount will also fill a 10″ quiche pan.

1 cup flour	1 tablespoon ice water
¼ teaspoon salt	1 teaspoon lemon juice
⅓ cup butter or margarine, chilled	2 cups dried beans or rice, if pre-baking shell
1 egg	

In bowl, stir together flour and salt. With knife, cut butter into ½″ pieces, dropping into flour mixture. Cut in butter until mixture resembles coarse crumbs (flour should look dry rather than moist). With fork beat together egg, water and lemon juice until blended; sprinkle over flour mixture. Toss with a fork, then hand gather particles into a ball. Wrap airtight and chill in the freezer 10 minutes. On lightly floured pastry board, roll out in a circle 1″ to 1½″ larger than pie tin or quiche pan. Fold dough in quarters and place in pan. Trim and crimp edges. With fork prick pastry about 12 times. For pre-baked shell, cover with a piece of waxed paper, then fill with beans. Bake at 425° 12 minutes. Cool slightly, remove beans (save for future shell baking); fill shell with filling desired. For completely baked shell, remove the beans as above, then continue baking until shell is golden brown.

Yield: 9″ shell

Chocolate Cookie Crumb Crust

This recipe can be varied by using 1 cup crumbs plus ½ cup finely chopped nuts.

1⅓ cups chocolate cookie crumbs   3   tablespoons melted butter or margarine

Let butter soften. Place a long piece of waxed paper on pastry board; stack cookies along center. Wrap, making a double fold in paper; tuck ends under. Roll fine with rolling pin, or roll out in a plastic bag. In a small bowl, with fork, mix the crumbs and soft butter or margarine until crumbly. Set aside 3 tablespoons of the mixture. With back of a spoon, press the rest in the bottom and up the side of a 9" pie plate, forming a small rim. Bake at 375°, 8 minutes. Cool as specific recipe directs. Sprinkle reserved crumbs on top.

Yield: 9" shell

A gingersnap crust is the same as above except increase margarine to 6 tablespoons.

Chocolate Crumb Crust

This is made with vanilla wafer crumbs with cocoa added. Handy to have if you lack the chocolate wafer crumbs.

1½ cups vanilla wafer crumbs   ⅓   cup cocoa
    (about 36 wafers)   ⅓   cup margarine, melted
⅓   cup powdered sugar

Pre-heat oven to 300°. Combine crumbs, sugar, cocoa and margarine. Press firmly on bottom and up sides of a 9" pie tin. Pour filling into crust (for fillings that have to be baked). Bake 30 to 35 minutes or until filling is set. Cool and chill. If a baked shell is desired, bake at 350° about 10 or 15 minutes or until lightly brown.

Yield: 9" crust

Cream Cheese Pastry Crust

This pastry also makes delicious tarts.

1½ sticks (¾ cup) unsalted butter, room temperature

½ pound cream cheese, room temperature

3 tablespoons sugar

½ teaspoon vanilla

2 cups all-purpose flour

Pinch of salt

In a bowl of an electric mixer or in a food processor, cream together the butter, cream cheese, sugar, salt and vanilla until mixture is light and fluffy. Add the flour and blend the dough until it is just combined. Form it into a ball, flatten it slightly, wrap it in waxed paper and chill it for 30 minutes or until it is just firm. Roll out as desired.

Yield: Double crust pie

Salads

Left to right:
Kyle, Eastman, Elyse and Ayla Landry

Asparagus Spears Vinaigrette

I like to use the young asparagus spears, if available.

Asparagus:
2   pounds fresh asparagus

Snap off tough ends of asparagus. Remove scales with vegetable peeler, if desirable. Cook asparagus in skillet in just enough water to barely cover, until crisp-tender. Drain but reserve ½ cup liquid. Place asparagus in a large, shallow casserole and set aside.

Vinaigrette:
½ cup asparagus liquid	1½ tablespoons lemon juice
½ cup sugar	1 teaspoon salt
½ cup cider vinegar	⅛ teaspoon pepper

Combine reserved asparagus liquid and remaining ingredients in a small saucepan. Bring to a boil, stirring constantly; pour over asparagus. Cover and chill 8 hours to blend flavors.

Yield: 8 servings

Asparagus and Tomatoes

A pretty salad to have for the Xmas holidays.

Asparagus:
1   pound fresh asparagus

Snap off tough ends of asparagus. Cook asparagus in skillet, in boiling water to cover, until crisp-tender. Drain and rinse with cold water to stop cooking. Chill.

Dressing:
½ cup plain yogurt	1 tablespoon minced fresh chives
2 tablespoons Dijon mustard	(optional)
2 tablespoons mayonnaise	⅛ teaspoon freshly ground
1 tablespoon fresh dill	pepper
or ½ teaspoon dried	Lettuce leaves
	Cherry tomatoes

Combine ingredients except lettuce and tomatoes; chill. To serve: Line salad plates with lettuce or greens of your choice, top with asparagus and yogurt dressing. Garnish with tomatoes.

Yield: 4 servings

Broccoli Salad

This is a pretty as well as delicious salad.

Salad:
4   cups fresh broccoli florets
2   cups sliced fresh mushrooms
1   (11 ounce) can mandarin
     oranges, drained

½   cup raisins
½   cup slivered almonds, toasted

Combine broccoli and rest of ingredients; add dressing, tossing to coat. Serve immediately.

Salad Dressing:
1   large egg
½   cup sugar
1½   teaspoons cornstarch
½   teaspoon dry mustard
¼   cup tarragon vinegar or white
     vinegar

¼   cup water
½   cup mayonnaise
3   tablespoons butter or
     margarine

Combine egg and next 3 ingredients in a non-aluminum saucepan; gradually add vinegar and water, stirring constantly with a wire whisk. Cook over medium heat, stirring constantly, until mixture thickens. Remove from heat and add mayonnaise and butter. Cover dressing with plastic wrap and chill.

Yield: 8 to 10 servings

Broccoli Slaw

Broccoli has so many vitamins in it. I use it often.

Slaw:
3   cups fresh broccoli flowerets
     (with about 1″ of stem)

Wash flowerets and place in salad bowl.

Dressing:
¾   cup cider vinegar
¾   cup vegetable oil
1   clove garlic, minced

2   teaspoons dried dillweed
¾   teaspoon salt

Combine vinegar and remaining ingredients; pour over broccoli, stirring gently to coat. Cover and chill at least 2 hours. Drain before serving, or serve with a slotted spoon.

Yield: 6 servings

Coleslaw with Grapes

I sometimes add a chopped red-skinned apple to this slaw for additional color, but it is great as is.

Coleslaw:
6   cups shredded white cabbage

Crisp cabbage for about an hour with ice cubes.

Dressing:
¾   cup cooked salad dressing
     (see below)
¾   cup dairy sour cream
1   tablespoon sugar

1   tablespoon vinegar
Salt and pepper
1   tablespoon chopped parsley
1½ cups seedless green grapes

Cooked Salad Dressing:
1   tablespoon flour
1   tablespoon sugar
½   teaspoon salt
½   teaspoon prepared mustard

½   cup water
3   tablespoons cider vinegar
1   egg, beaten
1½ tablespoons butter

In heavy saucepan, combine flour, sugar, salt and mustard. Gradually blend in water and vinegar. Cook over low heat, stirring constantly, until mixture thickens and boils. Boil 1 minute, stirring, then remove from heat. Add a little of cream sauce gradually to beaten egg, then combine with rest of sauce. Add butter and return to heat, stirring, for 3 minutes or enough to cook egg. Cool before combining with sour cream.

Mix together the salad dressing and sour cream. Add the sugar, vinegar and parsley, Chill to blend flavors. To serve, drain cabbage well and pat dry between paper towels. Pour dressing over cabbage. Add grapes, mix well and season with salt and pepper. Chill again before serving.

Yield: 8 servings

Marinated Tomatoes

For a buffet, I often serve these tomatoes on a platter for guests to help themselves, thus eliminating a salad plate.

6   medium tomatoes, sliced
⅓   cup vegetable oil
2   tablespoons lemon juice

1   teaspoon salt
½   teaspoon dried oregano
1   clove garlic, crushed

Place tomatoes in a 11"x 7"x 1½"Pyrex or ceramic dish. Combine oil, lemon juice, salt, oregano and garlic. Pour over tomatoes. Cover and chill before serving.
Yield: 10 to 12 servings

Green Bean and Tomato Salad

This low-calorie salad can take the place of a vegetable with a steak or roast beef dinner.

Salad:
1   (16 ounce) package frozen
     French-cut green beans

Cook green beans just a few minutes in an inch of water or until al dente. Drain and set aside.

Dressing:
¼   cup minced onion   ¼   teaspoon salt
1   small clove garlic, minced   ¼   teaspoon pepper
¼   cup olive oil   4   tablespoons grated Parmesan
2   tablespoons cider vinegar   cheese
½   teaspoon dried tarragon   Sliced tomatoes
¼   teaspoon dried basil

Combine onion, garlic, oil, cider vinegar, tarragon, dried basil, salt and pepper in a bowl; add beans, tossing to coat well. Chill, covered, about an hour. Sprinkle with Parmesan cheese and border with sliced tomatoes.

Yield: 6 servings

Melanie's Mango Salad

This is an unusual salad. It goes especially well with curry and chicken dishes. Adjust the amount of jalapeños to your taste. I only used 2.

Salad:
4 to 6 firm-ripe mangos   4   fresh jalapeños, seeded and
1   medium sweet onion, thinly   slivered, fewer or more to your
     sliced   taste

To prepare mangos, cut a slice off each end. Stand mango on larger flat end and cut from top to bottom in a rounded curve with a sharp knife to peel. Cut flesh away from the seed using the same technique. Slice from top to bottom in a rounded curve on either side of the seed. Cut remaining slices from the sides. Cut into small cubes. Combine mango and onion slices with jalapeños.

Dressing:
¼   cup salad oil   Salt and pepper to taste
¾   cup cider vinegar   Dash of sugar

Mix all ingredients together. Gently mix with mangos. Let stand, covered, in the refrigerator at least 1 or 2 hours before serving. You may serve it on salad greens, if you like. We served it in small bowls without greens.

Yield: 8 servings

Jellied Gazpacho

Gazpacho is a cold soup from Spain that contains fresh garden vegetables. It is served here as a molded salad with avocado cream.

Gazpacho:

2 envelopes unflavored gelatin
1 quart tomato juice, divided
¼ cup white wine vinegar
1 clove garlic, minced
¾ teaspoon salt
¼ teaspoon black pepper

1 cup peeled, chopped tomato, drained
½ cup finely chopped green pepper, blanched in boiling water for 5 minutes
¾ cup peeled chopped cucumber
½ cup chopped green onions

Sprinkle gelatin over 1 cup tomato juice in a medium saucepan; let stand until dissolved. Cook over low heat, stirring constantly, until gelatin is dissolved. Remove from heat; add remaining tomato juice, white wine vinegar and next 3 ingredients. Chill until the consistency of unbeaten egg white. Stir in tomato and next 3 ingredients. Spoon into 10 molds that have been rinsed in cold water, then drained; chill until firm. Unmold onto plates lined with lettuce. Top with avocado cream.

Avocado Cream:

½ cup sour cream
½ cup mashed avocado

Dash red pepper
Salt to taste

Combine all ingredients; stir until smooth. Yield: ⅔ cup.

Yield: 10 servings

Marinated Carrots Julienne

These add color to a dinner plate and are delicious.

1 pound carrots, scraped and cut into thin julienne strips about 2″ long

Heat 1″ of water in a saucepan to boiling. Add carrots; return to boiling. Cover and simmer until just tender. Do not overcook. Drain and combine with dressing in a bowl. Cover; refrigerate 8 hours, tossing occasionally.

Dressing:

½ cup olive oil
2 tablespoons white wine vinegar
1 teaspoon dried whole basil
¼ teaspoon finely minced garlic

½ teaspoon salt
Dash of freshly ground black pepper

Combine all ingredients in bowl or jar. Mix or shake well and pour over salad.

Yield: 6 servings

Melon Prosciutto Salad

Melon and prosciutto is served as an appetizer in Spain without a dressing. This salad can be served with either a poppyseed dressing or the lime vinaigrette given at the end of this recipe. Suit your own taste. I prefer the lime. It is not so sweet.

Salad:

3 cups cantaloupe balls (1 small cantaloupe)	4 ounces prosciutto, cut into strips
3 cups honeydew melon balls (1 small honeydew)	1 cup (4 ounces) shredded provolone cheese
	Lettuce leaves

Combine first 4 ingredients; toss together gently. Cover and chill. Either line salad plates with lettuce, top with mixture and ladle dressing over or line a salad bowl with lettuce, spoon in mixture and add enough dressing to moisten. Serve rest in bowl.

Lime Vinaigrette:

6 tablespoons olive oil	¼ teaspoon grated lime rind
8 tablespoons lime juice	Salt and pepper to taste
2 teaspoons honey	

Whisk all ingredients in a small bowl. Add salt and pepper to taste. Note: This dressing is good on any fruit salad.

Yield: 6 servings

Four ounces fully cooked, paper-thin ham slices can be substituted for the prosciutto, if necessary.

Helpful Hint: *8 ounces noodles (1" pieces) — 3 cups.*

Shrimp Pasta Salad

Salad:
5   cups water
1½   pounds unpeeled medium
     shrimp
1   (12 ounce) package vermicelli
3   hard boiled eggs, chopped
1½   cups chopped green onions

¼   cup chopped parsley
1   (2 ounce) jar diced pimento,
     drained
1   (10 ounce) package frozen
     tiny green peas, thawed and
     drained

Bring water to a boil; add shrimp and cook 3 to 5 minutes or until opaque. Drain well and rinse with cold water. Devein and chill. Break vermicelli into 3″ pieces. Cook according to package directions; drain. Place in a salad bowl and add shrimp, eggs, and next 4 ingredients; set aside.

Dressing:
1   cup mayonnaise
1   (8 ounce) carton sour cream
¼   cup lemon juice

1   tablespoon prepared mustard
1   teaspoon salt
¼   teaspoon pepper

Combine mayonnaise, sour cream, lemon juice, mustard, salt and pepper. Spoon over shrimp mixture; toss gently with a fork. Chill at least 2 hours. Serve on a lettuce-lined platter and sprinkle with paprika.

Yield: 8 servings

Spinach Rice Salad

Salad:
1   cup Uncle Ben's rice,
     uncooked
2   cups shredded fresh spinach
½   cup sliced celery

½   cup sliced green onions
6   slices lean bacon, cooked crisp
     and crumbled

Cook rice according to package directions. Drain and set aside in a bowl. When cool, add salad dressing and chill 2 hours. Stir in spinach and remaining ingredients into rice mixture. Serve immediately.

Dressing:
½   cup Italian salad dressing
1   tablespoon soy sauce

½   teaspoon sugar

Combine salad dressing, soy sauce and sugar in a large bowl. Stir in rice. Cover and chill 2 hours.

Yield: 6 to 8 servings

Shrimp and Orange Salad

My mother sometimes added diced apples to shrimp salad. Oranges are equally good.

Salad:

3	cups water	1	cup sliced ripe olives
1	pound unpeeled, medium fresh shrimp	5	cups torn Bibb lettuce
		5	cups torn leaf lettuce
2	oranges	2	green onions, sliced

Bring water to a boil; add shrimp. Cook only 3 or 5 minutes or until shrimp turn pink. Drain, then rinse with cold water. Peel and devein; set aside. Cut rind off of oranges being sure to remove all the white. Cut into 4 slices (about ½" thick), then cut slices into quarters. Add oranges, shrimp and olives to dressing; cover and chill at least an hour. To serve, toss salad greens with green onions and shrimp mixture. Serve immediately.

Salad Dressing:

3	tablespoons sherry wine vinegar or red wine vinegar	1	teaspoon sugar
		1	teaspoon grated orange rind
1	clove garlic, minced	⅓	cup olive oil

Combine first 4 ingredients in a large mixing bowl; gradually add olive oil, beating with a wire whisk until mixed well.

Yield: 8 servings

Spinach Apple Salad

A salad for a picnic as well as at home. Bring the dressing in a jar, torn spinach, apples and almonds in separate zip-top bags. (Pour enough dressing over sliced apples to thoroughly coat). Toss dressing with spinach and top with apples and almonds.

Salad:
1½ pounds fresh spinach   ½ cup sliced almonds, toasted
4   medium apples, unpeeled

Remove stems from spinach and wash in very salty water, tossing gently, then rinse under running water, place on paper towels and pat dry. Tear into bite-size pieces. Toss with enough dressing to coat, reserving remaining dressing; place spinach on serving platter. Core and slice apples. Toss in reserved dressing and arrange on spinach. Sprinkle with almonds.

Dressing:
⅔ cup vegetable oil   1½ tablespoons honey
⅔ cup raspberry vinegar   ¼   teaspoon salt
     (red wine vinegar can be   ⅛   teaspoon pepper
     substituted)

Combine first 5 ingredients in a jar; cover tightly and shake vigorously. Chill.

Yield: 12 servings

Wash spinach as well as squash or other vegetables in salted water. The salt makes the vegetables slick and the sand is removed with only the one washing.

Tomato Aspic

Tomato aspic has been around a long time, I know, but this Lemon Cream Dressing is a change. It is good on spinach and other vegetable salads. It does not separate on standing so can be made the day before using.

Aspic:

2   envelopes (2 tablespoons) unflavored gelatin
¼   cup cold water
½   cup boiling water
4   cups V-8 juice

1   teaspoon Worcestershire sauce
1   teaspoon salt
2   whole cloves
Juice of 1 lemon

Sprinkle gelatin on cold water and let soak 5 minutes; add boiling water and stir until gelatin is dissolved. In a saucepan, simmer the V-8 juice, cloves and salt for 15 minutes; strain. Add lemon juice, Worcestershire and dissolved gelatin. Pour into a 10″ ring mold or 6 individual molds that have been rinsed in cold water and drained upside-down. Chill and serve with lemon cream dressing.

Lemon Cream Dressing:

1   egg
2   tablespoons grated Parmesan cheese
1   clove garlic, minced

1½ teaspoons Dijon mustard
Salt and pepper to taste
½   cup salad oil
⅓   cup lemon juice

Combine egg, cheese, garlic, mustard, salt and pepper in blender, blend a few seconds. Add oil and lemon juice alternately, blending after each addition. Chill before using. Yield: about 1 cup.

Yield: 6 servings

In Mexico, limes are used instead of lemons. Lime juice can be used in this recipe, if lemons are not at hand.

Sweet-Sour Spinach Salad

Salad:
1 cup boiling water	¾ cup coarsely chopped
1 (6 ounce) package dried apricots or peaches	macadamia nuts or almonds, toasted
1 pound fresh spinach	

Pour boiling water over apricots that have been cut in half (cut peaches in fourths, if using). Let stand 30 minutes, then drain well and set aside. Remove stems from spinach, wash thoroughly and pat dry. Tear into bite-size pieces, set aside.

Dressing:
3 tablespoons cider vinegar	½ cup salad oil
3 tablespoons apricot preserves (peach preserves if using peaches)	

Combine vinegar and preserves in blender; process until smooth, scraping down sides once with a rubber spatula. With blender at high speed, add oil in a slow steady stream. Combine spinach, half of apricots, half of nuts and dressing; toss gently. Sprinkle with remaining apricots and nuts and dressing. Serve immediately to your happy guests.

Yield: 8 servings

Basil Vinegar

The flavor of basil vinegar can perk up anything from vinaigrettes, slaws, salsas, marinades and sauces. It is delicious on sliced tomatoes, hot turnip greens or green beans. Combine it with oil or mayonnaise, mix with chicken or seafood for a salad.

⅔ cup loosely packed fresh basil leaves	1 (17-ounce) bottle white wine vinegar
	Fresh basil sprig (optional)

Slightly crush basil with the back of a spoon. Place in a 1-quart jar. Bring vinegar to a boil and pour over basil. Cover and let stand at room temperature 1 to 2 weeks. Pour mixture through a wire-mesh strainer into a 4-cup liquid measuring cup, discarding the basil. Transfer to a bottle; add a fresh sprig of basil, if desired. Seal the bottle with a cork or airtight lid. Store in a cool, dark place up to 6 months.

Yield: 2 cups

Buttermilk Dressing

¾   cup buttermilk
½   cup olive oil

¼   pound Bleu cheese

In a food processor or blender, blend the buttermilk, oil and half the Bleu cheese for 30 seconds. Add the remaining Bleu cheese and blend for only 5 seconds.

Yield: 1¾ cups

Cottage Cheese Dressing

½   cup cottage cheese
1½ tablespoons fresh lemon juice
     or to taste
¼   teaspoon dried tarragon
Pinch of dried thyme

⅛   teaspoon celery salt
⅛   teaspoon pepper
⅓   cup salad oil
2   tablespoons water

In a blender or food processor blend the cottage cheese, lemon juice, tarragon, thyme, celery salt, pepper and water, scraping down the sides, until the mixture is smooth. With the motor running, add the oil in a stream and blend until mixture is emulsified.

Yield: ¾ cup

Creamy Mustard Salad Dressing

Serve over mixed salad greens or mixed fruit and greens.

¼   teaspoon powdered mustard
¼   teaspoon warm water
1   tablespoon flour
¼   cup salad oil
1   teaspoon salt

Pinch black pepper
⅔   cup water
1   teaspoon dillweed
½   teaspoon paprika
2   tablespoons cider vinegar

Combine mustard and warm water in a cup; set aside for 10 minutes. In a small saucepan, combine flour and oil. Cook, stirring constantly, over low heat until bubbly. Add salt, pepper, mustard mixture and ⅔ cup water. Bring to a boil. Reduce heat and cook, stirring constantly, until thickened. Remove from heat and stir in dill, paprika and vinegar. Cool, then refrigerate in a covered container until serving.

Yield: 1 cup

Ice Cream Peanut Butter Dressing

I ate this dressing on a hearts of palm salad at a restaurant in Florida. It is unusual but very good.

¼   cup mayonnaise
¼   cup vanilla ice cream

2   tablespoons chunky peanut
     butter
2   tablespoons pineapple juice

Mix peanut butter with mayonnaise, then fold in rest of ingredients. Store in a covered container in the refrigerator.

Yield: ½ cup

This recipe is easy to double, triple or whatever.

Pesto Vinaigrette

This is a very light dressing and can be used on any green salad. This dressing can also be used to dress cooked vegetables such as carrots, green beans or squash.

Vinaigrette:
¼   cup pesto sauce
1   cup olive oil, divided

½   cup white wine vinegar
Salt and pepper to taste

Mix all ingredients together with a wire whisk or blender.

Pesto Sauce:
1   cup olive oil, divided
¼   cup fresh basil
¼   cup fresh parsley leaves
4   cloves garlic

½   cup pine nuts or walnuts
¾   cup fresh basil
¾   cup fresh parsley leaves
¾   cup grated Parmesan cheese

Place ½ cup olive oil with ¼ cup basil and ¼ cup parsley and the garlic in the container of a blender. Blend until pureed, then add the rest of the basil, parsley, nuts and Parmesan cheese. Add remaining olive oil slowly. Blend until smooth.

Yield: 1¾ cups

The remainder of the pesto will keep in a covered container in the refrigerator for several days or can be frozen for a longer time. I first ate it in Nice with minestrone soup. It can also be added to potatoes when making twice-baked potatoes.

Red Wine Vinaigrette

When using red wine, always use a wine you would drink.

⅓   cup olive oil
2   tablespoons red wine vinegar
1   tablespoon red wine
½   teaspoon Dijon mustard

½   teaspoon salt
⅛   teaspoon freshly ground
     pepper

Whisk all ingredients in small bowl or shake in a jar with tight-fitting lid until blended. Whisk again before serving.

Yield: ½ cup

Walnut Oil Dressing

This is enough dressing for 1 pound mixed salad greens.

½   cup walnuts, toasted and
     broken up
3   tablespoons walnut oil or fruity
     olive oil
2   tablespoons fresh lemon juice

1   teaspoon honey
¼   teaspoon salt
⅛   teaspoon freshly ground
     pepper

With a wire whisk, mix oil, lemon juice, honey, salt and pepper in a bowl. Place greens and walnuts in serving bowl and pour dressing over, tossing to mix well.

Yield: ½ cup

Sauces

Bryan and Holly Graves

Alfredo Sauce — Low Calorie

2   cups low fat cottage cheese
3   tablespoons grated Parmesan
     cheese
2   tablespoons butter-flavored
     granules
½   cup evaporated skim milk

½   teaspoon chicken flavored
     granules
½   teaspoon dried basil
¼   teaspoon black pepper
Dash red pepper

Combine all ingredients in blender container; process until smooth, stopping to scrape down sides with rubber spatula. Pour into a small saucepan. Cook over low heat, stirring constantly, until thoroughly heated. Serve over pasta.

Yield: 2¾ cups

Black-eyed Pea Salsa Olé

1   (16 ounce) can black-eyed
     peas, drained
2   tomatoes, chopped
1   bunch green onions, chopped
1   tablespoon chopped parsley
3   tablespoons fresh lime juice

1   tablespoon olive oil
1 to 2 cloves garlic, minced
½   teaspoon ground cumin
     or to taste
¼   teaspoon salt
Leaf lettuce

Place black-eyed peas in a colander; rinse with cold water and drain. Combine tomatoes and next 7 ingredients in a medium bowl; stir in peas. Cover and refrigerate at least 4 hours or overnight. Place in a lettuce-lined bowl. Serve with tortilla chips.

Yield: 2½ cups

Helpful Hint: *Swish a lettuce leaf over the surface of sauces or soup to remove excess grease.*

Cream Cheese Sauce

This is a rich, versatile sauce. It can be used as is with shrimp, crabmeat or chicken. It is in my first cookbook under Spinach Lasagna. This sauce freezes well.

1⅓ sticks butter or margarine	6 to 8 ounces cream cheese, room
½ cup plus 1 tablespoon flour	temperature
4 cups whole milk	Salt to taste

Cream the butter and flour together in a small bowl.

This is beurre manié or kneaded butter. It is the easiest way I know of to make cream sauce in quantity. Heat milk in top of a double boiler over hot water. Gradually add pieces of the beurre manié to the hot milk, stirring constantly with a wire whisk until thickened and smooth. Remove from hot water and add the cream cheese in pieces, whisking again until smooth. Add salt and pepper to taste.

Yield: About 5 cups

Irene, a friend of mine, uses her imagination by adding water chestnuts, fresh mushrooms, a touch of garlic, white wine or vermouth, pimientos, etc. Improvise however you wish.

Mango Chutney

This is delicious served over Brie cheese.

1½ cups cider vinegar	1 tablespoon lemon juice
1¼ cups sugar	1 teaspoon minced fresh ginger
1¼ cups firmly packed dark brown	1 teaspoon ground cinnamon
sugar	1 teaspoon salt
3 cups peeled and coarsely	1 teaspoon mustard seed
chopped mango or peaches	½ teaspoon minced garlic
½ cup white raisins	¼ teaspoon ground red pepper

Bring sugars and vinegar to boil in 5-quart saucepan over high heat. Reduce heat to medium-low and add remaining ingredients. Simmer until mixture thickens slightly, 20 to 25 minutes. Cool; chutney will continue to thicken. Store in sterilized jars in the refrigerator.

Yield: 4½ cups

Marinara Sauce

¼ cup chopped onion
1 clove garlic
½ tablespoon olive oil
2 (14½ ounce) cans diced tomatoes

1 tablespoon lemon juice
1½ tablespoons dried Italian seasoning
1 bay leaf

Cook onion and garlic in olive oil in a Dutch oven or heavy skillet over medium heat, stirring, until tender. Add tomatoes and remaining ingredients. Bring to a boil; reduce heat to medium-low and cook, stirring occasionally, 20 minutes or until most of the liquid has evaporated. Remove and discard bay leaf.

Yield: 2½ cups

Salsa Fria

1 cup finely chopped onion
1 clove garlic, crushed
1 tablespoon olive oil
1 pound tomatoes, peeled and chopped
1 teaspoon sugar

2 or 3 large canned green chilies or jalapeños, finely chopped
Chili powder to taste
½ teaspoon oregano
Dash garlic salt

Sauté onion and garlic in oil until tender, but not brown. Add remaining ingredients. Bring to a boil and simmer gently about 15 minutes, stirring frequently. Serve hot or cold. This sauce can be incorporated in many dishes; is also tasty served on top of eggs.

Yield: 2 cups

Teriyaki Sauce

½ cup unsweetened pineapple juice
¼ cup soy sauce
2 tablespoons brown sugar

2 teaspoons cornstarch
¾ teaspoon ground ginger
1 clove garlic, minced

Combine ingredients in a saucepan. Bring to a boil; reduce heat, and cook 1 minute, stirring constantly, until thickened. Serve over chicken or fish.

Yield: ¾ cup

Vegetable Sauce

1	tablespoon cornstarch	¼	teaspoon salt
1	cup cold milk	⅛	teaspoon pepper
2	tablespoons butter or margarine		

Mix cornstarch and milk in heavy saucepan. Cook over medium heat, stirring constantly, until smooth. Add butter or margarine, salt and pepper. Serve over vegetables.

Yield: 1 cup

Sauce can be varied by adding chopped onions or garlic or herbs of your choice or Dijon mustard.

White Cream Sauce

2	tablespoons butter or margarine	¼	teaspoon salt
2	tablespoons flour	1	cup milk

Melt butter in saucepan over low heat. Blend in flour, salt, and dash of white pepper. Remove from heat. Add milk all at once and stir. Return to heat and cook quickly, stirring constantly, until mixture thickens and bubbles. Remove sauce from heat, then you may add ½ cup shredded Cheddar cheese or stir in ¼ cup dairy sour cream and ¼ cup crumbled Bleu cheese. This makes a medium cream sauce.

Yield: 1 cup

A thick sauce needs 3 tablespoons butter, 4 tablespoons flour and 1 cup milk. A thin sauce needs 1 tablespoon flour, 1 tablespoon butter and 1½ cups milk. Use a thick sauce for soufflés and croquettes, a thin sauce for soups or vegetables.

Chambord Melba Sauce

Place fresh, poached or frozen peaches in tall stemmed glasses, add vanilla ice cream and top with this sauce.

1	(10 ounce) package frozen raspberries	1	teaspoon cornstarch
½	cup currant jelly	⅓	cup Chambord liqueur
¼	cup sugar	½	teaspoon fresh lemon juice

Combine the raspberries, currant jelly, sugar and cornstarch in a saucepan. Stir over moderate heat until boiling. Then simmer gently for 10 minutes. Remove from heat and add the Chambord and lemon juice. Strain and chill before serving.

Chocolate Peanut Butter Sauce

This is delicious over ice cream or cake.

¾	cup chocolate sauce	¼	cup white corn syrup or enough to thin to sauce consistency
¼	cup crunchy peanut butter		

Mix all ingredients together and place in a jar. Cover and keep in the refrigerator.

Yield: 6 servings

Kahlúa Liqueur Custard Sauce

2	cups light cream	2	tablespoons instant espresso
2	large eggs		powder
¼	cup sugar	2	tablespoons Kahlúa

In a heavy saucepan, bring cream to a boil and remove pan from heat. Whisk the eggs and sugar in a bowl until mixture is combined well. Slowly add the scalded cream, whisking, and whisk in the espresso powder. Cook the mixture over moderately low heat, stirring constantly, with a wooden spoon, until it thickens, but do not let it boil. Remove pan from the heat and stir in Kahlúa. Strain the sauce through a sieve into a metal bowl set in a larger bowl with ice and cold water. Let it cool, stirring, then chill it, covered, at least 1 hour. Sauce will keep, covered, in the refrigerator for 2 days.

Yield: About 2 cups

Super Eggnog Sauce

This is a delicious sauce to serve over cake à la mode.

4	egg yolks, freeze whites for later use	1	cup half-and-half
		1	tablespoon dark rum
⅓	cup sugar		Dash nutmeg

Beat egg yolks with the sugar until thick. Add half and half and cook, stirring, in a double boiler until thick. Remove from heat, cool slightly, then add rum and nutmeg. Chill and serve.

Yield: 1 cup

Soups

Charles, Meagan and Emily Graves

Beef Soup with Little Dumplings

This is a Hungarian soup and can be served with or without the dumplings. It makes a full meal.

Soup:

2   tablespoons shortening
2½ pounds chuck, cut into
      1″ cubes
2   cups coarsely chopped onions
1½ teaspoons minced garlic
⅛   teaspoon caraway seeds
1   tablespoon salt
2   tablespoons sweet Hungarian
      paprika
2   quarts hot water

1   pound potatoes, peeled and
      cut into 1″ dice (3 cups)
1   green pepper, halved,
      deribbed and cut crosswise
      into ¼″ strips
2   medium-sized firm tomatoes,
      peeled and cut into 1″ pieces
6 to 7 medium carrots, scraped
      and sliced crosswise into thin
      rounds (2 cups)

In a heavy 4-quart casserole, melt shortening over moderate heat. Drop in the chuck cubes and brown on all sides. Stir in the onions and garlic and cook until onions are light brown, stirring constantly. Remove from heat. Wrap the caraway seeds and salt in a kitchen towel and crush them with a rolling pin, then add to casserole along with the paprika. Pour in enough hot water to cover meat 4″. Bring to a boil, then cover and simmer for 1½ hours. Add potatoes, green pepper, tomatoes and carrots and cook for 30 minutes longer. Taste for seasoning.

Little Dumplings:

2   eggs
½   cup flour

⅛   teaspoon salt

Just before serving the soup, prepare the dumplings. In a mixing bowl, combine eggs, flour and the salt. Beat together with a whisk until batter is smooth. Using a teaspoon, slide the batter into the simmering soup, a spoonful at a time. Simmer the dumplings for 2 or 3 minutes or until they rise to the surface. Serve the soup directly from the casserole or a large heated tureen.

Yield: 6 to 8 servings

As with other soups or stews, the flavor improves if made the day ahead. However, do not prepare the dumplings until soup is reheated.

Helpful Hint: 1 pound sliced or diced potatoes — 3½ to 4 cups.

Broccoli-Chicken Soup

I usually like to "cook from scratch", but this recipe was too easy to pass up.

¾   cup water
1   (10 ounce) package frozen
     chopped broccoli
1   (10¼ ounce) can cream of
     chicken soup

½   cup milk
⅛   teaspoon red pepper
½   cup grated Parmesan cheese

Bring water to a boil in a large saucepan; add broccoli. Cover, reduce heat and simmer until broccoli is tender. Add soup, red pepper and milk. Cook over medium heat, stirring constantly, until heated. Top each serving with Parmesan cheese. Taste for seasoning.

Yield: 1 quart

Cauliflower-Cheddar Soup

One of my granddaughters loves cauliflower. This is for her.

½   cup thinly sliced white part of
      green onions
1   tablespoon unsalted butter
1½ cups cauliflower flowerets
1½ cups chicken broth, homemade
      or canned

1   cup grated extra-sharp
      Cheddar cheese
2   tablespoons sliced white part
      of green onions for garnish

In a large heavy saucepan, cook onion in the butter over low heat, stirring, until it is softened. Add the cauliflower and the broth, bring the liquid to a boil and then simmer the mixture, covered, for 12 to 15 minutes or until cauliflower is tender. Add the Cheddar cheese, salt and pepper to taste. Cook the mixture, stirring, until the Cheddar cheese is melted, then puree the mixture in batches in a blender. Return soup to pan and heat over moderate heat, stirring, until it is piping hot.

Yield: 2 servings

Helpful Hint: *If you want to keep a large cut piece of cheese from molding,*
                   dip the cut end surface in melted paraffin.

Chicken and Sausage Gumbo

1	(3 pound) fryer cut in pieces	¼	cup flour
1	pound smoked sausage, cut into ¼" slices	1	quart chicken broth or 1 quart water and 3 chicken-flavored bouillon cubes
½	cup bacon drippings		
1	large onion, chopped	½	teaspoon salt
1	clove garlic, minced	½	teaspoon pepper
1	bunch green onions, sliced		Dash hot sauce
1	medium green pepper, chopped		Hot cooked rice

Brown the chicken and sausage in hot bacon drippings in a heavy casserole or Dutch oven. Drain well, reserving drippings. Sauté onion, garlic and green pepper in drippings until tender; drain well, reserving 2 tablespoons drippings. Add flour to drippings; cook over medium heat, stirring constantly, until roux is fairly brown. Gradually add broth to roux, stirring until well blended. Add salt and pepper, chicken, sausage, onion, and green pepper; cover and simmer 1 hour. Add hot sauce and taste for seasoning. Serve over rice.

Yield: 2½ quarts

I prefer to remove chicken from bones in fairly large pieces rather than having to struggle with bones when eating the gumbo. However, original recipe did not state this.

Chilled Pepper Soup

If you wish to make a dramatic presentation, serve this soup in hollowed out yellow peppers, garnished with chopped chives.

½	cup butter or margarine	1½	cups chicken broth
3	large sweet red peppers, sliced	3	cups buttermilk
1	cup chopped green onions	⅛	teaspoon white pepper

Melt butter in large saucepan. Add red pepper, onions and broth; bring to a boil. Cover, reduce heat and simmer, stirring occasionally, 30 minutes or until vegetables are tender. Pour mixture into container of blender or food processor and process until smooth, scraping down sides with spatula at least once. Pour through wire-mesh strainer into a large bowl to remove any lumps. You should have 3 cups liquid; stir in buttermilk and white pepper. Taste for seasoning and add salt, if necessary. Cover and chill at least 2 hours before serving.

Yield: 6 cups

Cold Cream of Squash Soup

A delicious addition to a summer luncheon or dinner.

2 tablespoons butter	6 cups chicken broth
¼ cup finely chopped onion	¼ cup fresh dillweed,
1 carrot, finely chopped	or ¼ teaspoon of dried
1 stalk celery, finely chopped	1 teaspoon salt
1½ pounds yellow squash, seeded and cut into ½" dice (3½ cups)	5 ounce can evaporated milk
1 medium potato, peeled and cut into ½" dice, (1 cup)	Whipped cream and slivered almonds for garnish

Melt butter in heavy 3- to 4-quart casserole over moderate heat. Stir in onion, carrot and celery. Cook over low heat until vegetables are soft; but not brown. Stir in squash and potato. Add chicken stock and bring to a boil, then reduce heat and simmer, partially covered, about 20 minutes or until squash and potato are tender. Strain contents through a sieve over a bowl, saving liquid. Puree vegetables in a food processor or blender. Add the puree to soup liquid and let cool to room temperature. Stir in dill, salt and evaporated milk. Taste for seasoning. Cover bowl with plastic wrap and refrigerate overnight or at least 2 hours until thoroughly chilled. Garnish with whipped cream and slivered almonds, if desired.

Yield: Serves 4 to 6

Cold Cream of Zucchini Soup

1 large onion, chopped	2 cups buttermilk, divided
3 tablespoons butter or margarine, melted	1 cup fresh parsley or cilantro, chopped and divided
3 pounds of zucchini, washed in salt water, then chopped	3 tablespoons lemon juice
	½ teaspoon salt
1 (14½ ounce) can chicken broth or equivalent of homemade	¼ teaspoon pepper

Cook onion in butter in a 3-quart saucepan over medium heat, stirring constantly, until tender; add zucchini and chicken broth. Bring to a boil; reduce heat and cook 15 to 20 minutes. Remove from heat; cool. Combine half of zucchini mixture, ½ cup buttermilk and ½ cup parsley in blender or food processor; process until smooth, stopping once to scrape down sides. Pour into a large bowl. Repeat process with remaining zucchini mixture, ½ cup buttermilk and parsley. Add to bowl and stir in remaining 1 cup buttermilk, lemon juice, salt and pepper. Taste for seasoning. Chill at least 8 hours. Garnish with parsley sprigs, if desired.

Yield: 8 cups

Cream of Brie Soup

This is a very rich soup so you will probably want to serve small servings as a first course. I usually serve an intermezzo between it and the entrée.

½	cup peeled and chopped onion	¾	pound Brie cheese, cubed,
½	cup thinly sliced celery		rind removed
4	tablespoons butter		Salt and pepper to taste
¼	cup flour		Chopped chives for garnish
2	cups whole milk		(optional)
2	cups chicken broth		

Place the butter in a 3-quart kettle. Over low heat, sauté the onion and the celery in the butter until limp. Stir in the flour. Remove from heat and add chicken broth and milk, using a wire whisk to mix well. Return to heat and simmer, stirring constantly, until soup thickens. Add the cheese. Stir until melted, then place in a food processor or blender and process until very smooth. Correct seasoning with salt and pepper. Serve very hot with a garnish of chives, if desired.

Yield: 6 servings

Lemon, raspberry or any tart sherbet in liqueur glasses is a good intermezzo. If I have homemade lemon sherbet, I scrape out the lemon rinds and serve the sherbet in them, no dishes to wash.

Cream of Carrot Soup

This is a pretty as well as nutritious soup. The calories can be lowered by using undiluted evaporated milk or even evaporated skimmed milk instead of the whipping cream.

2	tablespoons butter	2	tablespoons raw rice
¾	cup finely chopped onion		Salt
3	cups finely chopped carrots		White pepper
1	quart chicken stock,	½	cup whipping cream
	homemade or canned	1	tablespoon soft butter
2	teaspoons tomato paste		

Melt the butter in a heavy skillet or saucepan. Add the onions and cook over medium to low heat, stirring, until limp but not browned. Add carrots, chicken stock, tomato paste and rice. Lower heat to simmer and cook, uncovered, 30 minutes. Puree soup in a blender then put into another saucepan. Add the cream, then season with salt and pepper to taste. To serve: heat soup on low heat until it is simmering. Remove from heat and add remaining tablespoon butter. Ladle from a tureen at the table or into individual soup bowls.

Yield: 4 to 6 servings

Cream of Peanut Soup

We spent Easter one year in Williamsburg, Virginia. A version of this delicious soup was served to us at the Williamsburg Inn.

½   cup butter or margarine
4   celery stalks, chopped
1   large onion, chopped
¼   cup flour
2   (14½ ounce) cans chicken
    broth or homemade broth

1½ cups creamy peanut butter
¼   teaspoon pepper
½   teaspoon paprika
¼   teaspoon salt
2   cups whole milk
2   cups half-and-half

Melt butter in large saucepan; add celery and onion and cook over low heat, stirring constantly, until tender. Add flour, stirring until smooth; cook 1 minute, stirring constantly. Gradually add chicken broth; cook over low heat 30 minutes, stirring occasionally. Remove from heat; pour mixture through mesh strainer into a bowl discarding vegetables. Return to saucepan; stir in peanut butter and next 3 ingredients. Gradually add milk and half-and-half, stirring constantly; cook over low heat 5 minutes or until heated but do not boil. Taste for seasoning, then serve.

Yield: 7 cups

Cream of Spinach Soup

¼   cup boiling water
2   (10 ounce) packages frozen
    chopped spinach, thawed and
    drained
¼   cup minced onion
5   tablespoons butter or
    margarine

5   tablespoons flour
5   cups whole milk
1   teaspoon salt or to taste
Dash pepper
Monterey Jack cheese

Add boiling water to spinach and let stand until spinach is heated through, then puree in blender. Brown onion in butter and stir in flour. Cook until bubbly; add the milk, stirring rapidly, until thickened. Add spinach, salt and dash pepper. Ladle into cream soup dishes or bowls. When serving, put a teaspoon of coarsely grated Monterey Jack cheese on top.

Yield: 6 servings

Creamed Scallop Soup

A very rich but delicious soup.

2	tablespoons finely minced onion	4	tablespoons flour
1	quart diced fresh scallops, washed to remove sand	4	cups whole milk
			Salt and pepper
½	cup butter	1	cup heavy cream
			Slivered blanched almonds

Over medium heat, brown onion and scallops in butter, stirring so that scallops are evenly browned. Add flour and cook, stirring, until well blended. Remove from heat and add milk, then cook over low heat until thickened. Season with salt and pepper to taste. Add the cream just before serving, then reheat until very hot. Garnish with the slivered almonds.

Yield: 8 servings

Fresh Tomato Soup

This is another great summer soup. It was served to me as a first course at a luncheon given for my birthday, accompanied with crackers and Brie.

1	cup minced onion	2	tablespoons cornstarch
2	cloves garlic, minced	½	cup heavy cream
2	tablespoons butter or margarine	¼	cup snipped fresh dill or 1 teaspoon dried
2	pounds fresh tomatoes, peeled, seeded and chopped		Salt and pepper to taste
3¼	cups chicken broth, divided	1	large or 2 small tomatoes, peeled, seeded and chopped for garnish
2	tablespoons tomato paste		

In a large heavy stockpot or Dutch oven, sauté onion and garlic in butter until onion is soft but not brown. Add tomatoes and 1 cup of broth. Simmer 20 minutes, then place in a blender and puree. Return to stockpot, add 2 more cups of broth, tomato paste and cornstarch dissolved in ¼ cup broth. Bring to a boil, stirring constantly, then reduce heat and simmer, stirring occasionally, until thickened. Chill overnight. Just before serving, add cream, dill, chopped tomatoes and seasoning.

Yield: 6 to 8 servings

Shrimp Bisque

3	tablespoons butter	4	cups half-and-half
3	tablespoons finely minced onion	1	cup whole milk
		1	teaspoon salt
2	cups chopped raw shrimp		Dash white pepper
3	tablespoons flour	⅓	cup dry sherry

Melt the butter in a heavy saucepan; add the onion and sauté until soft but not brown. Add the shrimp and cook at low heat until shrimp are opaque. Remove the shrimp; add the flour and cook until bubbly. Add half-and-half and milk and cook until thickened. Return the shrimp, add salt and pepper then taste for seasoning. Let stand over hot water until ready to serve. Heat the sherry and float on top. It will mix in as it is served.

Yield: 6 to 8 servings

Shrimp and Green Chilie Soup

5	cups chicken broth	2	tablespoons butter or margarine
4	ounces tortilla chips (3 cups)		
1	pound fresh shrimp, peeled and deveined	1	medium onion, chopped
		2	cloves garlic, minced
2	(4.5 ounce) cans chopped green chilies	1	cup sour cream
		¼	cup cilantro or parsley
1	(10 ounce) can diced tomatoes		Shredded Monterey Jack cheese
			Shredded Cheddar cheese

Bring chicken broth to a boil in a large stockpot or Dutch oven. Add tortilla chips. Remove from heat and let stand 10 minutes. Coarsely chop shrimp and set aside. In food processor with knife blade in position, process half of broth mixture until smooth, stopping once to scrape down sides. Transfer mixture to another container. Repeat with remaining broth mixture. Return broth mixture to stockpot or Dutch oven and add green chilies and tomatoes. Melt butter in a large skillet over medium heat. Add shrimp, onion, and garlic; cook, stirring constantly, 2 or 3 minutes or until shrimp turn pink. Stir shrimp mixture into broth mixture and heat but do not boil. Stir in sour cream and cilantro and serve immediately. Sprinkle each serving with the Monterey Jack and Cheddar cheese.

Yield: 10 cups

Sour Grass Soup

This soup comes from Finland. Do not let the sauerkraut faze you. It is a delicious soup, especially in cold weather. Cold applesauce is sometimes served on the side. It is a pleasing contrast to the smoky flavor of the meat and sharpness of the kraut.

10	cups water	2	large potatoes, peeled and
1½	to 2 pounds smoked pork,		diced
	shredded or chopped	2	tablespoons chopped parsley
½	cup barley	1	(16 ounce) can sauerkraut,
3	carrots, peeled and sliced		drained
3	stalks celery, sliced		Salt and pepper
			Sour cream for garnish, if desired

Bring water to a boil in Dutch oven or large pot. Add smoked pork and barley. Simmer, uncovered, about 25 to 30 minutes. Add carrots, celery, potatoes and parsley. Return to a boil, then simmer 15 to 20 minutes longer. Add sauerkraut and cook just until heated through. Season to taste with salt and pepper. Serve topped with sour cream, if desired.

Yield: 6 servings

Stracciatella

This comes under the heading of healthful soups. For a bit of drama, present shallow soup bowls with spinach chiffonade at the table, then ladle the steamy broth into each bowl — a lovely way to begin a meal!

12	ounces fresh spinach leaves,	3	teaspoons fresh lemon juice
	trimmed, well rinsed and dried	6	cups chicken stock or canned
¾	cup grated Parmesan cheese,		broth
	freshly grated preferred		Salt to taste
	freshly ground black pepper,		Freshly grated Parmesan cheese
	to taste		for garnish
3	eggs		

Cut the spinach into chiffonade (very thin strips).

Divide it between the 6 soup bowls, and sprinkle with the Parmesan cheese and a grating of pepper. In a small bowl, beat the eggs and lemon juice together. Heat the chicken stock just to a boil, then remove it from the heat. Stir in the egg mixture, beating constantly, until broth is ribbony and slightly thickened. Add salt if needed. Ladle over spinach, and stir just until wilted. Serve with additional grated cheese.

Yield: 6 portions

This recipe may be increased or cut down to 2 or 4 portions.

Tomato Vegetable Soup

5	large carrots, grated	½	teaspoon soda
5	small onions, sliced	1	quart hot whole milk
5	tablespoons butter	½	cup warm half-and-half
¼	cup raw Uncle Ben's rice	Salt and freshly ground pepper
1	quart canned tomatoes, pureed		to taste

Over low heat, steam carrots and onions in butter, covered, until tender. Steam rice and add to vegetables along with tomatoes and soda. Add milk and half-and-half. Heat, but do not boil. Season with salt and pepper and serve.

Yield: 8 to 10 servings

White Bean Soup

This is similar to the classic minestrone soup, except with ham instead of beef.

1	cup dry beans (Great Northern, navy or white kidney)	¼	cup finely chopped celery
		½	teaspoon minced garlic
2 to 2½ quarts water		1½	teaspoons salt
2	tablespoons olive oil	Black pepper
½	pound cooked ham (about 2 cups cut up)	½	cup (1″ pieces) spaghetti
		Freshly grated Parmesan cheese
½	cup finely chopped onions		

In a 4-quart saucepan, bring the beans and 2 quarts water to a boil over high heat and boil them for 3 minutes. Remove from heat and let beans soak, covered, for 1 hour. Then drain the beans, saving liquid. Add enough water to make 2 quarts. Chop together the ham, onions, celery and garlic into very small pieces. This mixture is called batutto. Heat the olive oil in a large pot and stir in the batutto. Cook, stirring frequently, for 10 minutes or until it is lightly browned. Add the beans, liquid, and season with salt and pepper. Bring to a boil, then reduce heat and simmer, partially covered, for 1 to 1½ hours or until beans are tender. With a slotted spoon, remove about half the beans from the soup and puree them in a blender, then return them to the soup. Simmer over low heat, stirring constantly, for 2 minutes. Add the spaghetti and simmer 10 to 15 minutes, or until it is tender. Taste for seasoning, then ladle into soup bowls and sprinkle with the Parmesan cheese.

Yield: 4 to 6 servings

Helpful Hint: *1 pound kidney, navy or lima dried beans — 2½ cups.*

Vegetables

Ashley and Andrew Gray

Apple-Carrot Casserole

This is a not too sweet and colorful casserole. Pretty any time, but especially on a buffet table.

1	pound carrots, cut diagonally	4	medium cooking apples, peeled, cored and cut into ¼" slices
½	teaspoon salt		
½	cup water		
¼	cup sugar	¼	cup butter or margarine, thinly sliced, divided
2	tablespoons flour		
		¼	cup frozen orange juice mixed with ½ cup water

Mix flour and sugar together in a small bowl. Set aside. Combine carrots, salt and water in small saucepan. Cover and bring to a boil; reduce heat and simmer just until crisp-tender. Drain and set aside. Layer half of carrots, then half of apples in a lightly greased shallow 2-quart baking dish. (I use a 10"x 6"x 2" Pyrex dish). Sprinkle with half the flour mixture and dot with half the butter. Repeat layers. Drizzle with orange juice. Bake at 350° for about 35 minutes or until apples are tender, gently pressing apples down into syrup midway of cooking.

Yield: 8 servings

Asparagus Supreme

I like to use the young asparagus, if available, for this dish.

3	pounds fresh asparagus	¼	cup plus 2 tablespoons grated Parmesan cheese
¼	cup plus 2 tablespoons butter or margarine, melted		Paprika
¼	cup plus 2 tablespoons lemon juice		Lemon slices for garnish (optional)

Snap off tough ends of asparagus; Cook asparagus, covered, in a shallow skillet or pan in a small amount of water about 6 to 8 minutes or until crisp-tender. Drain. Arrange asparagus in a 12"x 8"x 2"baking dish. Combine butter and lemon juice and pour over asparagus. Sprinkle cheese and paprika over and place in 350° oven until hot. Garnish with thin lemon slices, if desired.

Yield: 12 servings

Asparagus-Tomato Stir-Fry

The traditional stir-fry utensil is a wok, its sloping sides and round bottom provide a large cooking surface. Since the bottom gets hot but the sides stay cool, foods that need no further cooking can be pushed up the sides.

1	pound fresh asparagus	4	green onions, bias-sliced into
1	tablespoon cold water		1" lengths
1	teaspoon cornstarch	1½	cups sliced fresh mushrooms
2	teaspoons soy sauce	2	small tomatoes, cut in thin
¼	teaspoon salt		wedges
1	tablespoon cooking oil		Hot cooked rice

Snap off and discard woody stems of asparagus. Bias-slice crosswise into 1½" lengths and set aside. (If asparagus spears are not slender and young, cook cut-up pieces, uncovered, in a small amount of boiling salted water about 5 minutes; drain well). In a small bowl, combine water and cornstarch; add soy sauce and salt and set aside. Pre-heat a wok or a large heavy skillet with deep sides over high heat for a few minutes; add cooking oil and heat a minute more. Stir-fry asparagus and green onion in hot oil 4 minutes. Use a long-handled spoon to lift food with a folding motion. Add mushrooms and stir-fry 1 minute more. Stir soy mixture again. Push vegetables up the sides of the wok; add soy mixture to center of wok. Let mixture bubble slightly, then stir in vegetables. Cook and stir until mixture is thickened and bubbly. Add tomatoes and heat through. Serve at once with cooked rice, if desired.

Yield: 6 servings

If you do not have a wok, a heavy skillet works equally well. Deep-fat frying can be done in a wok too. Since the bottom is smaller than the top, less oil is needed.

Baked Carrots

I love carrots, but it was not always so. When I was a little girl whose brothers had curly hair, but mine was straight, I was told that eating carrots would make my hair curl. Carrots have the vitamin beneficial to our eyes.

1½	pounds carrots, scraped and sliced diagonally	3	tablespoons packed brown sugar
½	teaspoon salt	3	tablespoons butter or margarine

Arrange carrots in a lightly greased 1½-quart casserole. Sprinkle with salt and sugar and dot with butter. Bake, covered, at 325° for 25 to 30 minutes or until carrots are tender.

Yield: 8 servings

Broccoli with Walnuts

This recipe is made in the microwave.

1½ pounds broccoli, separated
    into ¾" flowerets, the stems
    peeled and cut crosswise into
    ¼" slices
3   tablespoon butter

2   tablespoons minced walnuts
    or pecans
1   tablespoon dry bread crumbs
1   teaspoon grated lemon rind

In a shallow microwave-safe dish, combine broccoli with 2 tablespoons water and microwave it, covered with microwave-safe plastic wrap, for 3 minutes at high power, or until it is tender. Pour off any liquid and add butter, stirring to coat broccoli. Sprinkle the bread crumbs, grated lemon rind and walnuts over broccoli. Toss mixture to combine well and microwave it, uncovered, at high power for 30 seconds or until it is heated through.

Yield: 6 servings

Brown Rice Pilaf

Brown rice is very nutritious. Packaged brown rice is already washed and is parboiled in the processing which means that it cooks perfectly every time according to simple package directions. It has a nutty flavor and a chewy texture.

2   tablespoons cooking oil
1   cup brown rice
½   cup chopped onion
1   cup sliced celery
1   cup sliced carrot
1   (10½ ounce) can beef or
    chicken broth or equivalent of
    homemade

1¼ cups water
½   teaspoon dried rosemary,
    crushed
1   teaspoon salt
1   medium zucchini, diced
½   cup grated Parmesan cheese

Heat oil in a heavy 10" skillet. Add rice and sauté over medium heat 5 minutes, stirring frequently. Add onion, celery and carrot and cook until onion is tender. Add rosemary and salt. Place in a 3-quart round or oblong casserole. Heat broth and water to boiling and pour over. Stir with a fork, then cover tightly with a cover or foil and bake at 375° for 35 minutes. Remove from oven and mix zucchini in with a fork. Recover and bake for an additional 10 to 15 minutes or until zucchini is crisp-tender and rice is done. Serve sprinkled with the grated Parmesan cheese.

Yield: 5 to 6 servings

You do not have to explain to the family that this pilaf is good for them, the flavor speaks for itself.

Bulgur Dressing, Cynthia Bishop

This is a delicious dressing, sure to be relished by young and old.

1 cup bulgur	½ teaspoon dried basil leaves, crushed
2 cups water	
2 cups bread cubes, either stale or toasted	½ cup fresh mushrooms, sliced (optional)
½ cup celery, finely minced	½ cup chicken broth
½ cup onion, finely minced	2 beaten eggs
½ cup parsley leaves, finely minced	1 teaspoon baking powder
	⅛ teaspoon black pepper
¾ cups walnuts or pecans, chopped	Salt to taste

Bring water to a boil, add the bulgur, then lower heat and cook until water is absorbed, stirring frequently. Place in a large bowl and add rest of ingredients. Spray top of double boiler with Pam. Spoon in dressing and cook over hot water about 40 minutes. Serve with meat or fowl.

Yield: 6 to 8 servings

Leftovers are delicious with the addition of cooked chicken or turkey. Also, the addition of baking powder with other types of dressing makes a fluffier product.

Butternut Squash Puree

This recipe calls for maple-flavor syrup, for 120 calories per serving. If you are interested in saving even more calories, you may use low-calorie syrup. I like to use pure maple syrup and let the calories fall where they may.

2 medium butternut squash (about 1¾ pounds each)	½ cup maple-flavor syrup
1½ teaspoons salt, divided	6 tablespoons (¾ stick) butter or margarine

Cut each squash lengthwise in half; discard seeds. Then cut each squash half crosswise in about 1″ slices; cut off peel. In a 4- or 5-quart saucepot over high heat, in 1″ boiling water, heat squash and 1 teaspoon salt to boiling. Reduce heat to low; cover and simmer 15 minutes or until squash is fork-tender, stirring occasionally. Drain. In large bowl with mixer at low speed, beat squash, syrup, butter and ½ teaspoon salt until smooth, scraping bowl often with rubber spatula; spoon into warm bowl.

Yield: 10 servings

Cabbage Custard

This recipe will be eaten with relish. I served the cabbage prepared by the recipe at the bottom of this one to a first-time guest in our home. After asking for a second helping, he remarked that he disliked cabbage. He did not realize what he was eating!

2	pounds green cabbage	1	quart whole milk
1½	teaspoons salt	¼	teaspoon pepper
6	slightly beaten large eggs		

Slice cabbage coarser than for slaw. Parboil in a small amount of boiling water for about 6 minutes or until crisp-tender (do not overcook). Drain. Spread in buttered baking dish. Prepare the custard. Combine salt, eggs and pepper in a mixing bowl. Heat milk until little bubbles form around the edges of the pan. Add to eggs slowly, beating constantly with a wire whisk. Pour custard over cabbage without completely covering it. Bake at 325° until custard is set.

Yield: 10 servings

Try serving a head of cabbage, cut into wedges not quite all the way through, parboiled until crisp tender, then placed in a casserole and generously sprinkled with grated sharp cheese. Bake in a 325° oven until the cheese is melted.

Carrot and Green Pea Casserole

This is a recipe from the Guild Shop, a former project of the Women's Association of Trinity Episcopal Church in Houston. It is from Mrs. Thomas Guthrie.

2	cups cooked carrot pulp, about 1 pound carrots	2	tablespoons melted butter
1	cup English peas (frozen peas may be used)	1	teaspoon salt
		1	teaspoon onion juice
1	cup whole milk	1	cup cornflakes
3	eggs	¼	teaspoon pepper

Cook carrots until tender. Put in processor and process until smooth. Measure 2 cups into a bowl, add salt, pepper, onion juice and melted butter. Beat eggs slightly and add to milk. Mix with carrot mixture, then fold in peas. Place in a well-buttered 1½-quart casserole. Sprinkle with crushed cornflakes and bake at 350° for about 40 minutes or until set.

Yield: 4 servings

Helpful Hint: *½ pound cabbage, shredded — 4 cups.*

Butternut Squash Stir-Fry

This is another pretty casserole with several vegetables.

2	tablespoons vegetable oil	½	small onion, thinly sliced and
1	teaspoon olive oil		separated into rings
1	small butternut squash	1	clove garlic, minced
	(about 1 pound) peeled,	⅛	teaspoon ground ginger
	seeded and cut into ¼″ slices	1	tablespoon lemon juice
1	cup sliced celery	2	teaspoons honey
1	cup broccoli flowerets		

Heat oils in a large skillet; add squash and next 5 ingredients and stir-fry 5 minutes. Cover and cook 5 more minutes or until crisp-tender. Combine lemon juice and honey; pour over vegetables, tossing to coat. Serve immediately.

Yield: 4 cups

Easy Carrot-Sweet Potato Puree

If you cannot get the sweet potatoes in light syrup, use only 2 tablespoons brown sugar.

3	cups thinly sliced carrots	2	tablespoons fresh orange juice
1	(16 ounce) can sweet potatoes	½	teaspoon ground cinnamon
	in light syrup	⅛	teaspoon salt
¼	cup firmly packed brown sugar	¼	teaspoon vanilla

Cook carrots in boiling water for 15 minutes or until very tender; drain. Position knife blade in food processor bowl; add all ingredients. Process until smooth, stopping to scrape down sides. Serve immediately or put in casserole, cover, and place in a warm oven.

Yield: 6 servings

Green Beans with Dill

The garlic is skinned, but left whole, so do not be afraid of the amount.

3	pounds fresh young green	4	cloves garlic
	beans	1	tablespoon dried dillweed
1½	cups water	½	teaspoon salt
3	tablespoons olive oil	¼	teaspoon pepper

Wash beans, remove strings and ends,. Bring water to a boil in saucepan; add beans. Cover, reduce heat to medium and cook 10 minutes or until crisp-tender. Drain; plunge into ice water to stop cooking, then drain again. Heat olive oil in a wok or 2 large skillets; add garlic and cook, stirring constantly, until lightly browned. Remove garlic; add green beans and cook until heated. Add dillweed, salt, and pepper, tossing well. Heat and serve immediately.

Yield: 12 servings

Easy Scalloped Potatoes

I make this recipe often. It takes the minimum of preparation.

4	medium potatoes (about 2 pounds) scrubbed and cut into ⅛" slices (I leave the skins on but you may peel, if you prefer)	1	cup grated Cheddar cheese (sharp cheese is extra good)
		¼	teaspoon dry mustard
		1½	cups whole milk
		1	tablespoon flour
¼	cup finely minced onion	1	teaspoon salt
		¼	teaspoon black pepper

Place sliced potatoes in a buttered 8"x 11"x 2"baking dish. Cover tightly with foil, crimping edges well. This steams the potatoes. Bake at 400° for 20 minutes. Mix remaining ingredients, except cheese, in a bowl. Remove potatoes from oven, uncover, and pour milk mixture over. Sprinkle with grated cheese. Bake, uncovered, for another 20 minutes or until lightly browned and bubbly.

Yield: 6 servings

Grits Dressing

This is a dressing, not a stuffing, and is baked in a casserole dish.

3	cups regular grits, uncooked	1	cup chopped celery
1	cup flour	2	teaspoons poultry seasoning
1	teaspoon baking powder	1	teaspoon baking powder
½	teaspoon salt	2	large eggs, beaten
¼	teaspoon baking soda	1	(12 ounce) can evaporated milk
2	large eggs		
4	cups buttermilk	2	(14½ ounce) cans chicken broth or equivalent of homemade
2	tablespoons oil		
1	large onion, chopped		

Heat a well-greased 10" cast iron skillet in a 325° oven for 5 minutes or until hot. Combine grits, flour, baking powder, salt and soda in a large bowl; make a well in the center. Mix 2 eggs, buttermilk and vegetable oil and add to mixture, stirring just until moistened. Remove skillet from oven and pour in batter. Bake in 325° oven for 1 hour or until firm in center, but not browned. Cool and crumble. Combine crumbled bread, onion and remaining ingredients; pour into a greased 13"x 9"x 2"baking dish. Bake at 325° for 50 minutes or until firm. Serve piping hot with fowl of your choice.

Yield: 10 servings

Cynthia Bishop, a dear friend of mine, always adds baking powder to her stuffing. It makes them much lighter.

Green Beans with Herbs

Green beans seem to be the most liked vegetable next to potatoes.

2	pounds fresh green beans	½	teaspoon salt
1	small onion, sliced	½	teaspoon pepper
1	clove garlic, minced	¼	teaspoon dried whole
1	tablespoon olive oil		tarragon, crushed
¾	cup water		

Wash beans and remove strings. If young, leave whole; if large, cut diagonally in fourths or halves. Sauté onion and garlic in olive oil in a heavy saucepot or Dutch oven. Add beans and remaining ingredients. Bring to a boil; cover, reduce heat and simmer 20 minutes or until tender. Add additional water, if necessary.

Yield: 10 to 12 servings

If fresh beans are not available, canned ones can be used. However, open the canned ones at least an hour before you are using them. An official with the American Can Company gave me this hint. Letting the beans breathe removes some of the canned taste.

Green Beans with Lemon

⅓	cup chopped walnuts	1	tablespoon fresh rosemary
2	pounds fresh green beans		or ½ teaspoon dried
¼	teaspoon salt	1	tablespoon lemon juice
3	tablespoons butter or	2	teaspoons grated lemon rind
	margarine		

Spread walnuts on an ungreased baking sheet; bake at 300° for 10 minutes, stirring frequently. Set aside. Wash beans and remove ends. Cut in half and sprinkle with salt. Place in saucepan with a little water and steam until crisp-tender. Drain and set aside. Melt butter in a large skillet over medium heat; add green beans, walnuts, rosemary and lemon juice; cook until thoroughly heated, stirring constantly. Sprinkle with lemon rind. Serve immediately.

Yield: 8 servings

Helpful Hint: 1 pound green snap beans — 3 cups.

Lemon Herb Potatoes

This is a low calorie dish as skimmed milk is used and just a small amount of margarine. Potatoes are essential to our diet because of their calcium. However, whole milk or half-and-half may be used if you do not have to count calories.

6	(5 or 6 ounce) baking potatoes	1	teaspoon freshly grated lemon peel
⅓	cup chopped onion		
1	clove garlic, minced	⅛	teaspoon white pepper
2	tablespoons margarine	1	tablespoon fresh dill
½	cup skimmed or whole milk, warmed		or ½ teaspoon dried dill
		2	tablespoon chopped parsley

Bake potatoes. Cut off tops and scoop out insides into a bowl. Sauté onion and garlic in margarine until limp, but not brown. Add to potato along with the milk, lemon peel and pepper. Add salt to taste. Then add dill and parsley. Pile into potato skins. Sprinkle with paprika and bake at 350° until hot.

Yield: 6 servings

Mashed Potatoes with Pesto

I first ate pesto in Nice many years ago. It was served with minestrone soup. I have loved it ever since.

Pesto:

½	cup firm-packed fresh basil leaves	¼	cup (1 ounce) grated Parmesan cheese
¼	cup olive oil	1	small garlic clove

Process all ingredients to a smooth paste in a food processor; Set aside. (Can cover and refrigerate).

Potatoes:

6	baking potatoes, (2½ pounds) peeled and cut into large dice	1	tablespoon salt
6	tablespoons butter	4	quarts water
½	cup sour cream	½	teaspoon ground white pepper

Bring the 4 quarts of water to a boil in a large soup kettle; add the salt and potatoes. Boil until potatoes are tender, 15 to 20 minutes ; drain. Immediately transfer potatoes to a large bowl and mash until smooth. Place bowl over a saucepan of simmering water. Stir in butter and sour cream and pesto; season with salt and white pepper to taste. Place in serving dish.

Yield: 6 servings

Leftover Mashed Potatoes with Pesto can be made into croquettes. Mix the potatoes with one beaten egg; shape into patties. Dredge in flour or bread crumbs and pan-fry until golden.

Potato Cheese Casserole

This is rich, but very good!

3   pounds potatoes, peeled and quartered
½   cup (1 stick) butter
2   (3 ounce) packages cream cheese, softened
1   cup (4 ounces) grated Cheddar cheese, divided
1   (2 ounce) jar diced pimiento, drained

1   small green pepper, finely chopped (optional)
1   bunch green onions, finely chopped
½   cup grated Parmesan cheese
¼   cup milk
1   teaspoon salt

Cook potatoes in boiling water to cover, for 15 minutes or until tender; drain and mash. Add butter and cream cheese; beat at medium speed with an electric mixer until smooth. Stir in ½ cup Cheddar cheese and next 6 ingredients; spoon into a lightly greased 11" x 7" x 1½" casserole. Bake at 350° about 30 minutes, then spread remainder of cheese over and bake until cheese melts. If chilled, remove casserole from refrigerator and let stand at room temperature 30 minutes. Then bake at 350° 40 minutes or until thoroughly heated. Sprinkle remaining ½ cup Cheddar cheese; bake 5 minutes or until cheese melts.

Yield: 8 servings

Casserole may be made the day before and chilled in refrigerator.

Lemon Vegetables

A colorful and easy casserole of mixed vegetables.

4   small new potatoes, washed, unpeeled and sliced
2   carrots, cut into thin strips
2   yellow squash, cut into thin strips
1   zucchini, sliced

½   cup butter or margarine, melted
1   tablespoon grated lemon rind
3   tablespoons lemon juice
¼   teaspoon salt
⅛   teaspoon pepper

Arrange potatoes and carrots in a vegetable steamer, or in a large colander. Place colander in a large pot with just enough boiling water to barely cover bottom of colander. Steam 8 minutes, add yellow squash and zucchini. Cover and steam about 3 minutes or until crisp-tender. Place vegetables in a warm serving dish. Combine butter and remaining ingredients; pour mixture over vegetables, tossing gently.

Yield: 6 servings

Mountain Rice

⅔	cup Uncle Ben's rice, uncooked	3	ounces cream cheese, softened
2	cups boiling water	½	teaspoon salt
½	teaspoon salt	2	eggs
⅓	cup finely chopped onion	1½	cups milk
1	tablespoon margarine or butter	2	tablespoons chopped parsley leaves

Place rice in a 4-cup baking dish. Add the boiling water and the ½ teaspoon salt. Stir with a fork, then cover tightly with aluminum foil, crimping sides. Bake in a pre-heated 375° oven for 25 to 30 minutes or until water is absorbed and rice is done. Foil usually puffs up at this time. Sauté onion in margarine until limp, but not brown. In mixer, blend cream cheese and salt, then add eggs, one at a time, beating after each addition. Add milk and beat well. Add rice, onion and parsley. Pour into same baking dish which has been buttered. Bake at 350° about 35 minutes or until heated.

Yield: 8 servings

Party Rice

This is another recipe where the rice is baked along with other ingredients. It is delicious, especially with pork or poultry. Another plus is that, since it does not have a sauce, it can be served with a creamed or sauced entrée.

1¼	cups uncooked Uncle Ben's rice	½	cup slivered almonds, toasted
½	stick butter or margarine	¼	cup white raisins
2½	cups chicken broth	½	teaspoon salt or to taste
		¼	teaspoon pepper

Brown rice in butter. Add chicken broth, place in a lightly buttered shallow 2-quart casserole, cover tightly with foil, and bake at 350° for 40 minutes or until rice is tender. Add remaining ingredients and return to oven to warm, or press in a buttered ring mold. Unmold carefully onto serving plate. Center may be filled with fresh green beans, cut diagonally, cooked and buttered.

Yield: 6 to 8 servings

Helpful Hint: *Corn on the cob can be baked in the oven. Pull husks down and remove floss. Rewrap and place in a 400° oven for 30 to 35 minutes. Remove husks and either eat on the cob or remove kernels and sauté in olive oil and butter.*

Potato Cheese Pudding

This dish may be baked in a microwave oven. Cover potatoes with waxed paper; cook on high 10 minutes. Add milk-egg mixture; cover and cook 10 minutes or until custard is set and potatoes are tender.

4	medium potatoes (about 2 pounds) sliced very thin, peeled or not, as you please	¼	teaspoon pepper
		2	cups milk
¼	cup flour	4	large eggs, beaten
1	teaspoon salt	4	ounces shredded Cheddar cheese
½	teaspoon dry mustard	¼	cup minced onion

Spread potatoes in a 12"x 8"x 2"baking dish. Cover with foil; bake in pre-heated 350° oven 20 minutes. Meanwhile, mix flour, salt, pepper and mustard in a bowl. Gradually stir in milk until blended. Mix beaten eggs, cheese and onion in a small bowl. Add to flour-mixture, stirring to mix. Spoon over potatoes in baking pan. Bake, uncovered, 1 hour, then cover and bake 10 minutes longer until custard is set and potatoes are tender.

Yield: 4 to 6 servings

Quick-Soak Wild Rice

Wild rice grows naturally in the wilds of Canada and some places in the United States. This method of cooking is very convenient and retains the best of flavor and texture. Wild rice is low in fat content, high in protein and rich in vitamin B.

1	cup wild rice	3	cups water

Wash wild rice under cold running water. Bring water to a boil, add rice and parboil for only 5 minutes. Remove from heat. Let soak in the same water, covered, for 1 hour. Drain, wash and cook as directed in recipe. You can quick-soak rice in the afternoon, then bake and serve it piping hot at dinnertime.

Yield: 6 to 8 servings

1 cup wild rice yields about 4 cups cooked. If you wish to substitute some white rice in a dish, use at least half wild rice and half white rice.

Rice with Almonds

We used to serve this with our Raleigh House grilled chicken. It is also good with the Working Woman's Chicken in the index of this cookbook.

¼	cup butter or margarine	½	teaspoon salt
2	tablespoons minced onion	¼	teaspoon pepper
1	cup Uncle Ben's rice	¼	cup chopped parsley, optional
2½	cups beef or chicken broth	4	ounces slivered almonds

Melt butter, add onion and sauté 1 minute. Add rice and broth. Cover tightly with foil and bake at 350° for 45 minutes or until tender. Stir in nuts and parsley; taste for seasoning.

Yield: 6 servings

Rice Dressing

Toasting of the rice before cooking makes this unusual.

1	cup uncooked Uncle Ben's rice	2	tablespoons minced celery
2½	cups boiling water	2	cups coarse bread crumbs, toasted in a 300° oven
1	teaspoon salt		
6	tablespoons butter or margarine	1	teaspoon baking powder
2	tablespoons minced onion	1	well beaten large egg
2	tablespoons minced parsley leaves	2	teaspoons poultry seasoning

Spread rice in a shallow pan and toast until light brown in a 400° oven, stirring often to prevent burning. Spray a 1½-quart casserole with vegetable spray. Add rice, salt and the boiling water. Cover tightly with foil and bake in a 375° oven about 20 minutes or until tender. Melt the butter or margarine in a small skillet and sauté the onion, parsley and celery until tender. Combine the rice, bread crumbs and baking powder in a large bowl, add the sautéed vegetables, the egg and poultry seasoning. Bake in a shallow, buttered casserole for 20 minutes at 350°.

Yield: 8 to 10 servings

I always cook rice in the oven rather than in a saucepan — no gummy pot to wash.

Rice Casserole Olé

This casserole may be frozen before baking.

1½ cups uncooked Uncle Ben's
     rice
1   small green pepper, chopped
1   (4 ounce) can chopped green
     chilies, drained

½   cup chopped onion
1   stick butter or margarine
1   cup sour cream
½   pound Monterey Jack cheese,
     grated

Cook rice and set aside. Sauté pepper and onions in butter. Place in blender along with the green chilies and puree. Add sour cream and continue to blend. In a 1½-quart casserole, layer half the rice, then half of sour cream mixture, then half of the cheese. Repeat layers. Bake at 350° for 20 to 30 minutes or until cheese is melted.

Yield: 8 to 10 servings

Sausage-Apple Dressing

This dressing is delicious served with other entrées besides turkey. It is almost a meal in itself.

5   cups crumbled cornbread,
     baked and cooled
1   pound mild pork sausage
6   slices bacon
1   large onion, chopped
1   cup chopped celery
2   baking apples, peeled, cored
     and chopped

2   cups chicken broth
1   cup chopped fresh parsley
     leaves
½   teaspoon rubbed sage
1   teaspoon dried thyme
½   teaspoon pepper
¼   teaspoon salt

Cook sausage and bacon in a Dutch oven, stirring until sausage crumbles; drain, reserving 3 tablespoons drippings. Cook onion and next 2 ingredients in drippings over medium heat, stirring constantly, until tender. Combine sausage mixture, crumbled cornbread, chicken broth and remaining ingredients in a large bowl. Spoon into a lightly greased 13"x 9"x 2"baking dish. Cover with aluminum foil; bake at 350° for 30 minutes. Uncover and bake an additional 30 minutes.

Yield: 8 to 10 servings

Roasted New Potatoes

This is a low calorie recipe, 165 calories per serving.

2	pounds new potatoes, all of same size	½	teaspoon salt
4	cloves garlic, peeled and minced	¼	teaspoon pepper
2	tablespoons olive oil	¼	teaspoon thyme
		¼	cup chopped fresh parsley

Pre-heat oven to 375°. Combine potatoes, garlic, oil, salt, pepper and thyme in a bowl. Toss to coat evenly. Place potatoes in a single layer on a sheet of heavy foil. Fold foil over potatoes and crimp edges to seal. Bake on cookie sheet 1 hour or until potatoes are tender. Carefully open foil and sprinkle with parsley.

Yield: 6 servings

Scalloped Carrots

This is a great recipe to convert carrot haters.

2	pounds carrots, sliced		Dash of pepper
2	tablespoons butter or margarine	1½	cups milk
½	cup finely chopped celery	1	cup (4 ounces) grated Cheddar cheese
¼	cup finely chopped onion	1	cup soft bread crumbs
2	tablespoons flour	2	tablespoons butter or margarine, melted
¼	teaspoon salt	2	tablespoons chopped parsley
¼	teaspoon dry mustard		

Cook carrots in boiling salted water to cover, until barely tender. Set aside. Melt the butter in a heavy saucepan over low heat. Add celery and onion; cook, stirring often, until tender. Add flour and next 3 ingredients, stirring until blended. Cook 1 minute, stirring constantly. Gradually add milk; cook over medium heat, stirring constantly, until mixture thickens. Stir in cheese and carrots; spoon into a lightly greased 1½-quart casserole. Combine bread crumbs, butter and parsley; sprinkle over carrot mixture. Bake at 350° for 25 minutes.

Yield: 6 to 8 servings

Easy glazed carrots: just boil and drain fresh sliced carrots, leaving a little water in bottom of pan. Sauté carrots in water, then add a few pats of butter. They taste great, low calorie, too. Remember this tip, a little butter adds a lot of flavor.

Snow Peas with Bell Peppers

This adds attractive color to the dinner plate.

½	pound snow peas, strings removed	2	medium yellow bell peppers (¾ pound)
½	teaspoon salt	2	tablespoons olive oil
	Ice water		Ground black pepper
2	medium red bell peppers (¾ pound)	1	tablespoon softened butter

Bring 2 quarts water to a boil in a large saucepan with ½ teaspoon salt. Add the peas and cook just until water returns to a boil. Drain and immediately immerse in ice water. Drain and pat dry with paper toweling. (Can cover and refrigerate overnight). Core and slice peppers lengthwise into ⅛" julienne strips. Heat oil in a large skillet with ⅛ teaspoon salt and ⅛ teaspoon pepper. Add peppers and sauté over high heat, stirring constantly, until slightly softened, about 1 minute. Add the snow peas in 2 batches, stirring constantly until vegetables are heated through, about 1 minute longer. Remove from heat and stir in butter. Serve immediately.

Yield: 8 servings

Spinach-Wild Rice Casserole

You may assemble casserole, cover and chill 8 hours. Remove from refrigerator; let stand at room temperature 30 minutes, then bake as directed.

1	(6 ounce) package long-grain and wild rice mix	¼	cup butter or margarine (½ stick), melted
2	(10 ounce) packages frozen chopped spinach, thawed and drained	1	tablespoon chopped onion
		½	teaspoon dry mustard
2	cups (8 ounces) Monterey Jack cheese, grated	½	teaspoon salt

Cook rice according to package directions. Press spinach between two paper towels to remove excess moisture. Combine rice, spinach, and remaining ingredients; spoon into a lightly greased 2-quart shallow casserole. Bake, uncovered, at 350° for 35 to 40 minutes.

Yield: 6 servings

Spinach Pie

I sometimes serve a quiche as an appetizer. Three times this recipe can be made in a jelly roll pan (cookie sheet with a 1" rim). Roll pastry to a 18" x 15" rectangle. Place in pan and flute edges. Place in refrigerator until needed.

Filling:

1 (10 ounce) package frozen chopped spinach, thawed and drained well, pressing out extra moisture between paper towels	½ cup milk
	¼ cup minced fresh mushrooms
	½ cup minced onion
	½ teaspoon salt
	Dash pepper
3 eggs	⅛ teaspoon ground nutmeg
½ cup half-and-half	

Beat eggs in a large bowl; set aside. Combine half-and-half and next five ingredients in a small saucepan; simmer over low heat 1 minute. Slowly add hot mixture to eggs. Stir in nutmeg; add spinach. Pour into pre-baked cheese pastry. Bake at 400° for 15 minutes. Lower heat to 350° and bake until almost firm in center. As with baked custard, quiche firms up as it cools. Serve warm.

Cheese Pastry:

½ teaspoon salt	3 tablespoons shortening
1½ cups flour	2 tablespoons lemon juice
6 tablespoons (¾ stick) unsalted butter	1 to 2 tablespoons water
	½ cup grated Cheddar cheese

Cut butter and shortening into flour and salt. Add cheese, then lemon juice and enough water to make a dough. Fit into a 9" or 10" pie tin. Place a piece of foil or waxed paper in shell and add uncooked beans or rice or metal pellets made for this purpose. Bake at 425° for 10 minutes. Remove weights and bake for 5 minutes more until crust is just turning light brown.

Yield: 6 to 8 servings

If made in jelly roll pan, bake at 375° about 35 to 40 minutes or until almost firm in center. Cut into 40 squares.

Helpful Hint: *½ pound sliced fresh mushrooms equals 2½ cups.*

Sugar Snap Peas with Sweet Basil and Lemon

Sugar snap peas (not English peas) are one of my most favorite vegetables. I hope they are available in your area.

1	teaspoon olive oil	½	teaspoon grated lemon rind
¾	pound sugar snap peas	¼	teaspoon salt
¼	cup coarsely chopped fresh basil	¼	teaspoon white pepper

Heat oil in a nonstick skillet over medium heat. Add peas; stir-fry 3 minutes or until crisp-tender. Sprinkle with basil, lemon rind, salt and pepper; stir-fry 1 minute. Serve immediately garnished with lemon wedges, if desired.

Yield: 2 servings

Sweet Potatoes and Applesauce

2	cups cooked sweet potatoes, cut into ½" cubes	¼	cup firmly packed brown sugar
¼	teaspoon salt	2	tablespoons butter or margarine
1	(8 ounce) jar unsweetened applesauce	¼	teaspoon ground nutmeg

Place sweet potatoes in a buttered 1-quart casserole. Sprinkle with salt. Spoon applesauce over potatoes and sprinkle with sugar. Dot with butter and sprinkle with nutmeg. Bake at 350° for 30 to 35 minutes or until lightly browned.

Yield: 4 servings

Yams Praline

This recipe has no added sugar so it is not too sweet. It is flavored with praline liqueur, which I use often in breads, desserts and vegetables.

4	large yams (about 3½ pounds) unpeeled	1	teaspoon salt
¼	cup praline liqueur	⅛	teaspoon white pepper
¼	cup (½ stick) butter, melted		Toasted pecans or chopped parsley for garnish

Cook yams in boiling water to cover for 30 minutes or until tender. Drain and let cool to touch; peel. Mash yams; add praline liqueur and next 3 ingredients. Spoon into a 1½-quart shallow buttered casserole. Garnish with either toasted pecans or parsley. Serve immediately or chill. Place in a 350° oven to heat.

Yield: 6 to 8 servings

Sweet Potato or Baking Potato "Fries"

These "fries" are roasted in the oven.

2½ pounds sweet potatoes or
     regular baking potatoes,
     about 4 large
2   tablespoons cooking oil or
     olive oil, divided

1   teaspoon salt
¼   teaspoon freshly ground
     pepper

Pre-heat oven to 450°. Line cookie sheet with foil. Spread with 1 tablespoon oil. Cut potatoes lengthwise into ½"wedges. Transfer to a large bowl. Add the other tablespoon oil, salt and pepper and toss to coat. Spread potatoes in a single layer on prepared cookie sheet. Bake 25 to 30 minutes, until golden and crisp.

Yield: 4 servings

Sweet Potato Soufflé

This is a casserole to serve at Thanksgiving or Christmas when no one is counting calories.

Sweet Potatoes:

3   cups sweet potatoes
     (4 large potatoes) either boiled
     or baked, then mashed
¾   cup sugar
½   cup milk

½   stick margarine
¼   teaspoon salt
2   teaspoons vanilla extract
2   large eggs

Mix all ingredients in mixer bowl. Spoon into a buttered 3-quart casserole. Pour topping over casserole and bake at 350° 30 to 40 minutes.

Topping:

1   cup brown sugar, firmly
     packed
⅓   cup flour

1   stick margarine
1   cup chopped pecans
½   cup milk

Place all ingredients, except pecans, in saucepan. Bring to a boil, stirring constantly, add pecans before pouring over casserole.

Yield: 8 servings

Toasted Pecan Rice

This is a very easy casserole to make. The toasted pecans add a special touch. Toasted slivered almonds may be substituted and are equally good.

1	cup pecans, coarsely chopped	¾	stick butter
2½	cups Uncle Ben's rice, uncooked	1	teaspoon salt
		5	cups chicken broth

Toast pecans in a 300° oven until crisp. Sauté rice in butter over medium heat, stirring constantly, until light tan. Add salt and chicken broth and bring to a boil. Spoon into 13" x 9" x 2" casserole. Cover tightly with foil, crimping sides, and bake at 375° about 30 minutes or until rice is done. Remove from oven and fold in pecans.

Yield: 8 to 10

I always have chicken broth in my deep freeze. I buy necks or whatever parts of chicken that are on sale, boil them slowly until very tender. I strain the broth and put it in 2 to 4 cup containers. It is much cheaper than buying canned broth.

Twice-Baked Potatoes

Garlic is added to the potato pulp, a different taste treat.

3	large baking potatoes	⅓	cup sour cream
1	tablespoon vegetable oil	2	cloves garlic, crushed
2	tablespoons butter or margarine	½	teaspoon salt
		¼	teaspoon pepper

Scrub potatoes, then dry with paper towels. Rub evenly with the vegetable oil. Place in shallow pan and bake at 375° until soft to the touch. Remove from oven and cut in two lengthwise. Scoop out potato into a mixing bowl; add rest of ingredients and mix until fluffy. Taste for seasoning. Replace in potato shells and heat in a 350° oven until slightly brown.

Yield: 6 servings

These can be prepared early in the day and refrigerated. Increase warming time.

Wild Rice Casserole

This casserole is especially good with roasted duck and orange sauce.

⅔ cup wild rice, quick-soaked
3 cups boiling water
½ teaspoon salt
¼ cup chopped onion
1 cup fresh mushrooms, sliced
2 tablespoons butter
1 tablespoon flour

1 cup beef broth or chicken
   broth
½ to ¾ teaspoon salt
⅛ teaspoon pepper
⅓ cup thinly sliced or slivered
   almonds

Follow the quick-soak method to prepare rice for cooking. Then cook rice in the boiling water with ½ teaspoon salt until nearly tender, about 30 minutes. Sauté onion and mushrooms in butter. Blend in flour and cook until lightly browned. Add beef or chicken stock and cook over medium heat, stirring constantly, until thickened. Add salt and pepper and rice. Place in a buttered 1½- or 2-quart casserole. Sprinkle with almonds. Cover and bake in a 350° oven about 35 minutes or until hot.

Yield: 4 servings

Wild Rice Pilaf with Scallions

Quick-soak wild rice according to instructions in recipe in index of this cookbook, then proceed with this recipe.

1½ cups wild rice, quick-soaked
   and drained
1 tablespoon olive oil
3 cups chicken broth, canned
   or homemade

1 tablespoon lemon juice
   or to taste
⅔ cup thinly sliced scallions
   (green onions) including green
   part
Salt and pepper

Place olive oil in heavy saucepan or skillet, add rice and heat over moderate heat, stirring, until it is coated well. Add chicken broth and bring to a boil. Cook, covered, about 40 minutes or until tender and puffed. Drain, if necessary. Stir in lemon juice, scallion and salt and pepper to taste. Serve warm and enjoy.

Yield: 6 servings

Winter Vegetable Puree

My Mother cooked rutabaga in many ways, sometimes just boiled, drained then mashed with cream, dash of Worcestershire sauce and dash of Tabasco. Salt added to taste. This recipe brings back memories of my childhood.

1	pound potatoes, peeled and cut into 2" chunks	¼	cup butter or margarine (½ stick), cut up
1	pound carrots, peeled and cut into 1" chunks	½	cup half-and-half, heated
1	pound rutabaga, peeled and cut into 1" chunks	½	teaspoon freshly ground pepper
1½	teaspoons salt, divided	¼	teaspoon nutmeg
		2	teaspoons Worcestershire sauce

Combine vegetables in large saucepot with 1 teaspoon salt. Add enough water to come about 3" up sides of pot. Bring to a boil; reduce heat, cover and simmer until vegetables are tender, about 20 to 25 minutes. Drain. Transfer to a mixer bowl, add half-and-half and butter and beat until smooth. Add the remaining ½ teaspoon salt, the pepper, Worcestershire sauce and nutmeg. This can be made a little ahead of time, put in a covered casserole and warm in the oven.

Yield: 4½ cups

Zucchini-Tomato Skillet

1	small onion, chopped	¼	cup grated Parmesan cheese
¼	cup butter, melted	1½	teaspoons chopped fresh basil or ½ teaspoon dried
4	medium zucchini, sliced (about 1½ pounds)	¼	teaspoon salt
¼	pound fresh mushrooms, sliced	¼	teaspoon pepper
3	medium tomatoes, (about 1 pound) sliced	1	clove garlic, minced
3	tablespoons fresh parsley, chopped	1	cup (4 ounces) shredded Cheddar cheese

Cook onion in butter in large skillet over low heat, stirring constantly, until tender. Add zucchini and mushrooms; cook, stirring, 5 minutes or until crisp-tender. Add tomatoes, cook 1 minute or until heated, stirring often. Drain vegetables and return to skillet; gently stir in parsley and next 5 ingredients.

Remove skillet from heat. At this point, you may transfer to a casserole, if you wish, and finish in a 350° oven. Sprinkle mixture with cheese either in skillet or casserole. Cook either in skillet or in a 350° oven until cheese is melted.

Yield: 6 servings

Index

Index

Raleigh House
P. O. Box 2182
Kerrville, TX 78029-2182

Please send me _____ copies of *Raleigh House*   @ $19.95 each _____
Please send me _____ copies of *Raleigh House II* @ $19.95 each _____
Texas residents add 8¼% sales tax   @ $ 1.65 each _____
Postage and handling   @   2.00 each _____

Name _____

Address _____

City _____ State _____ Zip _____

Make checks payable to *Raleigh House*.

- -

Raleigh House
P. O. Box 2182
Kerrville, TX 78029-2182

Please send me _____ copies of *Raleigh House*   @ $19.95 each _____
Please send me _____ copies of *Raleigh House II* @ $19.95 each _____
Texas residents add 8¼% sales tax   @ $ 1.65 each _____
Postage and handling   @   2.00 each _____

Name _____

Address _____

City _____ State _____ Zip _____

Make checks payable to *Raleigh House*.

- -

Raleigh House
P. O. Box 2182
Kerrville, TX 78029-2182

Please send me _____ copies of *Raleigh House*   @ $19.95 each _____
Please send me _____ copies of *Raleigh House II* @ $19.95 each _____
Texas residents add 8¼% sales tax   @ $ 1.65 each _____
Postage and handling   @   2.00 each _____

Name _____

Address _____

City _____ State _____ Zip _____

Make checks payable to *Raleigh House*.

If you would like to see *Raleigh House* or *Raleigh House II* in your area, please send the names and addresses of your local gift or book stores.

If you would like to see *Raleigh House* or *Raleigh House II* in your area, please send the names and addresses of your local gift or book stores.

If you would like to see *Raleigh House* or *Raleigh House II* in your area, please send the names and addresses of your local gift or book stores.